SLAUGHTER
AT HALBE

SLAUGHTER AT HALBE

THE DESTRUCTION OF HITLER'S 9TH ARMY

TONY LE TISSIER

SUTTON PUBLISHING

First published in 2005 by
Sutton Publishing Limited . Phoenix Mill
Thrupp . Stroud . Gloucestershire . GL5 2BU

This paperback edition first published in 2007

British Library Cataloguing in Publication Data
A catalogue record for this book is available from the British Library.

ISBN 978-0-7509-4589-3

Typeset 10.5/13pt Photina.
Typesetting and origination by
Sutton Publishing Limited.
Printed and bound in England.

CONTENTS

Appendices

MAPS

ABBREVIATIONS

A	Army	How	Howitzer
Arty	Artillery	HQ	Headquarters
B/Bde	Brigade	Hy	Heavy
BF/Bye Fr	Byelorussian Front	ID	Infantry Division
C	Corps	Lt	Light
D	Division	M/Mech	Mechanized
Elms	Elements	Mor	Mortar
FWL	Forest Warden's Lodge	Mtn	Mountain
		Pol	Police
		Pz	Panzer
G/Gds	Guards	SA	Shock Army
GCC	Guards Cavalry Corps	R	Rifle
		Regt	Regiment
Gp	Group	UF/Ukr Front	Ukrainian Front
Gr	Grenadier		
Grn	Garrison	V	Volunteer

INTRODUCTION

Halbe, a small village of about 400 inhabitants in the Spreewald forests south of Berlin, was the eye of the needle through which, in late April 1945, the troops of the already defeated German 9th Army had to pass if they wished to escape Soviet captivity with a break-out to the west.

Some 40,000 people, soldiers and civilians, are said to have been killed in this tragic episode. Their story deserves to be told.

The increasingly vicious and destructive manner in which the war on the Eastern Front had been conducted by both sides left those German soldiers with experience of it in no doubt as to the kind of fate Soviet captivity would bring them, and provided a powerful incentive for engaging in this final desperate struggle to break out and seek captivity with the Western Allies.

Survivors' accounts give a chaotic picture, suggesting a large-scale loss of command and control in the military system that is not fully borne out by the surprisingly large number that got through to achieve their aim, despite the horrific casualties suffered in the process. Nevertheless, that there were some serious basic defects at command level cannot be denied.

I have been persuaded to attempt a study of these events by Horst Wilke, who survived the ordeal as a signals sergeant and was at one time business manager of the Halbe Memorial Sponsor Club (*Förderverein Gendenkstätte Halbe e.V.*), and gave me free access to the archives he had accumulated over the years. It was at this club's annual gathering in 1996 that I had the pleasure of meeting one of his Red Army opponents, Harry Zvi Glaser, who had actually fought in Halbe itself, and was now being fêted by his erstwhile enemies.

I am particularly indebted to my friends Dozent Dr Sc. Richard Lakowski and Oberst a. D. Dr Karl Stich, both military historians of the former German Democratic Republic, whose excellent work *Der Kessel von Halbe 1945 – Das letzte Drama* has proved an invaluable guide.

My own archives resulting from previous studies of the 1945 battles in and around Berlin (see *The Battle of Berlin 1945*, updated by feedback from the German edition as *Race for the Reichstag*, and *Zhukov at the Oder*), plus individual accounts related in *With Our Backs to Berlin* and *Death was our Companion*, yielded a wealth of useful information. Among my sources, I would like to name Erwin Bartmann and Rudi Lindner, the latter an officer cadet in the break-out who later became a major-general in the East German Army, Helmut Jürisch and the late Rechtsanwalt Günter G. Führling.

My thanks are also due to Lothar Schulze, who kindly allowed me the use of translations of the local eyewitness statements that he collated in his book *Der Kessel Halbe–Radeland*, and for his warning concerning the lingering traces of falsification of local history by the East German government in honouring their 'liberators' and attributing all blame and damage to the 'Fascist Wehrmacht'.

One factor in this connection is the reluctance to accept the fact that so-called *Seydlitz-Troops* were used in combat by the Soviets during the Berlin Operation, for official documentary evidence has yet to be found in either former East German or Soviet archives to support this claim. *Seydlitz-Troops* was the name given by the Germans to those turncoat prisoners of war who worked for the Red Army against their former comrades. The name came from General Walter von Seydlitz-Kurzbach, who had been captured at Stalingrad and had later become Chairman of the *Bund Deutsche Offiziere* (League of German Officers) and Vice-Chairman of the *Nationalkomitee Freies Deutschland* (NKFD – National Committee for a Free Germany), institutions set up by the Soviets, initially only for propaganda purposes. However, during the later stages of the war *Seydlitz-Troops* were also used to spy out German positions, issue false orders to retreating troops, and even engaged in combat under close Soviet supervision. General von Seydlitz totally disassociated himself from these activities, and was eventually exonerated by a West German court after the war.

I must also thank Rolf Kaim of the Kummersdorf Schiessplatz Museum for his assistance in my research, including locating the report by Willi Klär, and Werner Mihan for tracking down copies of the wartime maps of that area.

Above all, I am greatly indebted to the outstanding generosity of Wilhelm Tieke for allowing me to include translations of numerous survivors' accounts taken from his book *Das Ende zwischen Oder und Elbe*.

To assist the reader with the course of events described, I have endeavoured to illustrate the various aspects of the action with a series of maps and drawings incorporating as many of the place-names mentioned in the text as was feasible. Reference to the maps on which these names appear will be found noted in bold type in the index.

I would like to thank the various individuals whose names appear in the photo captions for allowing me to use the related illustrations. Evgeni Bessonov's photos originally appeared in his book *Tank Rider* (Greenhill Books, 2003, ISBN 1-85367-554-7). All illustrations which are not specifically credited are from my own collection.

ONE

PREPARING FOR 'OPERATION BERLIN'

21 APRIL 1999

When the Soviets launched Operation Berlin on 16 April 1945, Marshal Georgi Konstantinovitch Zhukov's 1st Byelorussian Front opposite Berlin, and Marshal Ivan Stepanovitch Koniev's 1st Ukrainian Front further south, faced the German 9th Army on the Oder River and 4th Panzer Army on the Neisse River respectively in overwhelming force.

For this final assault on the Third Reich, the Soviets had mustered the last of their manpower to fill the establishments of these two army groups and to provide them with all the equipment and supplies they needed. Additionally, substantial artillery formations from the Stavka (General Staff) Reserve had been placed at their disposal for the initial breakthrough battle. Excluding reserves and rear area troops, these forces amounted to:

	1st Byelorussian Front	1st Ukrainian Front
Men & Women	768,000	511,700
Tanks	1,795	1,388
Self-propelled guns	1,360	677
Anti-tank guns	2,306	1,444
Field guns (76-mm+)	7,442	5,040
Mortars (88-mm+)	7,186	5,225

1

	1st Byelorussian Front	1st Ukrainian Front
Rocket launchers	1,531	917
Anti-aircraft guns	1,665	945
Trucks	44,332	29,205
Fighters	1,567	1,106
Ground-attack	731	529
Bombers	1,562	422
Reconnaissance	26	91
Aircraft (total)	3,886	2,148[1]

In comparison, the opposing 9th Army could only muster some 200,000 men, 512 tanks and self-propelled guns (SPGs) of all kinds, and 2,625 artillery pieces, while air support was reduced to a minimum for lack of fuel for the aircraft available.

The statistics were such that the outcome of the Berlin Operation could be regarded as a foregone conclusion by the Soviets, but with different effects at either end of the rank structure. For the leadership, and that meant Josef Stalin, this entailed thinking and playing one step ahead of imminent victory, and for the rank and file seeing the war out, not taking unnecessary risks in combat, and making the most of their opportunities when not in action.

The attitude of the Soviet soldier since crossing the German frontier had proved a serious problem for the command. Encouraged to take revenge on the Germans by the Soviet press and radio for the outrages committed in the Soviet Union, they had indulged in endless atrocities of murder, rape, looting, arson and wilful damage, bringing about a serious collapse in army discipline. Consequently, the political departments in the command structure had a difficult task in motivating and inspiring the troops, apart from the necessary reimposition of discipline.

For Stalin the war had served to reinforce his position as leader of his country, in which role he would brook no potential rival, but it was inevitable during the course of the war that certain of his generals should have attracted public attention, and he now saw the opportunity to cut them down to size, the rival Marshals Zhukov and Koniev in particular. Zhukov did not like or particularly trust Koniev, the former political commissar turned professional soldier, and the latter's brief experience under Zhukov's command had led him to dislike Zhukov intensely. As Boris Nicolaevsky wrote in his book *Power and the Soviet Elite*, Stalin, with his great talent for exploiting human weaknesses, had:

> . . . quickly sized up Koniev and cleverly used his feelings towards Zhukov. If we trace the history of Stalin's treatment of the two soldiers, the chronology of their promotions and awards, we shall see that as early as the end of 1941 Stalin was grooming Koniev, the politician, as a rival whom he could play off against the real soldier, Zhukov. This was typical of Stalin's foresight and bears all the marks of his style. He confers honours on Zhukov only when he has no choice, but on Koniev he bestowed them even when there was no particular reason for doing so. This was necessary in order to maintain the balance between the 'indispensable organiser of victory' and the even more indispensable political counterweight to him.[2]

In fact Zhukov posed no threat to Stalin, whose authority Zhukov accepted without question, whether he thought Stalin right or wrong in his military decisions, in the same spirit in which Zhukov demanded total obedience from his own subordinates. Yet he had reason to be apprehensive for, as early as 1942, Stalin had sought some means of curbing Zhukov, tasking Viktor Abakumov, Head of the Special Department of the Ministry of the Interior (later to become SMERSH) with this. Although officially subordinate to Lavrenti Beria, Abakumov had direct access to Stalin, and began by arresting Zhukov's former Chief of Operations with the Western Front in an unsuccessful attempt to gain incriminating evidence. Although Zhukov was nominally Deputy Supreme Commander of the Soviet Armed Forces, Stalin retained all the power for himself. By the autumn of 1944 Stalin was becoming ever more openly critical of the directions Zhukov was giving to his subordinate fronts on behalf of Stavka, this time tasking Nikolai Bulganin, then Deputy Commissar for Defence, with finding some error or omission with which Zhukov could be charged. Eventually two artillery manuals were found that Zhukov had personally approved, without first clearing them with Stavka. An order was then distributed throughout the upper echelons of the command structure, openly warning Zhukov not to be hasty when serious questions were being decided. Zhukov's appointment as commander of the 1st Byelorussian Front then followed as a humiliating demotion, and placed him on a par with Koniev commanding the 1st Ukrainian Front. Consequently, Zhukov was now in a far from enviable position, being under constant threat of arrest.

With Zhukov's East Pomeranian and Koniev's Silesian clearance operations successfully completed, Stalin summoned them to Moscow to finalize the planning for the capture of Berlin. The matter was pressing because, despite the agreements reached at the Yalta Conference in February 1945 about the zoning of postwar Germany, the Soviet leaders generally expected that the Western Allies would try to get to Berlin ahead of them. The Soviets were fully aware of the political significance of taking the German capital, a point that General Dwight D. Eisenhower, Supreme Commander in the West, and his superior, General George C. Marshall in Washington, failed to grasp, despite urging from their British allies. On 28 March Eisenhower signalled Stalin to the effect that he had decided to disregard Berlin and direct his main thrust on the Erfurt–Leipzig–Dresden area and the mythical Alpine Redoubt.[3] Stalin had promptly and deceitfully replied approving these proposals and announcing his own intentions of a main thrust on Dresden with only subsidiary forces directed on Berlin. From German signal traffic the Western Allies had been alerted to the imminence of the Soviet offensive and had pressed Stalin for details, but it was not until the eve of the attack that he was to divulge the date to them, again emphasizing quite untruthfully that his main thrust would be in the south.[4]

General Sergei M. Shtemenko, Chief of the Operations Department of the Soviet General Staff, wrote about the preliminary planning for Operation Berlin:

The work of the General Staff in planning the culminating attacks was made extremely complicated by Stalin's categorical decision concerning the special role of the 1st Byelorussian Front. The task of overcoming such a large city as Berlin, which had been prepared well in advance for defence, was beyond the capacity of one front, even such a powerful front as the 1st Byelorussian. The situation insistently demanded that at least the 1st Ukrainian Front should be aimed additionally at Berlin. Moreover, it was, of course, necessary to avoid an ineffectual frontal attack with the main forces.

We had to go back to the January idea of taking Berlin by means of out-flanking attacks by the 1st Byelorussian Front from the north and north-west and the 1st Ukrainian Front from the south-west and west. The two fronts were to link up in the Brandenburg–Potsdam area.

We based all our further calculations on the most unfavourable assumptions: the inevitability of heavy and prolonged fighting in the streets of Berlin, the possibility of German counterattacks from outside the ring of encirclement from the west and south-west, restoration of the enemy's defence to the west of Berlin and the

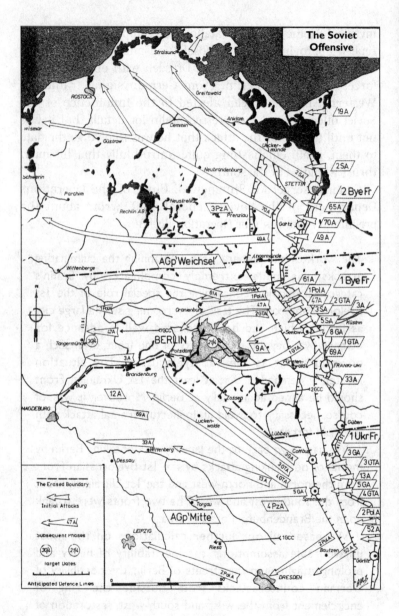

consequent need to continue the offensive. We even envisaged a situation in which the Western Allies for some reason might be unable to overcome the resistance of the enemy forces opposing them and find themselves held up for a long time.[5]

Zhukov arrived in Moscow on 29 March and saw Stalin that evening. Stalin gave him two days to sort out the final details of his plans with the General Staff. He and Koniev were to present their plans for Stavka approval on 1 April. Shtemenko then went on to describe the events of the 1945 Easter weekend in Moscow:

By this time the General Staff had all the basic ideas for the Berlin operation worked out. In the course of this work we kept in very close contact with the front Chiefs of Staff, A.M. Bogolyubov, M.S. Malin and V.D. Sokolovsky (later with I.Y. Petrov) and, as soon as the first symptoms appeared that the Allies had designs on Berlin, Zhukov and Koniev were summoned to Moscow.

On March the 31st they and the General Staff considered what further operations the Fronts were to carry out. Marshal Koniev got very excited over the demarcation line between his front and the 1st Byelorussian Front, which gave him no opportunity of striking a blow at Berlin. No one on the General Staff, however, could remove this obstacle.

On the next day, 1st April 1945, the plan of the Berlin operation was discussed at GHQ. A detailed report was given on the situation at the Fronts, and on Allied operations and their plans. Stalin drew the conclusion from this that we must take Berlin in the shortest possible time. The operation would have to be started not later than the 16th April and completed in not more than 12 to 15 days. The Front Commanders agreed to this and assured GHQ that the troops would be ready in time.

7

The Chief of the General Staff considered it necessary to draw the Supreme Commander's attention once again to the demarcation line between the two Fronts. It was emphasized that this line virtually excluded the armies of the 1st Ukrainian Front from direct participation in the fighting for Berlin, and this might make it difficult to carry out the operation as scheduled. Marshal Koniev spoke in the same vein, arguing in favour of aiming part of the forces of the 1st Ukrainian Front, particularly the tank armies, at the south-western suburbs of Berlin.

Stalin decided on a compromise. He did not completely abandon his own idea, nor did he entirely reject Marshal Koniev's considerations, supported by the General Staff. On the map showing the plan of the operation he silently crossed out the section of the demarcation line that cut off the Ukrainian Front from Berlin, allowing it to go as far as Lübben (sixty kilometres to the south-east of the capital) and no further.

'Let the one who is first to break in, take Berlin,' he told us later.[6]

In his memoirs, Koniev wrote of this event:

To me, in any case, the end of the boundary at Lübben meant that the rapidity of the penetration, as well as the speed and manoeuvrability of the operations on the right flank of our Front, might subsequently create a situation which would make our attack against Berlin from the south advantageous.

Could this halting of the boundary at Lübben have been designed to create competition between the two fronts? I admit that that could have been the case. At any rate, I do not exclude this possibility. This becomes all the more plausible if we think back to that time and recall what Berlin meant to us and how ardently we all, from soldier to

general, wished to see that city with our own eyes and
capture it by the force of our arms.

Naturally, this was also my passionate desire. I am not afraid
to admit this now. It would be strange to portray myself
during the last months of the war as a person devoid of
strong emotions. On the contrary, we were overflowing with
them.

As a matter of fact, the drawing of the line of demarcation
brought the planning of the operation to a conclusion. The
GHQ directives were approved.[7]

So this operation was to become not only a race against
time to beat the Western Allies to Berlin, but also a race
between the front commanders for the glory of taking the
enemy capital, and within the capital what to them was the
symbolic Reichstag building. Although it had been burnt out
twelve years previously and remained a desolate shell, its
significance to the Soviets was akin to that of the Kremlin in
their own country, as the centre of Nazi power.

Instead of the usual three to four months to prepare for an
operation of this magnitude, the Soviets could now only allow
themselves two weeks.

Stalin signed the directive approving Zhukov's plans for the
1st Byelorussian Front's operation on the night of 1 April and
Koniev's the following day. The directive for Marshal
Konstantin K. Rokossovsky's 2nd Byelorussian Front was not
issued for another week, for he was still heavily engaged in
mopping up the German forces remaining in East Prussia and
was not expected to launch his part of the Berlin operation
against the 3rd Panzer Army north of Berlin until 20 April.[8]

Zhukov's orders gave him the primary task of taking Berlin
by 21 April and pushing on to the Elbe by 1 May. Koniev
would support the Berlin operation by destroying the German
forces to the south of the city, and would have the secondary
task of taking Dresden and Leipzig, both important industrial

cities in the future Soviet Zone of Occupation. The 2nd Byelorussian Front would engage the German forces north of the capital, while other fronts further south would maintain pressure on the Germans to prevent the redeployment of strategic reserves to the Berlin area.[9]

The main problem for Zhukov in the breakthrough battle would be the clearing of the commanding Seelow Heights. He proposed doing this with a simultaneous attack from his bridgehead in the Oderbruch valley bottom by four reinforced combined-arms formations to clear breaches in the defences. This would enable his two tank armies to pass through and take Berlin in a pincer movement. The 2nd Guards Tank Army would penetrate the heart of Berlin from the north-east, while 1st Guards Tank Army would bypass Berlin and Potsdam to the south, pushing on to the west. A further two armies would conduct river crossings across the Alte Oder and Oder, press on to cover the northern flank and block off Berlin from the west. Meanwhile, 69th Army would cover the southern flank of the main attack while containing the Frankfurt-an-der-Oder garrison in conjuction with 33rd Army. The latter, with 2nd Guards Cavalry Corps, would break out of its own bridgehead, and together these two armies would push westward along the line of the autobahn with the objectives of Fürstenwalde and eventually Brandenburg. (This move, in conjunction with that of 1st Guards Tank Army, could also be interpreted as intended to forestall any attempt by Koniev to break into the city from the south.) The 3rd Army would form the front's second echelon, and 7th Guards Cavalry Corps the front reserve.[10]

However, as he reveals in his memoirs, Koniev was determined to get into Berlin, even though the GHQ directive for his front was somewhat vague on this point, reading:

The Front will organise and carry out an offensive operation aimed at routing the enemy group in the region

10

of Cottbus and south of Berlin. Not later than the 10th–12th day of the operation the Front will seize the Beelitz–Wittenberg line and advance further along the Elbe to Dresden. Subsequently, after the capture of Berlin, the Front will prepare for an attack against Lepizig.[11]

In his own orders to his front, Koniev inserted between the last two sentences of the above text: 'to bear in mind the possibility of using some of our forces of the right flank of the front to help the troops of the 1st Byelorussian Front in capturing the city of Berlin.' As he went on to explain in his memoirs:

> In the plan for the 1st Ukrainian Front the task of helping the 1st Byelorussian Front to capture Berlin was stated in a general way, but in the order issued to 3rd Guards Tank Army it was concrete:
>
> 'On the fifth day of the operation to seize the area of Trebbin, Zauchwitz, Treuenbrietzen, Luckenwalde . . . To bear in mind the possibility of attacking Berlin from the south by a reinforced tank corps and an infantry division of the 3rd Guards Army.'
>
> Thus, even before the operation began, one tank corps and an infantry division were earmarked for attacking Berlin from the south.
>
> It seemed strange and incomprehensible, when one was advancing along what amounted to the southern fringe of Berlin, to leave it deliberately untouched to the right of one's flank, particularly in circumstances when one had no preliminary knowledge of how things might work out in the future. The decision to be ready to deliver such an attack seemed clear, comprehensible and self-evident.[12]

In contrast to Stalin in the splendour of the Kremlin, Adolf Hitler, the Führer of the Third Reich and Supreme

Commander of the German Armed Forces, was exercising his authority from a new command bunker beneath the Old Chancellery building in the Wilhelmstrasse, into which he had moved on 16 January. He now lived and worked in an oppressive atmosphere of noisy air-conditioning and sweating concrete walls, with no distinction between night and day. The *Führerbunker* also suffered the serious defect of being inadequately equipped with communications facilities for its role. This was in part due to scale, for accommodation was extremely cramped in the *Führerbunker* itself, although more space could have been made available in the bomb-proof shelters beneath the New Chancellery building next door. However, the only communications facilities installed in the *Führerbunker* were a one-man switchboard, one radio transmitter and a radio telephone, which was dependent upon an aerial suspended from a balloon.[13]

The German Army's once powerful General Staff had been utterly broken by the purge following the unsuccessful assassination attempt against Hitler of 20 July 1944, and its representatives in Hitler's entourage were now mere sycophants. Permanently with Hitler in the *Führerbunker* was Field Marshal Wilhelm Keitel, nominal Chief of the Oberkommando der Wehrmacht (OKW – Armed Forces GHQ) with his headquarters in Berlin-Dahlem, but in practice acting as Hitler's personal chief of staff and issuing orders in the Führer's name. The OKW Chief of Staff, Colonel-General Alfred Jodl, and the Chief of Staff of the Oberkommando des Heeres (OKH – Army GHQ), General of Infantry Hans Krebs, were obliged to spend most of their time shuttling back and forth between the *Führerbunker* conferences and the secret wartime headquarters in the vast bunkers known as Maybach I and II respectively, some thirty kilometres south of the city at Zossen–Wunsdorf.[14]

One has only to read Colonel-General Heinz Guderian's book, *Panzer Leader*, to realize how intolerable Hitler's conduct as a commander was towards the General Staff and what pressure officers were placed under as a result of this. The essence of the problem lay in Hitler's Führer-system of unquestioning obedience to orders clashing with the General Staff's system of mutual trust and exchange of ideas, against a background of Hitler's class consciousness and genuine distrust of the General Staff following the failed putsch of 20 July 1944.[15]

Hitler's system of leadership was reflected in the state and composition of the German armed forces. One particularly confusing aspect was the use of corps and army headquarters taken out of reserve to command new formations to which they automatically gave their titles, irrespective of their composition or function. Thus, for example, V SS Mountain Corps commanded only one Waffen-SS formation and no mountain troops, and XI SS Panzer Corps consisted primarily of ordinary infantry units.[16]

The basic framework of the German ground forces was still that of the German Army, most commonly (though not strictly correctly) known by the overall title of the Wehrmacht. However, after the abortive coup of 20 July 1944, the Army had been seriously weakened by the great purge of officers that followed and by the Nazi leaders' distrust of the survivors. Political officers (*NS-Führungsoffiziere*) had been appointed to all units and formation headquarters for the purpose of promoting the Nazi spirit and to spy on possible dissidents.

Under the operational command of the Wehrmacht, although technically an entirely separate organization, was Heinrich Himmler's Waffen-SS, consisting of Panzer (armoured), Panzergrenadier (motorized infantry), cavalry and mountain formations, as well as foreign volunteer elements such as the 23rd SS Panzergrenadier Division *Nederland*. However, as a result of hard usage most of these formations were now drastically reduced in strength. Despite their elitism, by 1945 the various Waffen-SS units and formations were fully integrated into the Army's operational system.

Drastic measures had had to be taken to man the defences along the Eastern Front. Marsch (field replacement) battalions had been raised from police, fire brigade, customs and border guard resources, equipped with small arms and sent into combat to serve under their own officers, while sailors and airmen with little or no field training and inadequate equipment were drafted as infantry. Units of the Volkssturm (Home Guard) had also been used to bolster some formations, including some grenadier regiments raised from officer cadet schools.

Nevertheless, the continuing strength of the Wehrmacht lay in its tactical skills, its command system in the field, and its ability to reorganize quickly at all levels. Time and time again the Germans were able to trounce their opponents by means of their superior performance, despite a vast imbalance of numbers.

German field headquarters were kept small and well forward so as to maintain close contact with subordinate commanders, who in turn used experienced officers as their liaison links with those headquarters. Staff officers were highly trained and able to make quick decisions, for their philosophy was that the unexpected could always happen and one must be able to react decisively. Consequently there was a high degree of personal contact and mutual confidence in the command structure. For instance, it was the normal practice for newly appointed divisional generals and their chiefs of staff to attend a General Staff command course so as to practise working as a team before assuming their roles. The reason for this was that, although the commander took final responsibility, his chief of staff issued orders in his general's name and was entitled to make command decisions on his own authority when the general was away from headquarters. Also, the system of *Auftragstaktik* (mission-oriented command) left decisions as to how a given objective was to be achieved to the subordinate commander, thus achieving maximum flexibility of response to any given situation.[17]

However, on 21 January 1945 Hitler issued a Führer-Order severely limiting command initiative down to divisional level, and since then he had persistently interfered with the operations of the formations on his doorstep. Part of this Führer-Order read:

> Commanders-in-Chief, Commanding Generals and Divisional Commanders are personally responsible to me for reporting in good time:
>   a. Every decision to carry out an operation movement.
>   b. Every attack carried out in divisional strength and upwards that does not conform with the general directives laid down by the High Command.
>   c. Every offensive action in quiet sectors of the front over and above normal shocktroop activities that is calculated to draw the enemy's attention to that sector.
>   d. Every plan for disengaging or withdrawing forces.
>   e. Every plan for surrendering a position, a local strongpoint or a fortress.

Meanwhile Allied bombing had at last begun to make its mark on the battle front. Railway communications were being seriously disrupted so that supplies were not getting through, and ammunition states were running low. Most serious of all was the lack of motor fuel of all kinds, greatly restricting the number of armoured vehicles available for combat.

Disrupted communications included the troops' mail, which clearly had an effect on their morale. Those whose homes had not already been overrun had the worry of the continued bombing of the cities and the Western Allies encroaching from the west. They saw themselves as the last bastion against the Bolshevik hordes, and all lived in fear of Soviet captivity, for the ever increasing ruthlessness of the conduct of the war on the Eastern Front by both sides gave them little hope of mercy. Soviet atrocities in East Prussia served as a pertinent reminder of this, which Nazi propaganda did not fail to use to goad the troops on.

From the Baltic Sea to the Czech border, the German defences were organized into two army groups. Army Group *Weichsel* (Vistula), under Colonel-General Gotthard Heinrici, had the 4th Panzer Army covering the Oder between Stettin in the north and the mouth of the Finow Canal. From there down to Fürstenberg (today's Eisenhüttenstadt), masking Berlin, came the 9th Army, commanded by General of Infantry Theodor Busse. The final stretch was covered by the 3rd Panzer Army, commanded by General Fritz Herbert Gräser, of Field Marshal Ferdinand Schörner's Army Group *Mitte* (Centre).

In succession, 9th Army had the following formations deployed from north to south: CI Corps, LVI Panzer Corps, XI SS Panzer Corps, the Frankfurt Fortress Garrison of corps size, and V SS Mountain Corps. Next in line came V Corps of 3rd Panzer Army.

NOTES

1. *Soviet Military History Journal*, Moscow, April 1965.
2. Chaney, *Zhukov*, p. 307, quoting Nicolaevsky.
3. Eisenhower, *Crusade in Europe*, pp. 397–403; Montgomery-Hyde, *Stalin*, p. 525; Ziemke, *Battle for Berlin*, p. 64; Seaton, *The Russo-German War*, pp. 562–5.
4. Gosztony, *Der Kampf um Berlin*, p. 122 [quoting John Ehrmann, *Grand Strategy, October 1944–August 1945*, p. 142].
5. Shtemenko, *The Soviet General Staff at War*, pp. 317–18.
6. *Ibid.*, pp. 319–20.
7. Koniev, *Year of Victory*, p. 83.
8. Shtemenko, *The Soviet General Staff at War*, pp. 320–1.
9. Zhukov, *Reminiscences and Reflections*, pp. 346–51; *The Great Patriotic*

War of the Soviet Union [hereafter cited as GPW], pp. 376–8; Erickson, *The Road to Berlin*, pp. 531–5.

10. *GPW*, pp. 88–9; Erickson, *The Road to Berlin*, pp. 535–7. The role of the tank armies after the breakthrough is taken from a map used by General Ivanov in the 1993 film *Der Todeskampf der Reichshauptstadt* [Chronos-Film].

11. Koniev, *Year of Victory*, p. 82.

12. *Ibid.*, pp. 88–9.

13. Rocolle, *Götterdämmmerung – La Prise de Berlin*, p. 14; Guderian, *Panzer Leader*, pp. 323–5.

14. Toland, *The Last Hundred Days*, pp. 1118–19. These bunkers later accommodated the Soviet Army High Command in East Germany.

15. O'Donnell, *The Berlin Bunker*, pp. 40–3.

16. Tessin, *Verbände und Truppen der deutschen Wehrmacht und Waffen-SS*, with additional information on the Volksarmee from Tully. Note that the Germans used Roman numerals for their corps formation titles (including the unusual XXXX for 40) but not for their artillery corps. The Soviets did not use Roman numerals at all.

    Wilke, *Am Rande der Strassen*, states that on 15 March 1945 an instruction was issued dropping the word 'Panzer' from XI SS Panzer Corps' title and the word 'Mountain' from V SS Mountain Corps' title, but it appears that this was not implemented, as the formations concerned are referred to by their full titles in contemporary documents, as used in this text.

17. Timmons, 'Command and Control in the Wehrmacht'.

TWO

BREACHING THE
ODER–NEISSE DEFENCES

Simultaneously launching their attacks at 0500 hours Moscow time, 0300 hours local time, on 16 April 1945, the two Soviet fronts fought from widely differing base lines, with equally differing techniques, but both using enormous fire-power.

Marshal Zhukov's main blow was struck from an established bridgehead across a flat valley bottom to reach the bulk of the German defences strung out along the barrier of the 100-foot high Seelow Heights. To give himself an extra two hours of daylight in which to achieve his objectives, Zhukov had mustered 143 searchlights with a view to guiding and lighting the way for the advancing troops while blinding the enemy. Unfortunately, he had not tried out their use in conjuction with an artillery barrage. The result was night-blindness among his own troops, who were then silhouetted to the enemy against a milky mist. Furthermore, the opening barrage directed on the German forward positions was equally counter-productive, for Colonel-General Gotthardt Heinrici, the army group commander and an expert on such defensive operations, had correctly calculated the time of the attack and had had these positions evacuated during the night, so the damage caused by the bombardment only served to hamper the Soviet advance.

Marshal Koniev's attack, on the other hand, involved an assault river crossing, and his lengthy opening barrage set fire to the woods on the far bank, to the added distress of the defence. With the coming of daylight, he then had aircraft lay a smokescreen for a considerable distance up and down the river in order to conceal the actual crossing points, and by the end of the day his infantry had advanced 13 kilometres on a 29-kilometre front.

In his memoirs, Zhukov provided a detailed description of this first day of battle:

By about 1300 hours [Moscow Time] It was clear to me that the enemy defences on the Seelow Heights were still relatively intact and that we would be unable to take the Seelow Heights with the order of battle with which we had commenced the attack.

After seeking the advice of the army commanders, we decided to commit to battle both tank armies, in order to reinforce the attacking troops and ensure a breakthrough of the enemy defences.

At about 1500 hours I called Headquarters and reported that we had breached the first and second enemy lines of defence and that the Front had advanced up to six kilometres, but had encountered serious resistance from the Seelow Heights, where the enemy defences appeared to be largely intact. In order to reinforce the all-arms armies, I had committed both tank armies to battle. I went on to report that in my opinion we would breach the enemy defences by the end of the next day.

Stalin listened attentively to me and then said calmly, 'The enemy defences on Koniev's Front have proved to be weaker. He crossed the Neisse without difficulty and is now advancing without encountering any resistance of note. Support your tank armies' attack with bombers. Call me this evening and tell me how things develop.'

That evening I reported to him the difficulties we were experiencing on the approaches to the Seelow Heights, and said that it would not be possible for us to take these Heights before next evening. This time Stalin was not as calm as during my first telephone call.

'You should not have committed the 1st Guards Tank Army in the 8th Guards Army's sector, but rather where the Headquarters wanted.' Then he added: 'Are you sure you will take the positions on the Seelow Heights tomorrow?' Forcing myself to remain calm, I replied: 'Tomorrow, on the 17th April, the enemy defences on the Seelow Heights will be breached by evening. I believe that the more troops the enemy throws against us here, the quicker we will take Berlin, for it is easier to defeat the enemy on an open field than in a fortified city.'

'We will instruct Koniev to move Rybalko's and Lelyushenko's tank armies on Berlin from the south, and Rokossovsky to hurry his river crossing over the Oder and at the same time to strike past Berlin from the north,' Stalin said.

I replied: 'Koniev's tank armies are certainly in a position to make a rapid advance, and should be directed on Berlin. On the other hand, Rokossovsky will not be able to start his offensive from the Oder before the 23rd April, because he will not be able to manage the crossing of the Oder so quickly.'

'Goodbye!' said Stalin dryly, and rang off.[1]

Stalin was not to speak to Zhukov again during the course of the breakthrough battle, an obvious sign of his extreme displeasure with the way things were going. Marshal Zhukov was in deep trouble, and he knew it.

Despite the overall advance that could be claimed, the second day of battle proved as difficult for the 1st Byelorussian Front as the day before, with the casualty toll continuing to mount alarmingly. The rear areas had to be combed for any personnel capable of being redeployed as infantry to fill the gaps in the forward units, and concern at the consequences of the errors made in the planning and execution of this operation grew.[2]

The afternoon of the second day of battle saw the 1st Ukrainian Front's two tank armies successfully fording the Spree. That evening Koniev reported to GHQ by high frequency telephone from his advance command post, later to become his main headquarters, in Schloss Branitz on the southern outskirts of Cottbus, as he later related:

I was finishing my report when Stalin suddenly interrupted me and said:

'With Zhukov things are not going so well yet. He is still breaking through the defences.'

After saying this, Stalin fell silent. I also kept silent and waited for him to continue. Then Stalin asked unexpectedly:

'Couldn't we, by redeploying Zhukov's mobile troops, send them against Berlin through the gap formed in the sector of your Front?'

I heard out Stalin's question and told him my opinion:

'Comrade Stalin, this will take too much time and will add considerable confusion. There is no need to send the armoured troops of the 1st Byelorussian Front into the gap we have made. The situation at our Front is developing favourably, we have enough forces and we can turn both tank armies towards Berlin.'

After saying that, I specified the direction in which the tank armies would be turned and, as a reference point, named Zossen, a little town 25 kilometres south of Berlin and, according to our information, the Nazi GHQ.

'What map are you using for your report?' Stalin asked.

'The 1:200,000.'

After a brief pause, during which he must have been looking for Zossen on the map, Stalin said:

'Very good. Do you know that the Nazi General Staff HQ is in Zossen?'

'Yes, I do,' I answered.

'Very good,' he repeated. 'I agree. Turn the tank armies towards Berlin.'[3]

That same night, 17/18 April, Koniev issued the the following orders:

In accordance with the directive from the Supreme High Command, I order:

1. The Commander of the 3rd Guards Tank Army: on the night of 17 April 1945 the Army will force the Spree and advance rapidly in the general direction of Vetschau, Golssen, Baruth, Teltow and the southern outskirts of Berlin. The task of the Army is to break into Berlin from the south on the night of 20 April 1945.

2. The Commander of the 4th Guards Tank Army: on the night of 17 April 1945 the Army will force the Spree north of Spremberg and advance rapidly in the general direction of Drebkau, Calau, Dahme and Luckenwalde. By the end of 20 April 1945, the Army will capture the area of Beelitz, Treuenbrietzen and Luckenwalde, and on the night of 20 April 1945, Potsdam and the south-western part of Berlin. When turning towards Potsdam the Army will secure the Treuenbrietzen area with the 5th Guards Mechanized Corps. Reconnaissance will be made in the direction of Senftenberg, Finsterwalde and Herzberg.

3. The tanks will advance daringly and resolutely in the main direction. They will bypass towns and large communities and not engage in protracted frontal fighting. I demand a firm understanding that the success of the tank armies depends on the boldness of the manoeuvre and swiftness of the operation.

Point 3 is to be impressed upon the minds of the corps and brigade commanders.

Execution of the above orders will be reported.[4]

General Theodor Busse, commanding the German 9th Army, was aware of Koniev's success to his south. He later wrote of this:

On the evening of 17 April there was already a threat to our own far southern flank, which in a short time became such as to cause a withdrawal. Again HQ 9th Army, fully supported by Army Group, tried to reach the OKH with the plea that, because of the 9th Army's situation and in order to be able to hold on firmly to the boundary with the 3rd Panzer Army, it would be necessary to pull back before the front collapsed. All that the 9th Army got back was Hitler's sharp order to hold on to its front and to re-establish the position at the critical points with counterattacks.[5]

The third day of battle saw an improvement in the progress of Zhukov's troops, but at heavy cost once more. A German counterattack on the main line of advance, in which considerable casualties had been inflicted on the armour and infantry congesting the one road, pointed to a lack of pre-planning with regard to traffic control and infantry–tank cooperation, which was corrected by the issue of new orders that night. Then, on the fourth day, 9th Army's last lines of defence opposite Berlin were breached in two places and Zhukov's troops poured through, three days behind schedule. The Soviets had won, but the cost had been horrific, with an admitted 33,000 dead, but possibly more than twice as many, and 743 tanks and SPGs destroyed, that is one in four of those deployed, or the equivalent of an entire tank army. Moreover, the troops were exhausted.

Zhukov was obliged to revise his plans for the next phase,

the taking of Berlin. The 1st Guards Tank Army and the 8th Guards Army would continue as a combined force on the direct line along Reichsstrasse 1 to the city under Colonel-General Vassilii I. Chuikov, and there swing south over the Spree and Dahme rivers to encompass the southern suburbs along an arc extending from the Spree to the Havel. The primary objective was set as the Reichstag building, a distinctive, independently standing structure, still easily identifiable amid the chaos at the centre of the ruined city. Fate would determine which formation would actually take the building, for all the formations surrounding the city, except the 47th Army guarding the western flank, would be competing under front supervision. Zhukov was aware that Stalin had given his rival Koniev permission to send his tank armies towards Berlin on the night of 17 April, but still expected to have the city to himself, and part of Chuikov's task was to ensure this.[6]

On the German side, 9th Army had just been shattered for the second time in three months, all the reserves had been burnt up, some 12,000 men had been killed in the four days of fighting, and there was now no chance of re-establishing any force capable of standing up to the Soviet onslaught. LVI Panzer Corps was being driven back on Berlin in the centre, and was trying to make for the bridges across the Spree in the south-eastern corner of the city and so rejoin the bulk of the parent 9th Army, while in the north CI Corps was withdrawing northwards behind the temporary safety of the Finow Canal.

Hitler's insistence that 9th Army's right wing hold on to the Oder line had prevented any flexibility in the handling of the formations facing the Soviet attack. The bulk of 9th Army was now isolated south of the main thrust on Berlin and physically incapable of preventing the Soviet advance. General Busse summarized this last day in his postwar study:

The fighting on 19 April created a further yawning gap in the army's front. It was impossible to close the gaps. The wrestling by the army group and the [9th] Army for approval to break off had no success. The [9th] Army had decided that the LVI Panzer Corps should withdraw towards the Spree west of Fürstenwalde and east of Erkner so as to cover the XI SS Panzer Corps' left flank, and for the LVI Panzer Corps to cut away from the Spree sector east of Fürstenwalde/Erkner so that with them as a flank guard the Oder front could swing away south of Berlin.[7]

Clearly none of the German formation commanders involved had any intention of taking the battle into Berlin and defending the city by street fighting. They had fought the decisive battle and lost; now they were primarily concerned with preserving their remaining forces by maintaining a fighting front against the Soviets. However, a proper appreciation of the situation leading to an independent decision on a course of action was hampered by the current command structure and the limitations imposed on them by the system. But the critical point had been reached where the individual commanders had to accept that the regime was finished and that there was no longer any point in trying to continue the struggle, whatever orders might still come from above. The basic problem here was one of conscience in view of the seriousness with which the soldier's oath of allegiance was generally regarded, in this case the oath of loyalty to Adolf Hitler as head of state. Consequently, subsequent actions by many German commanders were to be dogged by individual struggles of conscience, bringing delays at considerable expense to their commands.

Meanwhile Koniev's tank armies, backed by three-quarters of Colonel-General S.A. Krasovsky's 2nd Air Army's aircraft, continued to make steady progress northward, although not fast enough to satisfy Koniev who was still hoping to get into

Berlin ahead of Zhukov. Apart from a few local Volkssturm units, there were no troops around to oppose the Soviets in this area and yet Colonel-General P.S. Rybalko's 3rd Guards Tank Army, concerned about the German forces on its right flank, made only about thirty kilometres on the 19th, in comparison with the fifty kilometres made by Colonel-General D.D. Lelyushenko's 4th Guards Tank Army. Koniev sent Colonel-General N.P. Pukhov's 13th Army to follow them up and secure their flanks and lines of communication.[8]

A member of the 4th Guards Tank Army commented:

> We forced the Neisse and Spree, reached Spremberg, Calau and Dahme. Everywhere we came across German refugees, but mostly prisoners of war and forced labourers from many countries, all asking for something to eat. We gave them what food we had.[9]

This advance by Koniev's forces had isolated V Corps from the remainder of 4th Panzer Army, so that on the evening of 19 April it was transferred to General Busse's command. Busse immediately ordered it to leave only a light screen in its positions along the Neisse and to cover his rear with a line of defence from north of Lübben to Halbe. He also took its 21st Panzer Division under his direct command, sending it to establish a line of defence along the chain of lakes between Teupitz and Königs Wusterhausen. However, this division had been seriously fragmented in the previous fighting, and the headquarters element under Lieutenant-General Werner Marcks brought little with it apart from Major Brand's 21st Armoured Reconnaissance Battalion, Artillery Regiment *Tannenberger* and some elements of the 192nd Panzergrenadier Regiment. Battlegroup *von Luck*, consisting of Colonel *von Luck*'s 125th Panzergrenadier Regiment and the remaining Panthers of the 22nd Panzer Regiment, was still engaged in the southern part of V Corps' area.[10]

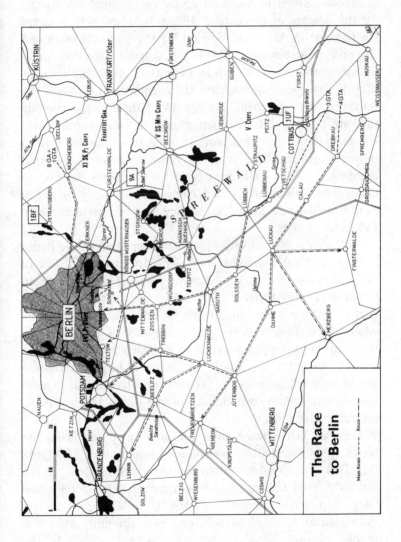

The Race to Berlin

Main Route ---- Recce ----

Hitler's 56th birthday, 20 April 1945, was the day he belatedly decided to make Army Group *Weichsel* responsible for the defence of the capital. Heinrici immediately assigned the task to 9th Army, but General Busse argued the point and the order was rescinded, the Berlin Defence Area remaining directly under Army Group Headquarters. With the remains of 9th Army coiling back on themselves in the south, the only resource now available was LVI Panzer Corps, already fully stretched and in imminent danger of losing contact with the formations on either side. In Heinrici's opinion, Hitler's instructions for 9th Army to remain on the Oder had condemned it to extinction and he therefore decided to concentrate upon saving 3rd Panzer Army north of Berlin from a similar fate, in essence leaving the problem of Berlin to LVI Panzer Corps.[11]

As a means of compensating for the depletion of the Berlin garrison, the *Friedrich Ludwig Jahn* Infantry Division of Reichsarbeitsdienst (RAD – Labour Service) personnel from General Walter Wenck's 12th Army was reassigned to the Berlin Defence Area but no one in Berlin seemed to know where the division was, or what it consisted of, and such was the state of communications that despatch riders had to be sent out to find it. Eventually the divisional headquarters was traced to a village north of Trebbin and Lieutenant-General Helmuth Reymann, commander of the Berlin Defence Area, set out to visit it.[12]

Koniev's forces were now approaching rapidly from the south against negligible opposition.[13] A column of 360 tanks and 700 other vehicles was reported moving north up the autobahn past Lübben.[14] Colonel-General Rybalko remained very concerned about his 3rd Guards Tank Army's vulnerability to flank attack, and kept dropping off road-blocks to seal off the Spreewald pocket, much to the annoyance of Koniev, who sent him the following signal:

> Comrade Rybalko, you are moving like a snail. One brigade is fighting, the rest of the army standing still. I order you to cross the Baruth–Luckenwalde line through the swamps along several routes and deployed in battle order. Report fulfilment. Koniev.[15]

With Koniev's exhortations urging it on, 3rd Guards Tank Army succeeded in covering sixty kilometres on 20 April, taking Baruth during the course of the afternoon and almost reaching Zossen before disaster struck.[16] The leading brigade of 6th Guards Tank Corps ran out of fuel and was then destroyed piecemeal by Panzerfausts.[17]

This occurred close to the Maybach bunker complex, where the bulk of the OKW and OKH staff had anxiously been awaiting permission to evacuate all day. The camp guard company, together with six to eight tanks from the nearby Wünsdorf training establishment, had been sent to block the crossroads at Luckau. By 0600 hours that morning, however, they were already reporting being bypassed by Soviet armour, and by nightfall the twenty survivors of the 250-strong unit were back in Zossen, apparently unaware of the cause of the delay in the Soviet advance. This, presumably, had been due to the intervention of local Volkssturm or Hitlerjugend (Hitler Youth) units.[18]

However, Koniev claimed that the Germans had pitted what he described as a tank training battalion, a brigade of assault guns, three labour and two construction regiments, two flying schools and units of the *Friedrich Ludwig Jahn* Division against his advance on Berlin.[19] The defence in this area is presumed to have been a battlegroup commanded by a Colonel Oertel, to which the 1st Grenadier Regiment of the *Friedrich Ludwig Jahn* Division had been sent by truck after the collapse on the Oder.[20] The tank training battalion he mentions was presumably an ad hoc unit raised by the tank school at Wünsdorf, while the brigade of assault guns would have been a battalion of SPGs, a deliberate misnomer used by the Germans at this stage of the war.

Permission was then received from the *Führerbunker* for the OKW and OKH staff to evacuate, but the staff packed up in such haste that there was no time to destroy any of the documents and equipment left behind, and the Soviets were able to take over these items intact next day. The convoy set off for Wannsee, a south-western suburb of Berlin, at about 1500 hours and immediately came under air attack, losing two of its vehicles. From Wannsee the OKW element was redirected to Krampnitz, north of Potsdam, and the OKH to the Luftwaffe Academy at Gatow. General Krebs moved permanently into the *Führerbunker* with General Wilhelm Burgdorf, Hitler's chief adjutant and head of the Army Personnel Office.[21]

Hans Lehmann witnessed the arrival of 3rd Guards Tank Army in Baruth on 21 April:

As a 14-year-old, I experienced the arrival of Soviet troops in Baruth, which went as follows: a file of tanks on the left, trucks on their right, and *panje* wagons[22] on both pavements.

Then Me 109s came from airfields north of Berlin at about 1530 and 1830 hours and attacked the enemy troops with bombs, cannon and machine-gun fire. Each attack lasted about half an hour, and there was some damage to the buildings on the western side of the main street. Several houses were also deliberately burnt down by the Soviets because they were drunk, careless, or they had pictures of Hitler hanging on the wall.[23]

On the left flank 5th Guards Mechanized Corps of 4th Guards Tank Army came up against some resistance in the Jüterbog–Luckenwalde area but was still able to cover forty-five kilometres in daylight, and one group pushed on through the night for a further thirty-five kilometres, until it reached the southern obstacle belt of the Berlin Defence Area.[24]

Jüterbog was an old garrison town with training areas, rifle ranges, schools of artillery and signals, an ammunition factory and depots, two airfields at Jüterbog Damm and Altes Lager, and military hospitals. The airfields had already been attacked by Soviet aircraft on 18 and 19 April, as had the Fuchsberg barracks complex and the railway workshops on 19 April. Next to the large Werk A ammunition factory was a camp for some 1,600 American, British and Norwegian prisoners of war, and another large camp for forced labourers. Guards Lieutenant Feodor Ivanovitch Shartshinski of the 51st Guards Tank Regiment was to be awarded a posthumous 'Hero of the Soviet Union' decoration after he was shot by the camp guards while attempting to liberate the labour camp with eight other scouts on 22 April.[25]

It seems that, while 11th Guards Mechanized Brigade was left to subdue the town, 13th Guards Mechanized Brigade was ordered to push on northwards to Luckenwalde, while the orders given to 10th Guards Mechanized Brigade on 20 April read:

To take the village of Niebel on the morning of 22 April and, in the second half of that day, the town of Treuenbrietzen by a flank attack. A firm defence is then to be established in the area Niebel–Treuenbrietzen.[26]

That evening, 20 April, General Reymann returned to Berlin with the news that the *Friedrich Ludwig Jahn* Division, while forming up on the parade ground at the Wehrmacht's main ammunition depot at Jüterbog that day, had been surprised and scattered by Soviet tanks. Some of the men from the two infantry regiments had been saved but nearly all the artillery had been lost and the divisional commander, Colonel Klein, had been captured.

Shortly afterward General Krebs telephoned instructions to send this division together with the Wünsdorf Tank Unit to drive back the Soviet spearheads approaching Berlin from the south. These *Führerbunker* orders, committing the remains of two badly shattered regiments and a handful of tanks that had already been destroyed to repulse two tank armies, Reymann could only ignore, and he ordered the survivors back to Potsdam.[27]

Meanwhile General Busse was trying to cover the exposed northern flank of his truncated 9th Army as best he could. A Soviet thrust on Fürstenwalde threatened the rear of XI SS Panzer Corps, whose 169th and 712th Infantry Divisions, together with the Frankfurt Garrison, were still trying to hold on to their forward positions east of the Spree. Busse only had the remains of the *Kurmark* and *Nederland* SS Panzergrenadier Divisions to cover this exposed sector and to counter the Soviet thrusts along his front. Inevitably the infantry divisions began to reel back to the south-west as the situation rapidly deteriorated, while the Panzergrenadier divisions fought to keep the escape routes open over the Spree east of Fürstenwalde. In order to cover the Spree west of this point, part of the 32nd SS Volunteer Grenadier Division *30. Januar* was pulled out of the line to establish a screen from Fürstenwalde to the Müggelsee (lake) south of the Oder–Spree Canal – Spree River barrier.[28]

Frieda Schulze, a farmer's wife, described what it was like in one of the villages in the path of the fighting:

> Early in the afternoon on 20 April a leaflet was passed from house to house in Radeland with the following information: 'Route 96 is occupied by Russian troops. Not possible to get through, you have to flee through the woods.'
>
> We quickly packed the most important items and fled into the woods together, not knowing where we should go. We spent a night there. During that night German infantry went past us in a westerly direction. We asked one of the

Radelanders whether we could come with them and got the reply: 'You must be tired of life!'

When we went back the following day, 21 April, we found Soviet soldiers already in the village. White flags had been raised the previous day instead of the Swastika for Hitler's birthday. From that day the fighting at Radeland kept flaring up and was sometimes heavy. The village changed hands three times. Early each day and in the evenings I left our shelter in the cellar and went out into the yard to feed the cows, which were all there and only driven away by Soviet soldiers when the fighting was over. One day German soldiers were living in our potato cellar, and the next day Soviet soldiers. The worst time for the fighting was 25 and 26 April, when the barns of Farmers Brückmann and Piesker went up in flames as a result of a Soviet air attack.[29]

NOTES

1. Zhukov, *Reminiscences and Reflections*, pp. 366–7.
2. Ziemke, *Battle for Berlin*, p. 83.
3. Koniev, *Year of Victory*, p. 105.
4. *Ibid.*, pp. 197–8.
5. Busse, 'Die letzte Schlacht der 9. Armee', p. 165.
6. Chuikov, *The End of the Third Reich*, p. 164.
7. Busse, 'Die letzte Schlacht der 9. Armee', p. 165.
8. Koniev, *Year of Victory*, pp. 111–12.
9. V.A. Roldugin, quoted in the Kreisleitung Jüterbog booklet, p. 50.
10. Von Luck, *Gefangener meiner Zeit*, p. 272, Tieke, *Das Ende zwischen Oder und Elbe*, pp. 144, 171; Gosztony, *Der Kampf um Berlin*, p. 207 [citing Steiner, *Die Freiwilligen*, p. 228].
11. Gosztony, *Der Kampf um Berlin*, pp. 228–9, including quotation from *Der grundlegende Befehl des Führers vom 21. April 1945* (National Archives, Washington DC).
12. Kuby, *The Russians and Berlin 1945*, p. 105 (quoting Colonel Refior, an officer of the Berlin Defence Area staff); Tieke, *Das Ende zwischen Oder und Elbe*, p. 214.

    Six months' service with the Reichsarbeitsdienst was a statutory preliminary to military service and included generous amounts of drill, marching and discipline in its programme. Towards the end of the war, RAD units were inevitably armed and incorporated into the military.

13. Novikov, 'The Air Forces in the Berlin Operation', p. 93. 'We did not know that the enemy had so few troops to defend this boundary and expected strong opposition.'

14. Kortenhaus, *Der Einsatz der 21. Panzer-Division*, p. 131.

15. Zhukov, *Reminiscences and Reflections*, p. 609 – but not mentioned in Koniev!

16. Koniev, *Year of Victory*, p. 115.

17. Some 40 years later at Spandau Allied Prison the author discussed this episode with Soviet Army officers, who regarded this incident as common knowledge.

18. Tieke, *Das Ende zwischen Oder und Elbe*, p. 184, says that there was about a battalion of clerks and drivers from Zossen and three tank-hunting brigades mounted on bicycles, whom he presumes were Hitler Youth units.

19. Koniev, *Year of Victory*, p. 122.

20. Gellermann, *Die Armee Wenck*, p. 35.

21. Gosztony, *Der Kampf um Berlin*, pp. 193–5 [citing Gerhard Boldt's *Die letzten Tage der Reichskanzlei*, p. 49]; Ryan, *The Last Battle*, p. 234; Schramm, *Kriegestagesbuch des OKW*, pp. 1289, 1438–9; Tieke, *Das Ende zwischen Oder und Elbe*, p. 147, says originally twelve tanks had set off from the Kummersdorf Training Area nearby.

22. The horse-drawn cart used by the Soviets to carry the soldiers' personal gear.

23. Schulze, *Der Kessel Halbe–Baruth–Radeland*, pp. 29–30.

24. Kuby, *The Russians and Berlin 1945*, p. 97; Koniev, *Year of Victory*, p. 115.

25. Kreisleitung Jüterbog booklet, pp. 12–15.

26. *Ibid.*, p.12 [citing Major-General A.P. Riasanski, *Im Feuer der Panzerschlachten*, Moscow, 1975, p. 179 ff.].

27. Refior Berlin Diaries, p. 20, Federal Military Archives Freiburg, RH 53-3-24; Koniev, *Year of Victory*, p. 122; Tieke, *Das Ende zwischen Oder und Elbe*, p. 183; Gellermann, *Die Armee Wenck*, p. 35.

28. Tieke, *Das Ende zwischen Oder und Elbe*, pp. 129–80.

29. Schulze, *Der Kessel Halbe–Baruth–Radeland*, pp. 43, 45.

THREE

9TH ARMY ENCIRCLED

21 APRIL 1945

The opportune arrival of Lieutenant-General A.A. Luchinsky's 28th Army from the 2nd Byelorussian Front on the night of 20 April enabled Koniev to fill the gap between 3rd Guards Tank Army pushing on Berlin and 3rd Guards Army both besieging Cottbus and engaged with the German V Corps beyond it as far north-west as Baruth. He therefore allocated the 28th Army all his available transport with instructions to send one division, the 61st Guards Rifle Division, to the support of the 3rd Guards Tank Army, and to deploy two other rifle divisions in the woods around Baruth by the evening of 21 April. The rest of the army was to deploy between Zossen and Baruth by 23 April. This screening force was to block off 9th Army's exit routes with strong defences against tanks and infantry to thwart any possible break-out to the west or south-west. Koniev was also very conscious of the vulnerability of his tank armies on the main communications route, the Dresden– Berlin autobahn.

Baruth, the nodal traffic point on the east–west flow of the Baruther Urstromtal (glacial valley) with its swamps and streams, was recognized as the critical exit point for a German break-out from the Spreewald.[1]

Much as he would have liked to concentrate on Berlin, Koniev had other urgent responsibilities, as he described:

35

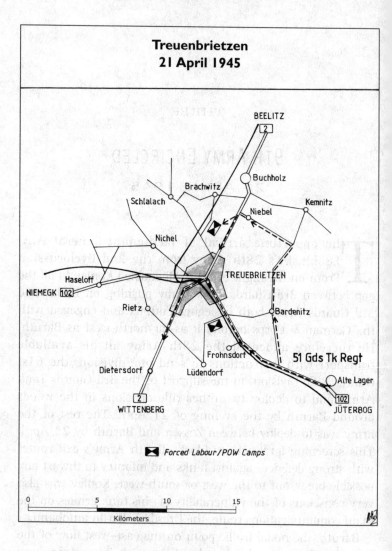

Treuenbrietzen
21 April 1945

BEELITZ
2

Buchholz

Brachwitz

Schlalach

Kemnitz

Niebel

Nichel

TREUEBRIETZEN

Haseloff

NIEMEGK 102

Rietz

Bardenitz

Frohnsdorf

51 Gds Tk Regt

Dietersdorf

Lüdendorf

Alte Lager

2

WITTENBERG

102

JÜTERBOG

⚔ *Forced Labour/POW Camps*

0   5   10   15

Kilometers

The difficulty of my position, as commander of the front, was that operations were developing simultaneously in several directions and each of these directions required attention and supervision. Fighting for Cottbus was still going on in the north, while in the centre, after the liquidation of the Spremberg area of resistance, our troops were confidently advancing towards Berlin and the Elbe. On our left flank, however, in the Dresden direction, we were still having a hard time of it, and this distracted me very much from our main attack.

Koniev was also responsible for 6th Army besieging Breslau well in his rear, but there he could urge restraint. He also sent his Chief of Staff, General Petrov, to deal with his problems on the southern flank.[2]

By evening the leading elements of 3rd Guards Tank Army had come close to the outer sections of the Berlin Defence Area, and some of their scouts reached Königs Wusterhausen from the south, thereby effectively completing the encirclement of the German 9th Army. Although, as they were on the other side of the water complex from Colonel-General Chuikov's 8th Guards Army, the troops of the two Soviet fronts remained unaware of their proximity to each other.[3]

Meanwhile 4th Guards Tank Army's 5th Guards Mechanized Corps continued to be heavily engaged in the Jüterbog area. The vanguard of 10th Guards Mechanized Brigade, having bypassed the town through the woods to the north during the night, reached the northern perimeter of the Altes Lager at daybreak and was met by fire from anti-tank guns, SPGs and Panzerfaust-armed infantry, which were shortly reinforced by the arrival of a troop of tanks coming from Treuenbrietzen. The brigade commander, Colonel V.N. Buslaiev, then sent off 51st Guards Tank Regiment to secure the right flank in the Niebel– Treuenbrietzen area, while the main body engaged the Altes Lager defences. These were overrun by the end of the morning with Soviet claims of four German tanks and two armoured personnel carriers (APCs) destroyed. Some large camps were then discovered nearby containing prisoners of war and forced labourers from Russia, Poland and France.

The local Volkssturm units, which had been deployed in defence of Treuenbrietzen the previous evening, disbanded themselves on the morning of 21 April, leaving the town's anti-tank barriers open and unguarded. The first of 51st Guards Tank Regiment's tanks arrived at 1700 hours and by 1900 hours twelve had passed through the town heading for Wittenberg with about a company of infantry on board. The inhabitants had expected American, not Russian troops, and some had already hung American flags from their windows, but these were soon replaced with white ones when the locals realized the identity of the intruders. Some elements of the *Friedrich Ludwig Jahn* Division, which were in the town, hastily withrew to the western outskirts after losing an SPG and then came under Soviet artillery and mortar fire. They then mounted a counterattack, but this was repulsed with the loss of two tanks.

While this was going on, another part of Lieutenant-Colonel E.I. Grebennikov's 51st Guards Tank Regiment took Niebel without a fight that afternoon after having bypassed Treuenbreitzen well to the east.[4]

On 3rd Guards Tank Army's line of advance on 21 April 1945 we have this account from Willi Klär, from Kummersdorf Gut, where the German Army's main artillery testing ranges were located. The complex included barracks, workshops, stores, a secret atomic and chemical warfare research laboratory complex, its own railway station and sidings, as well as some military and civilian accommodation. However, apart from the military families living on site, most of the civilians employed here lived in the main village, a new settlement resulting from the increased activity arising from

Hitler's military expansion and located a kilometre away to the north-east off the Sperenberg road. (This should not be confused with the main village of Kummersdorf, which lies immediately beyond Sperenberg several kilometres north of the military installation, although 'Kummersdorf' to most German soldiers meant the ranges at Kummersdorf Gut.)

Our village was spared the bombing attacks on Berlin. Only once an aerial mine landed near the railway level crossing near Schönefeld village and some incendiaries landed between the water tower, market garden, barracks and our village, but did little damage. The aircraft came from the direction of Luckenwalde, where they had dropped some bombs. A house and seven barns were set on fire in the nearby village of Horstwalde by incendiaries dropped by the same aircraft.

There were no proper air raid shelter facilities for those living in the village or near the ranges, only the cellars of their houses and some slit trenches covered with concrete slabs and sand. There was one in front of the old folks' home. The constant air alerts were frightful and made the people exhausted, putting their nerves on edge.

On 20 April 1945 all the men and youths still remaining in the village were rounded up to stop the advance of the Red Army, which had already reached Baruth. During the night of 20/21 April the Volkssturm had to dig foxholes in the cleared ground beyond Lindestrasse, Birkenallee and Am Ring. They were supposed to stop the tanks with their rifles.

Soldiers were deployed on the ranges from the forest warden's lodge, where the command post was located, along the main road to Schönefeld. The first enemy tanks approached the Königsgraben on the Horstwalde road early on the morning of 21 April.

An engine-less Tiger tank and a 75-mm anti-tank gun had been deployed in defence of the bridge over the

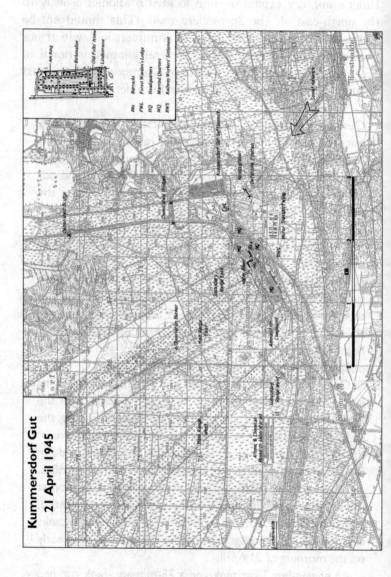

**Kummersdorf Gut
21 April 1945**

Königsgraben but, after a brief exchange of fire, the crews abandoned them in face of the overwhelming numbers of the enemy.

None of the modern weapons being tested on the ranges were brought into use on 21 April, or our losses would have been even greater.

The soldiers deployed on the ranges also abandoned their positions after a short exchange of fire. Most of the local inhabitants who had been deployed in the defence outside the village were captured. Some died a hero's death and a few were able to escape, withdrawing to the Elbe, only to return home a few weeks later exhausted and half-starved.

Some of the ammunition stores were blown up as the Red Army approached on 21 April, as were the two industrial railway bridges over the main line to Sperenberg, and the industrial railway bridge over the main road to Sperenberg, in order to check the advance.

Three teenage youths, a young woman and four men over normal military age were killed during the fighting on 21 April. Most of the women and children had already fled on the evening of 20 April, or in the early hours of 21 April, to the observation bunker on the east range and remained there for a few days, returning to their homes once things had quietened down.[5]

Orders from Hitler for 9th Army, which were received by Heinrici at 1720 hours, were to hold on to the existing defensive line from Cottbus to Fürstenberg, and from there to curve it back via Müllrose to Fürstenwalde. At the same time a strong front was to be established between Königs Wusterhausen and Cottbus, from which repeated, vigorous and coordinated attacks were to be made, in cooperation with 12th Army, on the deep flank of the Soviet forces attacking Berlin from the south.[6]

General Busse's Spreewald concentration now became a focus of round the clock attention for Air Chief Marshal A.A. Novikov, who devoted a large part of the resources of his 2nd, 16th and 18th Air Armies to the harassment of the 9th Army pocket, with as many as 60 to 100 aircraft in action at a time.[7]

With 9th Army were tens of thousands of refugees from Germany's eastern provinces who had been camping out in the woods since their arrival in the area during the winter. The Nazi Party authorities had been reluctant to initiate evacuation for fear of being accused of defeatism, with the consequence that civilians continued to remain in the combat area until the Soviet onslaught caught them out, as General Busse himself complained.[8] However, fear of the Soviet invaders led to evacuation on a vast scale where no stable front existed, as in the preceding winter when the Soviet forces had swept across from the Vistula to the Oder. Many of the refugees seeking shelter in the Spreewald came from the part of Germany east of the Oder, including the Warthegau province, part of which had been seized from Poland in 1939 and re-settled with ethnic Germans from the Baltic states, other parts of Poland, Bessarabia and Romania.[9] Organising themselves in community-related treks, these refugees took what they could of their worldly possessions in horse-drawn wagons, or pulled them along in the four-wheeled type of handcart then common to German households for conveying heavy loads. The refugees were mainly women, children and the elderly, all able men of military age having long since been taken into the armed forces, and all others up to the age of 60 having more recently been conscripted into the Volkssturm.

In February 1945 the Nazi Party authorities had established a system for passing these refugees on, allowing them to stay overnight in the villages on their route but having them move on by 1000 hours the next day, only those who had fallen ill being allowed to remain. Halbe itself was accommodating about 1,000 refugees per night.[10] It seems that a large number of those who had no relatives to head for, or who had chosen not to leave their fate to the authorities, had decided to camp out in the comparative safety of the Spreewald.

With the collapse of the 9th Army front, the number of existing refugees was greatly augmented by those fleeing their homes from the Fürstenwalde–Frankfurt–Cottbus area as the troops withdrew. Although there was sufficient food for everyone, internal communications rapidly deteriorated, and troops and civilians became hopelessly mixed in their predicament as the perimeter of the pocket contracted. Ammunition and fuel were in particularly short supply and when the artillery began running out of shells on 21 April, Colonel-General Heinrici at Army Group *Weichsel* advised General Busse to find some means of disengaging from the Soviet forces and to forget Hitler's orders about holding on to the Oder.[11]

Consequently, General Busse started making preparations for a break-out as suggested by Heinrici. The redisposition of the newly acquired V Corps was part of his plan. As soon as the Frankfurt garrison could withdraw into his lines, V Corps and V SS Mountain Corps were to start a simultaneous withdrawal from their Oder/Neisse positions in two bounds, going back on either side of Friedland to the line Staupitz–Beeskow–junction of the Spree and the Oder–Spree Canal.[12]

The imminent danger to his northern flank caused Busse to decide to use Colonel-General Helmuth Weidling's LVI Panzer Corps with the SS Panzergrenadier Divisions *Nordland* and *Nederland* to establish a screen along the line of the Spree west of Fürstenwalde, behind which those of his formations still on the Oder could withdraw westwards, but he was unable to bring himself to issue the necessary orders as this would have been in defiance of Hitler.[13] He thus remained dependent upon the thinly spread 32nd SS Volunteer

Grenadier Division's battlegroup deployed south of the Spree to cover his north-west flank.

Part of Lieutenant-General Werner Marcks' scattered 21st Panzer Division arrived opportunely in the Halbe area, and was sent to establish a new line of defence along the chain of lakes between Teupitz and Königs Wusterhausen facing west. As the men drove north through the Spreewald, they caught glimpses of the Soviet forces moving parallel to them on the autobahn. Marcks only had with him what remained of the 1st, 5th and Workshop Companies of the 22nd Panzer Regiment, Major Brand's 21st Armoured Reconnaissance Battalion, the two battalions of the 125th Panzergrenadier Regiment and the 1st Company of the 192nd Panzergrenadiers, elements of the 220th Armoured Engineer Battalion, the staff and two battalions of the 155th Armoured Artillery Regiment *Tannenberger*, and the 305th Army Flak Battalion.[14] The remains of the 10th SS Armoured Reconnaissance Battalion *Frundsberg*, which was following these elements of 21st Panzer Division, then took up north-facing defensive positions just outside Königs Wusterhausen.[15]

Ernst-Christian Gädtke, then serving with the 32nd SS Tank-Hunting Battalion in Riessen, near Fürstenberg, gives us some idea of the atmosphere in the ranks as 9th Army's withdrawal began:

> At 0500 hours we were alerted and ordered to prepare to move off. As we packed up the rumours started flying around. The Russians were said to be before Berlin.
>
> At roll-call we were given no explanations as usual, only confirmation that the Russians were before Berlin and that we were to defend it. We left at 0530 hours for Fürstenwalde and Rauen.
>
> In the damp, foggy, early spring morning, our tank-hunting company with its four assault guns rattled off to the west, complete with the supply section.

After the highly-charged garrulousness of the previous day, a grim silence now reigned. The speech had been knocked out of us, and the silence was quite profound. No one dared say what he was thinking or feared, as everyone now accepted the terrible truth that defeat was inevitable. Nevertheless, the step in thinking from foreboding to certainty was one that I did not take. I continued to do what I had been doing for so long now, as did so many others; I just suppressed what I didn't want to accept.

So our journey to the west was somewhat despairing, grim and silent. The morning was foggy and became cloudy, remaining like that all day. The engines thundered monotonously, the tracks rattled, squeaking and screaming whenever we took a bend. We crouched down dumb and grim-faced in our hatches. The gun was overloaded and packed with infantry, who crouched under their tent-halves and clung on as usual. Everything was grey. We drove through villages and small market towns – there, too, everything was dull and grey. People stood on the streets in Müllrose, watching us pass with doubt and uncertainty. Could we have dispelled their anxieties and fears as we passed through, or were we no longer any use as defenders of the fatherland? We should have looked back at them full of confidence, but we couldn't.

By afternoon we were in Rauen. The Russians were said to be already in Fürtstenwalde, north of the Spree.[16]

In his diary, SS-Lieutenant Bärmann of the same unit gave some indication of the confusion arising out of the redeployment on the northern flank of 9th Army that day. He wrote that the battalion command post was first established in Bad Saarow that morning, then moved back east to Alt Golm. He conducted a reconnaissance of the road from Alt Golm to Saarow, finding the route blocked with troops of all kinds who did not know what was ahead of or behind them.

He then drove west to Friedersdorf to try and locate Battlegroup *Krauss* (based on 32nd SS Division's tank-hunting battalion) but it had already moved on. On his way he met SS-Captain Paul Krauss, commander of the battalion, in Niederlehme and went on with him to Wernsdorf.[17]

Behind the lines, Märkisch Buchholz was declared a fortress and prepared for all-round defence. Of vital importance here were the three bridges leading out of the town where the River Dahme connected with the Dahme Flood Canal that helped drain the Upper Spreewald. One was on the Halbe road next to the weir on the upper stretch of the canal and two across the lower stretch leading into the Hammer Forest, one of which carried Reichstrasse 179.

Meanwhile a Waffen-SS unit occupied Halbe and expressed its intention to defend the village, come what may. The local Volkssturm unit had already prepared an anti-tank barrier on the east–west running high street, and another on the street south leading to Teurow. The inhabitants prepared for the coming fighting, realising that their village lay on the main route to the west. Many prepared dugouts in the woods around, or prepared to take to their cellars, while concealing their valuables by burying them in boxes.[18]

NOTES

1. *GPW*, p. 381; Koniev, *Year of Victory*, pp. 121–2.
2. Koniev, *Year of Victory*, p. 124.
3. *Ibid.*, p. 122.
4. Kreisleitung Jüterbog booklet, pp. 13–19.
5. *Ortschronik von Kummersdorf Gut*, a handwritten document supplied by Rolf Kaim to the author.
6. Lakowski/Stich, *Der Kessel von Halbe 1945*, p. 42 [citing Federal Military Archives 19 XV/10, Sheet 60].
7. Novikov, 'The Air Forces in the Berlin Operation', p. 95; Wagner, *Der 9. Fallschirmjägerdivision*, pp. 355–6.
8. Busse, 'Die letzte Schlacht der 9. Armee', p. 157.

9. Noakes & Pridham, *Nazism 1939–1945*, pp. 935–6.

10. Führling, *Endkampf an der Oderfront*, p. 105.

11. Thorwald, *Das Ende an der Elbe*, pp. 88–9.

12. Lakowski/Stich, *Der Kessel von Halbe 1945*, p. 42 [citing Federal Military Archives 19 XV/10, Sheet 71f].

13. *Ibid.*, pp. 39–40.

14. Kortenhaus, *Der Einsatz der 21. Panzer-Division*, pp. 133–4.

15. Tieke, *Das Ende zwischen Oder und Elbe*, p. 173.

16. Gädtke, *Von der Oder zur Elbe*, pp. 26–7.

17. Tieke, *Das Ende zwischen Oder und Elbe*, pp. 172–3.

18. Führling, *Endkampf an der Oderfront*, p. 105.

FOUR

DESTROY THE 9TH ARMY

22 APRIL 1945

At 1100 hours on Sunday, 22 April, General Heinrici telephoned General Krebs to say that, unless 9th Army was allowed to withdraw, it would be split in two by nightfall. This time his words must have had some effect, for at 1450 hours Krebs telephoned back with permission for the Frankfurt Garrison to abandon the city and fall back on the 9th Army, thus allowing some adjustment to the army's over-extended dispositions.

At this stage the 9th Army's northern flank was still firm from Frankfurt to a Soviet bridgehead north of Fürstenwalde. From there a battlegroup of the 32nd SS Volunteer Grenadier Division *30. Januar* provided a light screen as far as Wernsdorf at the western end of the Oder–Spree Canal.

That evening, with his normal supply routes severed, General Busse sent the following message to Army Group *Weichsel*:

> Last possibility of resupply for the army checked by breach at Grünau. Thus initiated relief measures invalidated. Supply only by air or air drop.[1]

In turn, Army Group *Weichsel* reported the loss of Cottbus after a day's heavy fighting. V Corps' front for two kilometres to the north of there was under heavy pressure, and on 9th Army's northern front the Soviets had reached as far as the Berlin–Frankfurt autobahn. Rapidly diminishing stocks of fuel and ammunition were making things extremely difficult for 9th Army.[2]

LVI Panzer Corps had by now been forced back to the south-eastern corner of Berlin and its troops were already crossing the Spree at Köpenick with a view to rejoining their parent formation. However, during the retreat the corps had lost contact with 9th Army. Turncoat German *Seydlitz-Troops* working for the Soviets had been particularly active during the withdrawal in disseminating false orders for the troops to reassemble at Döberitz, west of Berlin, and other locations outside the city, and the rumour then spread that the corps had withdrawn to Döberitz.[3] When General Busse and Hitler heard of this that evening, they both ordered Weidling's arrest and execution.

At a conference with his divisional and regimental commanders held at his corps headquarters in the eastern suburb of Kaulsdorf, Weidling told them that General Busse had threatened to have him shot if he failed to link up with 9th Army, and that Hitler had threatened him with the same fate if he did not go to the defence of the city. They all agreed that to go into the city would mean the end of the corps, and decided that they should try and hold on to their present positions in the south-eastern suburbs to enable 9th Army to withdraw in their direction.[4] This was an astonishing decision in that the participants were showing an unusually independent line of thought in rejecting the demands of both their superior headquarters and implementing their own solution to 9th Army's predicament. However, this was to come to nothing next day over a point of personal honour, as we shall see.

A further consequence of the *Seydlitz-Troops'* activities was that, when 20th Panzergrenadier Division was later allocated to the defence of the Wannsee area, only 90 men turned up with their divisional commander, the rest having gone on to Döberitz immediately west of Berlin, from where they eventually reformed as an armoured brigade under 3rd Panzer Army. Others were misdirected to regroup at Güterfelde east of Potsdam, and many of those who followed these false orders were caught by the Soviets in Marienfelde.[5]

At 1900 hours Hitler summoned Keitel and Jodl for another conference, at which he formally announced his intention of committing suicide in the event of the city falling to the Soviets, rejecting all their protestations.[6] He then turned to his maps and began discussing possible means of saving the situation. It was agreed that 12th Army had nothing to fear from the Americans, who clearly had no intention of crossing the Elbe, and therefore 12th Army's units could afford to turn their backs on the river and march to the relief of Berlin. Simultaneously 9th Army could send its strongest infantry division westward to meet up with 12th Army, mopping up any Soviet formations encountered on the way, and then make a joint thrust on the capital. Field Marshal Keitel would deliver the orders to General Wenck of 12th Army in person, while Jodl would see to the organization of the OKW staff at Krampnitz in preparation for their move to Plön, from where they would serve both Grand Admiral Dönitz, commanding the German forces in the north, and Hitler. General Krebs would remain as Hitler's military adviser. The conference broke up at about 2000 hours.[7]

The departure of Keitel and Jodl left only General Krebs and his aide, Major Bernd Freiherr Freytag von Loringhoven, representing the General Staff in the *Führerbunker*, so a third officer, Cavalry Captain Gerhard Boldt, was summoned from the OKW at Krampnitz to assist with the preparation of situation reports for presentation to Hitler.[8]

That night Moscow issued a directive ordering 1st Byelorussian and 1st Ukrainian Fronts to surround the German group south-east of Berlin by 24 April at the latest and to prevent 9th Army's forces breaking out towards Berlin or the west by all means. The withdrawal of the bulk of 9th Army into the Spreewald had not been anticipated in the planning for Operation Berlin, so this major development had now to be contended with on the move. A German concentration of this size could not be ignored.

Marshal Koniev reacted the same night, ordering:

• 28th Army will secure its troops standing in front of Berlin with two divisions along the sector Bohnsdorf–Mittenwalde–Teupitz, organize a stable defence to the east, and prevent any attempt by 9th Army to break out through its rear to the west or south-west.
• 3rd Guards Army will attack 9th Army.
• 3rd Guards Tank Army will occupy Buckow (in south-east Berlin) and take measures to link up with the forces of 1st Byelorussian Front in the rear of 9th Army.

To comply with Moscow's instructions, Marshal Zhukov issued the following directive:

• 3rd Army, hitherto in the front's second echelon, is to attack in the direction Wildau–Brusendorf–Jühnsdorf–Michendorf and immediately to secure the sector Gosen (south of Erkner) – Hartmannsdorf (Lower Spreewald) – Winkel (west bank of the Spree).
• 2nd Guards Cavalry Corps is to attack southwards in the direction Busch [Buchholz?] – Leibsch and attain the sector Krausnick–Leibsch–west bank of the Scharmützelsee and, with a front facing east, prevent the forces of 9th Army withdrawing to the west.
• 69th Army is ordered to attack southwards with its right wing, occupy the sector Scharmützelsee–Bad Saarow–Ketschendorf, and prevent a withdrawal of elements of 9th

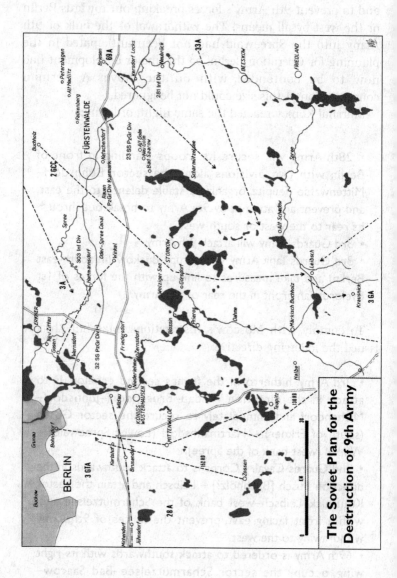

The Soviet Plan for the
Destruction of 9th Army

Army to the west and north-west. Its left wing is to attack in the general direction of Briesen–southern tip of the Scharmützelsee.
• 33rd Army is to attack generally in a south-westerly direction with its right wing on Beeskow–Alt Schadow and tie down the enemy troops by active engagement.[9]

Zhukov's orders to 3rd Army show how totally ignorant he was of Koniev's progress and deployment when he issued them, for occupying the line Wildau–Michendorf was the role he had originally intended for 1st Guards Tank Army in securing the southern approaches to Berlin. On the other hand, Koniev's directive would appear to reflect his preoccupation with the attack on Berlin, in which he was hoping to beat Zhukov to the prize of the Reichstag, whereas Zhukov was now sufficiently confident in his advance on the city centre to allocate resources and plan the destruction of the 'Frankfurt–Guben group' in some detail, while still trying to block Koniev from Berlin.

By pushing forward the bulk of 69th Army, together with 3rd Army from his second echelon, Zhukov was applying pressure on the truncated 9th Army from the north and also protecting the southern flank of his thrust on Berlin. By evening his 3rd Army had a bridgehead across the Spree south of Erkner and was probing down to the Oder–Spree Canal, where the 32nd SS Volunteer Grenadier Division *30. Januar* was hastily trying to establish a defensive screen.[10]

The arrival of advance units of Colonel-General Rybalko's 3rd Guards Tank Army in the southern outskirts of Berlin on 23 April was the high point of Koniev's day. It would take another day for the remainder of the army to catch up and prepare to cross the major obstacle of the Teltow Canal, for which he ordered an attack on the morning of 24 April. In addition to the infantry reinforcements already allocated, he sent 10th Breakthrough Artillery Corps and 25th

Breakthrough and 23rd Anti-Aircraft Artillery Divisions, which were to travel by night to avoid detection. He also allocated 5th Air Fighter Corps of 2nd Air Army in support. In the meantime 3rd Guards Tank Army was to secure the suburb of Buckow on its right flank and to try and establish contact with 1st Byelorussian Front, whose troops were expected in that area.[11]

Koniev had beaten Zhukov to the southern suburbs of Berlin, but he needed to use the 23rd to amass sufficient strength for his attack on the city proper next day, which he intended to supervise in person. A major threat to his lines of communication having been removed with the elimination of the Cottbus defence, 3rd Guards Army was now ordered to turn its attention to the western flank of the German 9th Army.[12]

The redeployment of forces on 9th Army's northern front as a defensive screen proved to be too weak and too late to be effective. Although Battlegroup *Krauss* had reached the Oder–Spree Canal at Wernsdorf and SS-Major Egger's 1st Battalion, 86th SS Grenadier Regiment, had reached Neu Zittau the day before, the Soviets arrived soon afterwards and forced a crossing near Neu Zittau, thus bypassing Wernsdorf and obliging SS-Captain Krauss' troops to fall back on Königs Wusterhausen via Niederlehme.

However, this withdrawal was not all one-sided, as SS-Second Lieutenant Porsch of Tank-Hunting Company *Dora II* of the 500/600th SS Punishment Battalion wrote:

> We still had several nuts to crack, tanks as well as Russian infantry. Ehlers bagged his 14th, Schuler his 12th, myself my 17th, the company its 125th. During a reconnaissance near Neu Zittau we took 30 prisoners, and finally Ehlers and myself captured a Soviet battalion headquarters, 14 officers, including some women.[13]

At the railway station in Königs Wusterhausen *Krauss* found an ambulance train that had already been attacked several times by Soviet aircraft that had no respect for the Red Cross. His own troops were under fire from a column of T-34s that were firing at anything that moved, including civilians trying to help the wounded, so he withdrew to Prieros.[14]

Further east the 561st SS Tank-Hunting Battalion, together with 1st Battalion, SS-Regiment *Falke*, deployed in the Biegen–Pillgram area, launched a counterattack on Rosengarten, opening and holding open a breach in the Soviet cordon around Frankfurt through which the garrison was able to evacuate that night.[15]

NOTES

1. Busse, 'Die letzte Schlacht der 9. Armee', pp. 166–7.
2. Lakowski/Stich, *Der Kessel von Halbe 1945*, p. 50 [citing Federal Military Archives 19 XV/10, Sheet 71f and 19 XV/10, Sitrep of 22 April 45, Sheet 213].
3. Colonel von Dufving, Weidling's chief of staff, told the author that he may inadvertently have been responsible for some of these rumours through having ordered all the corps' non-combatant troops to Döberitz on 18 April.
4. Discussions between the author and Herr Fritz-Rudolf Averdieck and other survivors of the 20th Panzergrenadier Division; Engelmann, *Geschichte der 18. Panzergrenadier Division*, pp. 645–6; Tieke, *Das Ende zwischen Oder und Elbe*, p. 244.
5. Kuby, *The Russians and Berlin 1945*, p. 108; Tieke, *Das Ende zwischen Oder und Elbe*, pp. 216–17; Wagener, *The Soviet Air Forces in World War II*, p. 63.
6. Trevor-Roper, *The Last Days of Hitler*, pp. 160–1; Gorlitz, *The Memoirs of Field Marshal Keitel*, p. 202; Thorwald, *Das Ende an der Elbe*, pp. 116–17.
7. Trevor-Roper, *The Last Days of Hitler*, pp. 161–2; Gorlitz, *The Memoirs of Field Marshal Keitel*, pp. 202–3; Thorwald, *Das Ende an der Elbe*, pp. 118–19.
8. Von Loringhoven interview in the film *Der Todeskampf der Reichshauptstadt* [Chronos-Film].
9. Lakowski/Stich, *Der Kessel von Halbe 1945*, p. 48.

10. *GPW*, p. 381.
11. Koniev, *Year of Victory*, pp. 131–2.
12. *Ibid.*, pp. 128–9, 132.
13. Wilke archives.
14. Tieke, *Das Ende zwischen Oder und Elbe*, pp. 188–91.
15. *Ibid.*, pp. 186, 192.

FIVE

12TH ARMY TO THE RESCUE
23 APRIL 1945

Field Marshal Keitel reached General Wenck's headquarters in the woods east of Magdeburg with some difficulty at about 0100 hours on 23 April. Wenck's 12th Army, whose boundary extended from the junction of the Havel and Elbe Rivers in the north to below Leipzig in the south, consisted of the following formations:

XXXIX Panzer Corps, under Lieutenant-General Karl Arndt, which had been sent into the Harz Mountains to support 11th Army and had been virtually destroyed within five days. Its remnants had only been re-assigned to 12th Army on 21 April.
XXXXI Panzer Corps, under Lieutenant-General Rudolf Holste, which was based near Rathenow, and consisted of miscellaneous units, some of which were survivors of the Rhine battles.
XX Corps, under Lieutenant-General Carl-Erik Koehler, which was currently engaged in containing the minor American bridgeheads near Zerbst and consisted of:
  Theodor Körner RAD Infantry Division
  Ulrich von Hutten Infantry Division
  Ferdinand von Schill Infantry Division
  Scharnhorst Infantry Division
XXXXVIII Panzer Corps, under General Maximilian Freiherr

von Edelsheim, which constituted the army reserve near Coswig, and consisted mainly of miscellaneous units culled from the Leipzig and Halle areas.[1]

Keitel first briefed Wenck on the general situation as he knew it, and then gave him Hitler's orders for 12th Army. Keitel waited for Wenck to draft out his orders, as he wanted to take a copy with him back to the *Führerbunker* and he also wanted to deliver the orders in person to General Koehler's XX Corps, which was to provide the bulk of the attacking force. At dawn he reached one of Koehler's infantry divisions, which was already preparing for the operation, and addressed the assembled officers.[2]

The 12th Army's specific orders read:

By extensively disregarding the Elbe defences between Magdeburg and Dessau and on the Mulde front between Dessau and Grimma, an assault group of at least three divisions is to be formed in the area west and south-west of Treuenbrietzen with the task of striking at the Russian forces attacking Potsdam and the southern outskirts of Berlin along the line Jüterbog–Brück towards Zossen and Teltow ... 9th Army has orders to hold the line Cottbus–Peitz–Beeskow and, if necessary, to keep east of the line Lübbenau–Schwielochsee, in order to release forces for an attack towards Baruth from the east.[3]

What Keitel failed to realize was that Wenck, unlike his immediate superiors, had formed a very clear appreciation of the situation and had no illusions about the future, which he saw as a simple choice between captivity in either the east or the west. There was no doubt in his own mind which was preferable and he regarded his primary task as that of holding a door open for a general exodus from what would become the Soviet Zone of Occupation.

It became obvious to me that this man [Keitel] and with him the Supreme Commander-in-Chief [Hitler], whom he advised, were long since out of touch with what was happening in this war. After consulting with my staff, I decided to go my own way from then on. We had already started to do so some weeks before, when we stopped demolition squads from destroying supply depots in our area. Now, however, was the time to lead the army guided solely by what we knew ourselves. We could not free Berlin with our forces, but we could help vast numbers of people by opening a way to the west for them with a determined attack. By attacking from the Belzig area towards Potsdam, it would be possible to free the 20,000 troops encircled there. It did not seem impossible for 9th Army to get out of its pocket after such a thrust. Apart from this, the columns of refugees moving behind our front to the west would gain a few extra days time in which to reach the Elbe and escape the Russians.[4]

Wenck was fortunate in that many supply barges from all over the country had been trapped and stranded in his sector, so that he had no shortage of supplies, including motor fuel. Although he dutifully reported all this, no attempt was made by the OKW to have this windfall distributed.[5]

By 1100 hours Keitel was back in Krampnitz, where he conferred with Jodl and had a brief rest before they set off for the Chancellery together. At the afternoon war conference Keitel reported to the Führer on his trip and General Krebs announced that 12th Army was already on the move. Hitler asked if 9th and 12th Armies had established contact yet, but there was no information available on this point and Krebs was directed to tell 9th Army to get on with it. Before departing, Keitel again tried, without success, to persuade Hitler to leave Berlin.[6]

This conference clearly illustrates the air of fantasy in

which Hitler and his staff operated and which Keitel did nothing to dispel. He must have been fully aware that neither army was ready to act immediately and yet said nothing to this effect. In fact, Wenck did not expect to be ready until the 25th, by which time his formations would be redeployed for the attack and he hoped to have recovered some of his armour from west of the Elbe to assist him. In the meantime Wenck was acutely conscious of the threat from the south-east, where 1st Ukrainian Front was making rapid progress in his direction.

At 1300 hours the signal authorising 9th Army's withdrawal was sent by Army Group *Weichsel*. General Busse purportedly used this order to implement his own intended and already initiated redeployment towards the west without openly opposing Berlin. To this end, he reported the following measures taken in fulfilment of his task that day:

1. Withdrawal of the eastern and north-eastern fronts on the general line Burg–Butzen–Schwielochsee–Spree in one move during the night of 23/24 April.

2. V Corps to take over command of the eastern front from the right wing (Königs Wusterhausen) to Burg inclusive. V SS Mountain Corps to take over command of the eastern front from Burg to the Kersdorf locks (2 km west of Briesen) . . .

3. Released forces: 342nd Infantry Division, one reinforced battlegroup from 35th SS Police Division (deployed until now north of Guben), one battlegroup from the Frankfurt Fortress Garrison (about two regiments) already with XI SS Panzer Corps. No artillery as yet.

4. For the intended assault group to unite with 12th Army within the sense of the new plan: 21st Panzer Division's battlegroup, 342nd Infantry Division, elements 35th SS Police Division, one SS armoured reconnaissance group (105th SS Armoured Reconnaissance Battalion of V SS Mountain Corps under SS-Major Fucker). Earliest start 25 April.[7]

Busse later claimed: 'Thus my headquarters had freedom to adjust its forces itself with a view to a rapid redeployment for a break-out to the west.' However, his subsequent behaviour indicates that he was in fact still attempting to comply with superior orders. Unlike Generals Heinrici and Wenck, he failed to see that his primary concern should have been the fate of his men and the accompanying refugees dependent upon him.

The problem here was that Busse, like many of his contemporaries, basically owed his successful military career to Hitler, to whom he was now in thrall, a situation further exacerbated by the consequences of the failure of Colonel Claus Graf Schenk von Stauffenberg's assassination plot of 20 July 1944, which had imposed an even greater subservience on commanders and the General Staff. A major obstacle to independent action, as previously mentioned, was the personal oath of allegience to Adolf Hitler that the obsequious commander-in-chief, General Werner von Blomberg, had imposed on the Wehrmacht immediately following the death of President von Hindenburg on 20 August 1934, which many continued to think of as binding, even when the failure and criminality of the regime had been exposed.

Busse had enlisted in the German Army as a potential officer in December 1915 and ended the First World War as a substantive second lieutenant. His war service had obviously attracted official attention, for he had been awarded the Knight's Cross with Swords of the Hohenzollern Order, the Kaiser's equivalent of the British royal family's Victorian Order. His subsequent service with the Reichswehr saw painfully slow progress with promotion to captain not achieved until 1933, but then came rapid acceleration to major in 1936, lieutenant-colonel in 1939 and full colonel in 1941, by which time he was on the General Staff. He then served as Chief of Staff to Army Groups *Süd* and *Nordukraine* on the Eastern Front, achieving the rank of major-general and then lieutenant-general in 1943, and being awarded the

German Cross in Gold on 24 May 1942 and the Knight's Cross on 30 January 1944. Busse had been given command of 122nd Infantry Division in July 1944, and then, on 1 August 1944, I Corps with Field Marshal Ferdinand Schörner's Army Group *Nord*, which was trapped on the Courland peninsula and condemned to extinction by Hitler's refusal to allow evacuation. He would therefore have been mightily relieved to have been flown out and then given command of the shattered 9th Army as a general of infantry on his own home ground around Frankfurt on 21 January 1945.[8]

The withdrawal of Busse's troops from their eastern and southern fronts was relatively well protected by the geographical features, particularly the dense waterways of the Lower and Upper Spreewald areas, which formed an 'L' from Leibsch via Lübben to Cottbus. The Soviets were unable to follow closely enough to endanger the German troops. However, V Corps' 342nd Infantry Division, fighting an isolated action in the Burg–Cottbus area, was overrun that afternoon. Meanwhile, V Corps headquarters, which had been made responsible for 9th Army's southern flank on 22 April, reported having established a perimeter defence along the line Löpten–Teupitz–Halbe, south of which a regiment of 35th SS Police Division held the line down to Lübben with the Engineer Training Battalion beyond.

The Soviets were able to gain the south bank of the Spree near Fürstenwalde, and also to close up to the Oder–Spree Canal. The remains of the 561st SS Tank-Hunting Battalion held fast on the autobahn east of Fürstenwalde in the Biegen, Briesen and Kersdorf areas, enabling the Frankfurt Garrison and the remains of 286th Infantry Division and SS Regiment *Falke* to get through. The 712th Infantry Division was still holding out at Petershagen, the 169th at Alt Madlitz, and Battlegroup *Nederland* at Falkenberg. Elements of the *Kurmark* Division prevented Soviet penetration of the woods on either side of the Scharmützelsee.[9]

It was different on the northern flank, where conditions had become worse since the withdrawal of LVI Panzer Corps into the capital. Despite constant counterattacks being mounted, not all the planned lines could be held. In some areas the hard-pressed divisions and battlegroups had to withdraw as much as ten or fifteen kilometres before they could hold.

A soldier of the 32nd SS Motorized Artillery Regiment, which had been covering the withdrawal from just north-east of Beeskow, described the situation:

> The concerned expressions, but also the good wishes of the civilian population, gave us many problems. The civilian bush telegraph was faster than our marching speed. They knew that Ivan was only a few hundred metres behind us. We were often begged to take on the protection of a place, and civilian clothing was offered us. With very heavy hearts, we marched on with our unit. Many old soldiers watched us with tears in their eyes.[10]

That evening HQ 9th Army, which had already issued its orders for the withdrawal, received revised orders to: '. . . hold on to the largest possible area between the autobahns leading to Berlin from Frankfurt and Cottbus, and to cooperate with 12th Army's attack from Treuenbrietzen to the north-east against the Soviets attacking Berlin from the south.'[11]

To do this would mean holding fast on the northern flank in the first case, something which was already beyond 9th Army's ability. General Busse, whose staff had meanwhile moved from Bad Saarow to the Scharmützelsee railway station at the southern end of the lake, later wrote:

> The traverse of a distance of 60 kilometres as the crow flies to the 12th Army, right through the rear communications

area of 1st Ukrainian Front's northern wing, would only have been possible providing the thrust was so rapid that the enemy were unable to mount effective countermeasures. The troops would have had to keep moving day and night. They could only have done this if the effectiveness of the strong Russian air and tank forces could possibly be reduced. The wide expanse of woodland from Halbe via Kummersdorf to north of Luckenwalde offered the only possibility for this. This became more apparent with 12th Army's disappointing announcement that it was not attacking to the east, but to the north, towards Beelitz, so there was no longer any question of a thrust being made to meet us. Nevertheless, the High Command still ordered that 9th Army, following a successful break-out, was immediately to wheel and attack the rear of the enemy on the southern outskirts of Berlin. This order 9th Army neither heeded nor acknowledged.

We had to go about things in accordance with our intention to get as many troops away as possible from the Russians' grasp. Our firm resolve was to breach the encirclement on either side of Halbe and break through to south of Beelitz using the cover of the woods.[12]

The 21st Panzer Division was now deployed south from Karlshof, two kilometres north-west of the autobahn junction, with a series of strongpoints stretching to the west of Ragow and Mittenwalde down to Teupitz, and was heavily engaged all day. On its right, the land link to Berlin was reduced to a corridor barely four kilometres wide and already under artillery surveillance. Behind them in Königs Wusterhausen were the remains of the 32nd SS Volunteer Grenadier Division's battlegroup, which had been forced out of Wernsdorf and Niederlehme on the Spree–Dahme line by Chuikov's troops.[13] A field hospital in the town, many of whose citizens were already displaying white flags, came under repeated attack from Soviet aircraft.[14]

During the day elements of 128th Rifle Corps of the Soviet 28th Army continued to arrive to take part in the operation but one formation, 152nd Rifle Division, was caught up near Mittenwalde in what was thought to be a break-out attempt by 9th Army. Whatever the cause, 152nd Rifle Division was still fighting in the Mittenwalde area that night and does not appear to have rejoined its parent formation for another day or two. The two other corps of 28th Army, 3rd and 20th Guards Rifle Corps, were also heading north towards Berlin, but were diverted to assist with the encirclement of 9th Army. As an additional safeguard, 25th Tank Corps was moved into the area of Duben as a mobile reserve.[15]

The 4th Guards Tank Army continued closing in on Potsdam and closing the gap with 1st Byelorussian Front's 47th Army encircling Berlin from the north, but made no attempt to cross the line of the Havel, which seems to have been its operational boundary. The 6th Guards Mechanized Corps split off at Beelitz, wheeling west towards Brandenburg and Paretz (near Ketzin), taking Lehnin that day.[16]

By the end of 23 April the Soviet 13th Army had almost reached the Elbe at Wittenberg. Koniev decided to detach its 350th Rifle Division to 4th Guards Tank Army to assist with the screening of Potsdam, and to take over its reserve corps at Luckau as his front reserve and locate it at Jüterbog, where it would be more centrally placed to meet anticipated contingencies.[17]

Further south the bulk of 5th Guards Army closed up to the Elbe around Torgau on a wide front that day, thus cutting the remains of the Third Reich in two. Koniev decided to leave only 34th Guards Rifle Corps in that area to await the arrival of the Americans on the opposite bank, and pulled back 32nd Guards Rifle and 4th Guards Tank Corps into the second echelon prior to striking a counterblow at the German forces on his southern flank. These had now penetrated some thirty kilometres towards Spremberg, separating the 52nd and 2nd Polish Armies and creating havoc in their rear areas.[18]

Although he had just sufficient troops to cope with this emergency in the south, it is clear that Marshal Koniev's forces were extremely finely stretched at this stage. His active northern front extended in a great loop from Cottbus in the east to Wittenberg in the west, via Berlin, Potsdam, Brandenburg and Beelitz, and he had only a very small reserve in the centre to counter the real threat posed by the German 9th and 12th Armies.[19] It was therefore even more remarkable that he should personally concentrate, with the key members of his front staff, solely on 3rd Guards Tank Army's penetration of Berlin and the race for the Reichstag.

That evening Lieutenant-General Gerhard Engel's *Ulrich von Hutten* Infantry Division set off from the River Mulde with two grenadier regiments, supporting artillery and SPGs, in convoys of vehicles confiscated from construction battalions, factories, rear area units and Nazi Party sources, acting in accordance with orders to establish as big a bridgehead as possible in the Wittenberg area and to hold on as long as possible against the advancing Soviet forces.[20]

The LVI Panzer Corps' headquarters had moved across the Spree and the southern branch of the Teltow Canal during the night into the suburb of Rudow. Sometime during the day, General Weidling's chief of staff, Lieutenant-Colonel Theodor von Dufving, telephoned an old friend from his cadet days, Colonel Hans Refior, now on the Berlin Defence Area staff, to ask for news. Refior was surprised when von Dufving told him that the corps was seeking to rejoin 9th Army and had no intention of defending the capital, but enabled von Dufving to re-establish contact with 9th Army Headquarters. General Weidling then spoke to the chief of staff, Colonel Hölz, who gave him orders to secure 9th Army's northern flank.

From another source Weidling learnt that a general had been sent to Döberitz to arrest him on Hitler's instructions, so he tried to contact Krebs for an explanation. Eventually he was summoned to report to the *Führerbunker* at 1800 hours, where he saw Krebs and General Burgdorf. They received him most coolly at first, but once they had heard his account they agreed to put his case to the Führer immediately.[21] Weidling then told them that he was moving his corps south towards Königs Wusterhausen that night in support of 9th Army in accordance with General Busse's instructions, but Krebs said that these orders would have to be cancelled as LVI Panzer Corps was needed in Berlin. Weidling saw Hitler shortly afterward and was shocked by the Führer's appearance and obvious deterioration. When he emerged from this interview, Krebs informed him that, with immediate effect, he was to take over the defence of the city's south-eastern and southern defence sectors with his corps. LVI Panzer Corps would not be rejoining 9th Army.[22]

NOTES

1. Gellermann, *Die Armee Wenck*, p. 97.
2. Wenck, 'Berlin war nicht mehr zu retten', p. 64; Gorlitz, *The Memoirs of Field Marshal Keitel*, pp. 203–4; Tieke, *Das Ende zwischen Oder und Elbe*, pp. 196–7.
3. Lakowski/Stich, *Der Kessel von Halbe 1945*, p. 44 [citing Federal Military Archives RH 2/337, Sheet 8f, 23 April 45].
4. Wenck, 'Berlin war nicht mehr zu retten', p. 64; Gellermann, *Die Armee Wenck*, pp. 80–3; Ryan, *The Last Battle*, p. 351.
5. Gellermann, *Die Armee Wenck*, p. 48; Ryan, *The Last Battle*, p. 443.
6. Gorlitz, *The Memoirs of Field Marshal Keitel*, p. 205.
7. Lakowski/Stich, *Der Kessel von Halbe 1945*, p. 46 [[citing Federal Military Archives RH 19 XV/10, Sitrep of 22 April 45, Sheet 15].
8. Bradley, Dermot, Karl-Friedrich Hildebrand & Markus Röverkamp: *Die Generäle des Heeres 1921–45*.
9. Tieke, *Das Ende zwischen Oder und Elbe*, pp. 194–5.
10. Stang/Arlt, *Brandenburg im Jahr 1945*, p. 99.
11. Busse, 'Die letzte Schlacht der 9. Armee', p. 167.
12. *Ibid.*
13. Kortenhaus, *Der Einsatz der 21. Panzer-Division*, p. 134.
14. Tieke, *Das Ende zwischen Oder und Elbe*, p. 190.
15. Koniev, *Year of Victory*, p. 135.

16. *Ibid.*, p. 135.
17. *Ibid.*, p. 137.
18. *Ibid.*, pp. 137–41; Komornicki, *Polnische Soldaten stürmten Berlin*, pp. 128–34.
19. Koniev, *Year of Victory*, p. 124.
20. Gellermann, *Die Armee Wenck*, p. 78.
21. Weidling, 'Der Todeskampf', p. 42; Gorlitz, *The Memoirs of Field Marshal Keitel*, p. 221; Tieke, *Das Ende zwischen Oder und Elbe*, pp. 216–18. Ryan's interview notes with Refior, von Dufving Archives.
22. Weidling, 'Der Todeskampf', pp. 42–5; Willemer, p. 19; Tieke, *Das Ende zwischen Oder und Elbe*, p. 224.

SIX

THE SOVIETS CLOSE IN

24 APRIL 1945

On 24 April Colonel-General Vassilii Chuikov's 8th Guards Army, with 1st Guards Tank Army under its command, and therefore Marshal Zhukov's strongest striking force, was busy side-stepping to the west to get into position to attack Berlin from the south. However, its plans were unexpectedly modified as the result of a surprise encounter, which must have created a tremendous upheaval at front and army command levels. At about 1030 hours, while some of Chuikov's troops were traversing Schönefeld Airfield, they unexpectedly came across several tanks from 3rd Guards Tank Army, thus linking up with 1st Ukrainian Front. According to Chuikov, Zhukov did not apparently learn of this encounter until the evening and then acted disbelievingly, insisting that Chuikov send officers to discover what units of 1st Ukrainian Front were involved, where they were located and what their objectives were.[1]

If, as it appears, this was Zhukov's first intimation of Marshal Koniev's participation in the battle for the city itself, we can imagine the consternation this report must have caused. Apart from the blow to Zhukov's pride, this incident clearly demonstrates the lack of communication between the Soviet leaders and their continuing mutual distrust. Having had his hand revealed, Stalin then laid down the inter-front

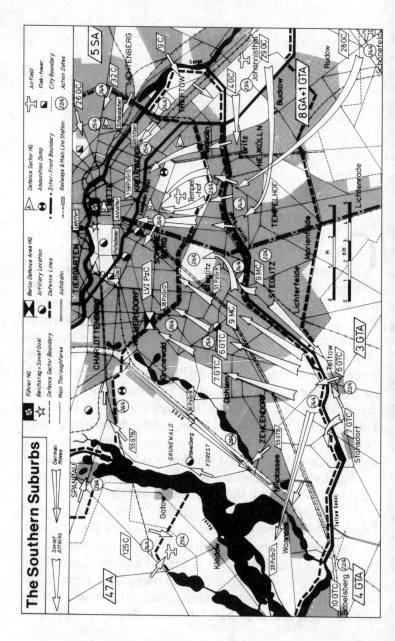

The Southern Suburbs

Führer HQ
Berlin Defence Area HQ
Reichstag = Soviet Goal
Artillery Location
Sovet Attacks
German Moves
Defence Sector Boundary
Main Thoroughfares
Defence Sector HQ
Ammunition Dump
Inter-Front Boundary
Railways & Main Line Station
Airfield
Flak-tower
City Boundary
Action Dates

boundaries, which were to run from Lübben through Teupitz, Mittenwalde and Mariendorf to the Anhalter railway station. Within the city, this meant the distinctive line of the railway leading north from Lichtenrade.

Koniev had obviously been aware of the GHQ order laying down the new inter-front boundaries on the night of the 22nd. When he issued his orders for the attack across the Teltow Canal he deployed 71st Mechanized Brigade on the right flank tasked with establishing contact with 1st Byelorussian Front. The boundary line, when extended beyond Anhalter station, passed well to the east of the Reichstag, giving him the opportunity of reaching it first from the south. Somehow this GHQ order had been withheld from Zhukov, although it had been effective from 0600 hours (Moscow time) on the 23rd, and his balance of forces and reported reactions to the news of this encounter on Schönefeld Airfield clearly demonstrate how unprepared he was for this eventuality.[2]

Significantly Chuikov states, '. . . 8th Guards Army, in whose front of advance formations of 1st Guards Tank Army were also operating, was diverted by order of the front commander to the north-west against the central sector of Berlin.'[3] This diversion led to Chuikov's 28th and 29th Guards Rifle Corps having to wheel sharply right through Rudow, Buckow and Lichtenrade into Mariendorf.[4]

Although Air Chief Marshal Novikov was responsible for coordinating air activity for the overall Oder–Neisse theatre operation with 2nd, 16th and 18th Air Armies under command, and was surely aware of the relative positions of the two fronts on the ground, he does not seem to have kept Zhukov informed on this point, possibly because Stalin forbade it.

Then, at about 1230 hours, the infantry of both fronts met near the Schönefeld autobahn junction, and later in the day Colonel-General A.V. Gorbatov's 3rd Army of 1st Byelorussian

Front linked up with 1st Ukrainian Front's 28th Army at Teupitz, thereby completing the encirclement of 9th Army.[5] Some small groups of German troops tried to break through 28th Army's lines between Mittenwalde and Teupitz during the day, but without success.[6]

Koniev joined Colonel-General Rybalko on the southern bank of the Teltow Canal to observe 3rd Guards Tank Army's assault crossing. For this he had amassed no fewer than 1,420 guns, of which 400 were aimed over open sights, at the unprecedented density of 650 guns per kilometre, to fire a 55-minute opening bombardment. The importance he attached to this operation is obvious. When the attacks on either flank failed for various reasons, he pushed everything through the central successful bridgehead at Teltow.[7]

Meanwhile, in its general advance on Potsdam, 4th Guards Tank Army had split, with 6th Guards Mechanized Corps heading west for Brandenburg, whose outskirts were reached that day, 10th Guards Tank Corps in the centre taking the eastern suburbs of Potsdam, and 9th Guards Mechanized Corps attempting a crossing into Wannsee. When this operation failed, this corps was also pushed across the Teltow bridgehead at Koniev's suggestion.[8]

The Soviet 13th Army reached Wittenberg on the Elbe that afternoon but ran into the *Ulrich von Hutten*, *Theodor Körner* and *Scharnhorst* Infantry Divisions, which reacted so violently that Koniev was led to believe that Wenck's 12th Army was launching its anticipated counterattack, and therefore called in part of 5th Guards Mechanized Corps and 1st Air Assault Corps to assist. In fact General Wenck was not yet ready to launch an attack, but the news of the fighting caused some concern to 4th Guards Tank Army.[9] The *Ulrich von Hutten* Infantry Division retook Wittenberg by evening, established its headquarters there and deployed around the town.

The Soviet formations here were up against improvised but relatively strong German forces. The troops were mainly young recruits drawn from various training establishments in the area but they were led by experienced instructor officers and NCOs, and some of their equipment had come straight off the manufacturing lines. The *Ulrich von Hutten*'s 3rd Tank-Hunting Battalion ran out of fuel that day, but was given a tip-off about the local Nazi Party chief's private store of 40,000 litres, which was promptly confiscated for the benefit of the division.[10]

Further south the intervention of the 5th Guards Army group under Koniev's chief of operations, who, in addition to the chief of staff, had been sent to resolve the situation, succeeded in checking Field Marshal Schörner's disruptive drive towards Spremberg. However, several more days of hard fighting were to ensue before the Germans were driven back.[11]

That day 2nd Air Army moved all but its bomber bases forward across the Neisse, the bombers still having ample range for continuing operations in support of 1st Ukrainian Front.[12]

There was also a surprise development in 33rd Army's sector, where the bridgehead had been firmly contained by V SS Mountain Corps against all attempts to break out since the beginning of the operation. That morning the 2nd Brigade of the Dnieper Flotilla laid a smokescreen across the Oder opposite Fürstenberg and supported an attack by marine infantry and some troops of 33rd Army on the town. The withdrawal of V SS Mountain Corps had already begun, so there could not have been much resistance, if any, to this assault.[13]

The 9th Army withdrawal that had started on 23 April continued smoothly enough on the southern and south-eastern sectors of the perimeter, where the Soviet attackers were unable to follow up fast enough. When the last of 21st Panzer Division had passed through Münchehofe, an engineer company set up a roadblock at the entrance to the village, using Goliath mini-tanks filled with explosives to be detonated beneath enemy tanks.[14] The situation was more complicated on the northern sector, where the pressure from the Soviets was more direct, and on the eastern sector the combat team based on 32nd SS Field Training and Replacement Battalion and commanded by SS-Captain Frenken of 32nd SS Engineer Battalion was having to fight a desperate battle on the line Ahrensdorf– Behrensdorf.[15]

During the night of 24/25 April, 21st Panzer Division withdrew to the line of the chain of lakes between Teupitz and Prieros, while 32nd SS Division's battlegroup pulled back to the Prieros area on the right flank. At the same time, 21st Panzer Division's 155th Armoured Artillery Regiment *Tannenberger* unilaterally decided to break out, requisitioning fuel from 21st Armoured Reconnaissance Battalion and heading off in a north-westerly direction without informing anyone. Nothing is known of this formation's fate, but its departure left a gap in the lines and a lot of anger among those remaining.[16] A crisis in morale was brewing, as Major Brand, commanding 21st Armoured Reconnaissance battalion, reported:

> The artillery staff of the *Tannenberger* commandeered my fuel and fled via Ketsin to the north-west. Through lack of fuel my own unit was reduced to 70 per cent effectiveness, so future attempts to make a motorized break-out on our own would prove futile.
>
> Resistance was only coming from the armoured divisions, the SS and, in the beginning, units from the city. There was no longer any operational direction higher than division. Units with unpopular officers were running away. Death sentences were no longer being carried out. From the orders given, the High Command was clearly demanding the constant sacrifice of our army, which was why our operational tasks made no sense. Everyone, from the leaders of reconnaissance units to senior staff officers, was in the dark about what was going on.
>
> The question arose whether to flee with one's troops on

one's own responsibility, or stay with the parent division – a question of conscience. I sent my adjutant, Second Lieutenant Kielhorn, home to his mother in Berlin by the last remaining route, as he was an only child. One hour later the ring was closed.

The results were simply incredible chaos: hassle, no sleep, no supplies, contaminated drinking water, unbelievable casualties, the encirclement constantly closing in, ferocious enemy air attacks, and massive artillery bombardment. During this phase there was a visible sinking of morale in my own unit. The chief of staff, Major Renner, had already fled. Unit leaders took control. The generals were no longer exercising their authority.[17]

The battles on the pocket perimeter that followed saw the deaths of thousands and were a nightmare for the survivors. Small groups of armoured vehicles with escorting infantry, such as the remains of 502nd SS Heavy Panzer and 10th SS Armoured Reconnaissance Battalions, were to play a prominent part in the Storkow–Bad Saarow area. There was no continuous front and fighting was taking place everywhere, though the intention was to conduct an orderly withdrawal from one line to another. Counterattacks brought temporary success, checking but not stopping the Soviet advance. Soviet penetrations in the flanks and rear could not be prevented.

Heinz Deerberg, then a twelve-year-old boy, reported on his experiences:

We were fleeing (to nowhere in particular) in a small group with all our vital belongings in a handcart along a woodland track, presumably near Prieros. Crouching down on both sides of the track were German soldiers without badges of rank or the eagle and swastika emblem, and armed with Soviet drum-magazine submachine guns, clearly *Seydlitz* people setting a trap for German soldiers. Several hundred metres further on were the first Russians. A young soldier, or officer, mounted on a horse, was looking around, spying out the land and relieving the refugees of their valuables and watches.[18]

The complete air superiority of the Soviets and other factors made conditions for the German troops even worse. Organized convoys and units became entangled with leaderless groups of soldiers on foot; refugee groups with their horse-drawn carts and handcarts, and wounded in all kinds of vehicles were all making their way westwards on the country roads and woodland tracks of the Spreewald. The 16th Air Army alone flew 2,000 sorties on 24 April. Tanks and SPGs were knocked out, ammunition trucks blown up, and whole groups of people killed or wounded by direct hits, as well as many military and privately owned horses.[19] Because of the constant Soviet pressure and the little or complete lack of reconnaissance by the Germans, most sectors and assembly areas remained ignorant of what was going on around them. Even 9th Army HQ lacked a proper overview.

At the end of 24 April the OKW summarized:

In the difficult, wide-reaching redeployment of the 9th Army, the enemy is thrusting with strong encircling attacks from the east and north, making it hard to release forces for the break-out to the west.

Deep breaches west of Fürstenwalde and the lateral movement of LVI Panzer Corps to the Teltow Canal have led to a further worsening of the situation for 9th Army. The supply situation for infantry and anti-tank ammunition is exceptionally tense.

There are overwhelming attacks to the west by the enemy on 9th Army from a bridgehead west of Fürstenwalde.

Göllmitz, the Langedamm forest warden's lodge and Rauen have been lost. An enemy thrust south has been checked on the northern edge of Kolpin.[20]

NOTES

1. Chuikov, *The End of the Third Reich*, p. 164; Kuby, *The Russians and Berlin 1945*, pp. 52–3. Tieke, *Das Ende zwischen Oder und Elbe*, p. 201, gives the time of encounter as 0900 hours. Zhukov does not even mention it! According to Koniev's *Year of Victory* this was 23 April, but it is quite clear from the accounts of both Zhukov and Chuikov that it must have occurred on the 24th.
2. Koniev, *Year of Victory*, p. 131. The new inter-front boundaries followed the main railway lines into Berlin, being clearly discernible to the troops on the ground, however badly damaged the environment, then crossed the Landwehr Canal to the Anhalter railway station. Any extension of that line left the Reichstag clearly to the west and in Koniev's path. (Here I disagree with both Ryan, *The Last Battle*, p. 354, and Erickson, *The Road to Berlin*, p. 586, for the reasons stated.) North of the canal Zhukov could now only approach the Reichstag from the east, north or west. Chuikov's group, originally intended to cover the whole southern arc of the city, could now, however, concentrate a disproportionately powerful punch on the eastern flank of that arc in competition with the 3rd Guards Tank Army. From then on one suspects that Zhukov must have pushed Chuikov deliberately to block Koniev's route to the Reichstag, thus causing the forthcoming changes in the inter-front boundary of 28 April with a *fait accompli*.
3. Chuikov, *The End of the Third Reich*, p. 163.
4. *Ibid.*, pp. 159–60.
5. Lakowski/Stich, *Der Kessel von Halbe 1945*, p. 50.
6. *Ibid.*, p. 53.
7. Erickson, *The Road to Berlin*, pp 587–8.
8. Koniev, *Year of Victory*, p. 156.
9. *Ibid.*, pp. 158, 161; Wagener, *The Soviet Air Forces in World War II*, p. 350; Erickson, *The Road to Berlin*, p. 592.
10. Gellermann, *Die Armee Wenck*, pp. 78–9.
11. Koniev, *Year of Victory*, p. 140.
12. Chernayev, 'Some Features of Military Art in the Berlin Operation', p. 105.

13. Zhukov, *Reminiscences and Reflections*, p. 610.

14. Fleischer, 'Der Kessel von Halbe'.

15. Wilke notes in the hands of the author.

16. Kortenhaus, *Der Einsatz der 21. Panzer-Division*, p. 135.

17. Brand, in the author's *Death Was Our Companion*. Ketsin is not identified on maps of this area, but this could be a misspelling of Ketzin, north-west of Potsdam, where the Soviet encirclement of Berlin was completed on 25 April.

18. Schulze, *Der Kessel Halbe–Baruth–Radeland*, pp. 18, 20.

19. Lakowski/Stich, *Der Kessel von Halbe 1945*, p. 60.

20. *Ibid.*, p. 60 [citing Federal Military Archives RH 19 XV/10, Sheet 332].

SEVEN

NO LUCK FOR VON LUCK

25 APRIL 1945

This was the day of the historic link-up of the Soviets and the Americans on the Elbe, when 5th Guards Army's 58th Guards Rifle Division encountered patrols from 69th US Infantry Division of 1st US Army near Torgau. All that remained of the Third Reich was thus split horizontally in two. Another significant development that day occurred when troops of both Soviet fronts completed the encirclement of Berlin, meeting north-east of Potsdam. Now there were two encirclements for them to deal with, the 'Berlin Group' and the 'Frankfurt–Guben Group', as they called them.[1]

Meanwhile Marshal Koniev had the three armoured corps of 3rd Guards Tank Army with their infantry and artillery reinforcements advancing steadily through the southern suburbs of the city aimed directly at the Reichstag, detaching only 55th Guards Tank Brigade to cover the exposed left flank through the Grunewald Forest and move on into the Olympic Stadium area of Charlottenburg. However, there were problems, as he related:

In street fighting it is generally hard for aircraft to operate with any degree of precision. Everything is in ruins and is shrouded in flame, smoke and dust. From the air it is generally difficult to make out anything at all.

From Rybalko's reports I understood that there were instances when he was suffering losses inflicted by our own air force. It was not easy to ascertain which front's aircraft were bombing our own troops in the turmoil of the street fighting.

It is always a bitter shock when, by some mischance, one is suddenly hit by one's own people and suffers losses. It was especially painful during the fighting for Berlin, since reports of this kind kept coming in all day, apparently not only to me, but also to Zhukov.

The commands of both fronts applied to GHQ to clear up the problems of troop coordination so that unnecessary argument could be avoided.

The GHQ directive established a new boundary running through Mittenwalde, Mariendorf, Tempelhof and the Potsdamer Railway Terminal. All these points, as the military documents put it, were inclusive for the 1st Ukrainian Front.

That was in the evening. By the time the line of demarcation had been established a whole corps of Rybalko's army was far beyond it in a zone which was now under the jurisdiction of the 1st Byelorussian Front. This corps had to be withdrawn from the centre of Berlin and deployed outside the new line of demarcation. But this was easier said than done. Anybody who fought in that war will understand how hard it was psychologically for Rybalko to withdraw his tankmen back inside the line of demarcation.[2]

It is interesting to note that the fronts had to apply to GHQ to sort out this problem, being incapable of doing so themselves, the hostility between the two commanders being too great. However, the change of inter-front boundary still left the Reichstag within Koniev's reach, as a subtended line from this boundary shows, there being no designated end line across the front of the troops advancing from any direction.

In the early hours of the morning 13th Army's reserve corps suffered a severe rebuff from the *Friedrich Ludwig Jahn* Infantry Division when it tried to regain Wittenberg. The Soviet infantry had been hastily trucked forward from Jüterbog without armoured support and were just leaving their forming-up areas when the German troops ran into them while expanding their own perimeter. In this surprise encounter the Germans came off best, driving the Soviets back ten kilometres by midday. The fighting continued all day. The Soviets brought up some T-34 tanks and tried to force their way in along the various streets leading into the town, but the German flak gunners formed a 'hedgehog' and used their 88-mm guns in the anti-tank role to hold them at bay. The German division then received orders to disengage and to move to Jeserigerhütten, where it was to prepare to attack eastwards. This was achieved by launching a series of sharp counterattacks before withdrawing.[3]

There was also some fierce fighting around Treuenbrietzen with a German penetration south of the town eastwards towards Bardenitz, but by 1500 hours this had been driven back to the southern outskirts of Treuenbrietzen by elements of 13th Army assisted by 5th Guards Mechanized Corps' artillery, whose commander, Colonel Nikolai P. Dyakin, was killed in the action.[4]

Oblivious to the conditions under which the German forces were operating, Hitler was planning the relief of his capital and re-ordering the command structure. In future OKW was to be responsible for overall operations under his instructions. His orders would be passed through the Chief of the General Staff of the OKH, General of Infantry Krebs, who was with him. OKW would deal directly with 12th Army and Army Group *Weichsel* with 9th Army. The main task of OKW was: 'By attacks with all forces and means and greatest speed to re-establish broad contact with Berlin from the north-west, south-west and south and thus bring the battle for Berlin to a decisive victory.'[5]

That day Hitler told General Weidling, now commanding the Berlin Defence Area:

> The situation will improve. The 9th Army will come to Berlin and deliver the enemy a blow with General Wenck's 12th Army coming up from the south-west. This blow will be delivered against the southern flank of the Russian troops attacking Berlin, and from the north will come units under Steiner's command to attack the Russian northern wing. These strikes will change the situation to our advantage.[6]

In numerous urgent telephone conversations, Krebs demanded, on Hitler's orders, counterattacks by 12th Army, SS-General Felix Steiner's corps north of Berlin, and even by 9th Army. Krebs was fully aware of the impossibility of executing these orders, and was only passing them on to calm Hitler down. Although completely out of touch with reality, the orders signed by Krebs were still being sent to 9th and 12th Armies for action.

General Wenck's orders for his 12th Army concentrated on the reception of the break-out elements of 9th Army. He had begun the day before with the deployment of a weak security screen against the southern flank of 1st Ukrainian Front as his XX Corps assembled and marched on the Beelitz–Niemegk area. This thrust towards Beelitz and Potsdam was to have some initial success, but brought no relief to the Berlin situation, except to provide a source of hope to the encircled population and defenders.

Major-General Ernst Biehler's Frankfurt-an-der-Oder garrison at last succeeded in breaking through to 9th Army, a full three days after receiving Hitler's permission to do so. General Busse could now begin to concentrate his troops for a break-out attempt to the west. Whether he was mentally

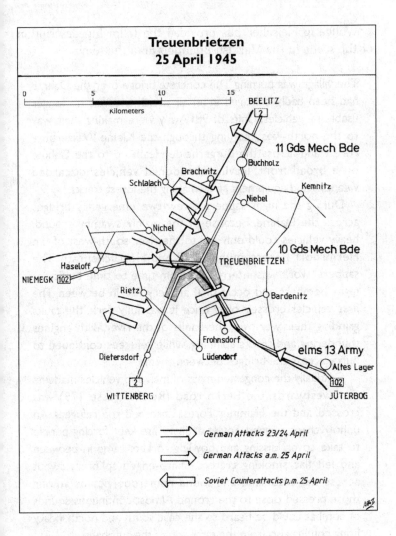

Treuenbrietzen
25 April 1945

German Attacks 23/24 April

German Attacks a.m. 25 April

Soviet Counterattacks p.m. 25 April

prepared to act in defiance of Hitler's orders, however, remains doubtful. Meanwhile his pocket was being harassed day and night from both land and air, and it was time to act if the people in his charge were to have a chance of escaping death or capture at the hands of the Soviets.[7]

83

Wolfgang Fleischer has provided the following description of the scene in the Märkish Buchholz area that day:

The village was burning. The concrete bridge over the Dahme had been badly damaged in an air attack and was no longer usable by vehicles. Units of 9th Army were making their way to the north-west, coming through the Kleine Wasserburg Forest and across the Bürgerheide Heath up to the Dahme on a broad front, leaving abandoned vehicles, discarded weapons and equipment strewn along the forest tracks.

During the night sappers threw two emergency bridges across the Dahme. Because of the mainly swampy ground, heavy vehicles could only get to the river south-west of the Hermsdorf [Grossemühle] Mill and Herrlichenrath. The sappers' work was interrupted from time to time by Soviet night bombers and occasional artillery fire in between. The first vehicles crossed over once it was fully dark, the tanks grinding their way over the banks of the river with engines thundering and tracks spinning, while refugees continued to hurry across the bridges between them.

Gradually the congested mass of men and vehicles made its way westwards, the Berlin road (Reichsstrasse 179) was crossed, and the Hammer Forest absorbed the refugees. An unholy chaos reigned. Soviet artillery fire kept forcing people to take cover. Hissing and howling rockets came in between and left flat, smoking craters. Sharp-edged splinters swept across the woodland and found numerous victims among those pressed close to the ground. Almost continuous sounds of combat could be heard to the east, south and north, heavy firing coming also from the direction of the autobahn.

Having crossed the Dahme, the units of 9th Army moved along the Berlin road and through the Hammer Forest to Halbe. With daylight the Soviet ground-attack aircraft would be engaging the encircled troops again, making movement even more difficult. The columns became stuck at the crossroads east of Klein Köris. Several II-2s flew along the road, firing with their machine guns and rockets, the ammunition belts and cartridges clattering down on the road surface, the tracer bullets biting into vehicles, horses and human bodies.[8]

In the woods of the Halbe area were now concentrated the remains of XI SS Panzer Corps, V SS Mountain Corps, the Frankfurt fortress garrison, and V Corps, with in all the remnants of one tank and 13 infantry divisions, plus a number of independent units. Also with them were a large number of sick and wounded, as well as refugees, Wehrmacht employees, female flak and signals auxiliaries, forced labourers, prisoners of war, and even concentration camp inmates. The exact number of people surrounded in the Halbe pocket has never been calculated with any exactitude, but estimates vary from 150,000 to 200,000.

According to 9th Army's rear area commander, Lieutenant-General Friedrich-Gustav Bernhard, there were some 50,000 fighting troops and 10,000 Volkssturm personnel in the pocket and 'including rear service units, there were up to 150,000 men in the pocket. Also in the pocket were the whole headquarters of 9th Army under General Busse and his staff, the commanders and staff of XI SS Panzer Corps, V SS Mountain Corps and V Corps, as well as senior officers of the rear area services.'

Soviet accounts reckoned that the German force amounted to 11 regiments, 4 brigades, 71 battalions, one artillery regiment, 5 artillery battalions, 1 tank regiment, 1 tank battalion and the Frankfurt fortress garrison. Some, certainly exaggerated, Soviet accounts also include figures of over 2,000 guns and mortars and about 300 armoured vehicles in the pocket.

There would be little sense in attempting a comparison of strengths between the opponents, as no reliable figures are available for the German side. Witness accounts give subjective impressions and are seldom based on documentary

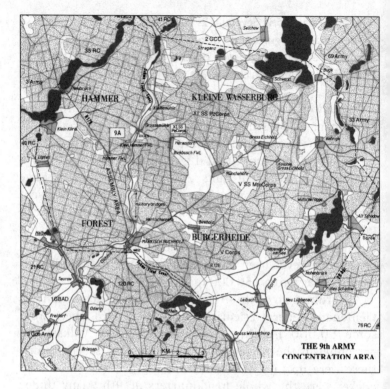

THE 9th ARMY
CONCENTRATION AREA

evidence available today. Apart from this, only definitive comparisons at an exact time and place would have any value, as the strengths of the surrounded group varied daily, if not by the hour, for the worst. Accordingly all figures given serve only as a rough indication.

What is certain is that, after a week of heavy fighting, defence and retreat, the German formations were down to seldom more than half their original strengths and equipment holdings, bearing in mind also Soviet claims that German units on the Oder and Neisse fronts had suffered up to 80 per cent losses. Taking into consideration that the heavy artillery pieces and static flak batteries would have had to be blown up and abandoned in the retreat, there were probably fewer than 1,000 guns and mortars available in the pocket, all with extremely limited supplies of ammunition. A similar situation applied to the armoured vehicles. In contrast to the Soviet figures, 9th Army reported to army group headquarters on 24 April that V Corps had 79 tanks of all kinds and XI SS Panzer Corps had 36. No figures were given for the other formations or units. In fact it now seems that there was possibly a maximum of 250 armoured vehicles in all, but only between 150 and 200 of these would have been available for combat. The acute and ever-worsening fuel and ammunition situations made things even worse for the encircled troops.

The following were in the pocket just before the final encirclement:

Northern Front

On the general line Königs Wusterhausen–Wolziger See–Storkow–Bad Saarow–Berkenbrück:

XI SS Panzer Corps with the staff of the *Kurmark* Panzergrenadier Division and several battlegroups; battlegroups of the 303rd, 169th and 712th Infantry Divisions; the *Schill* regimental battlegroup with the 2nd Battalions of the 86th and 87th SS Grenadier Regiments; en route the *Kurmark* battlegroup with the 1st Battalions of those regiments; Battlegroup *Hengstmann*; elements of the 32nd SS Tank-Hunting Battalion; 502nd SS Heavy Panzer Battalion; 561st SS Tank-Hunting Battalion; 23rd SS Panzergrenadier Division *Nederland* (HQ and one battlegroup), 21st Panzer Division's battlegroup; the Dora II tank-hunting commando.

Eastern Front

On the general line Burg–Butzen–Schwielochsee–Beeskow:

V SS Mountain Corps; 32nd SS Volunteer Grenadier Division *30. Januar* (HQ plus one battlegroup from the 32nd

SS Field Training and Replacement and 32nd SS Fusilier Battalions); 391st Security Division (HQ and elements); 286th Infantry Division (HQ and elements); *Becker* regimental battlegroup with elements of other units from the Müllrose–Beeskow area; the remains of 505th Corps' corps troops as well as a battlegroup formed of mixed artillery and flak gunners from static units from near Merz.

Southern Front
Along along the general line of Halbe–Krausnick–Lübben:
V Corps with the remains of the 35th SS Police, 275th, 214th and 342nd Infantry Divisions; elements of 36th SS Grenadier Division; a battlegroup of 10th SS Panzer Division; elements of 6th SS Gendarmerie Battalion.

There were no prepared defensive positions available for the encircled troops, so they used natural obstacles, or quickly improvised defensive positions in villages, barns and other suitable features. Often the encroaching enemy forced them into small pockets within the greater encirclement. The fighting along the pocket's perimeter also continued remorselessly. The 1st Byelorussian Front was able to gain some 10–15 kilometres in various sectors that day, and 9th Army was unable to prevent the further constriction of the encirclement, especially in the north and north-eastern sectors.[9]

Ernst-Christian Gädtke, who was now on foot with his unit's supply section, having had to abandon his assault gun due to engine failure, continued his story:

Without being disturbed by the enemy, we reached the edge of Niederlehme at dawn and came to a thin line of defence almost totally occupied by Hitler Youth under a young second lieutenant.

We passed through the village and, just before the Neue

Mühle locks, were accosted by a sergeant-major, who ordered us to dig trenches facing east in the gardens along the street and to prepare for an attack. What had happened to the rest of our unit, nobody seemed to know, nor what the rendezvous was. We tried to get across the lock bridges, but there were some military police sentries standing on them, letting nobody cross.

So we dug in, protected by a hedge running along the edge of the street, from where we could see the eastern exit. But nobody came all day long, and it became boring for us crouching in our holes and staring at the street, so we wandered around the gardens and looked into the cellars of the houses there, where women and old men, inhabitants of the village, were sitting crammed close together. Anxious questions everywhere: 'When are the Russians coming?' 'What will they do to us?' There were some wounded soldiers among them.

The day passed quietly.

Then, suddenly at dusk, it all changed. Sounds of fighting from the north, exploding shells, the dry crack of tank guns. Individual groups of soldiers hurried past and somebody shouted: 'The Russians are coming! Everyone back! The bridges are being blown!'

We jumped up and ran back to the bridges, where the second lieutenant from early that morning was. 'Stop!' he screamed, 'Stop! Don't blow the bridges! My youngsters are lying up there in front on the edge of the village. You can't leave them there!' But the engineer captain wouldn't budge. 'It doesn't matter to me what happens to those kids. Get over now or not at all, we are blowing now!'

We rushed across the bridges past the second lieutenant, who turned round and slowly went back.

Hard behind the bridges stood both of our two remaining guns on either side of the street with their engines running. Relieved, we jumped aboard and drove off to Prieros. The bridges went up behind us with a powerful bang.

That night of 25 April we found accommodation in a school at Prieros. For the first time in days we slept on straw, deep and sound.[10]

The situation for the surrounded soldiers and civilians was becoming more desperate by the hour. The troops' freedom to manoeuvre was becoming less and less. They were now completely cut off from their supply lines and attempts at air supply produced less than at any time in the war. Soviet fighter aircraft and anti-aircraft fire were too strong and the German air transport facilities too weak. Fuel and ammunition were in even shorter supply than they had been on the Oder.

Available sources on the attempts to resupply the encircled forces by air give a stark picture. As early as 0710 hours on 25 April, 9th Army radioed the Air Liaison Officer at Army Group *Weichsel*: 'To Flivo: Friedersdorf available but no machine has landed yet. Get them going immediately!' A little later, at 0750 hours, another message followed that included: 'The army has been left in the lurch by air supply despite available airfield and lighting facilities. Urgently request for night of 26th in Kehrigk area. Location by coordinates with codewords follows.' At 1850 hours that same day the Air Liaison Officer sent the following reply: 'The fifth transport aircraft crossed the airfield for 30 minutes at 0300 hours, but saw no lights.' A few minutes later he reported: 'The next air drop by six aircraft on the southern edge of the airfield will start from the north. Later landings by further aircraft too risky.' Finally the quartermaster department of Army Group *Weichsel* reported that 75 tons of air supplies had been loaded for 9th Army that day. Apart from these details, this signal read:

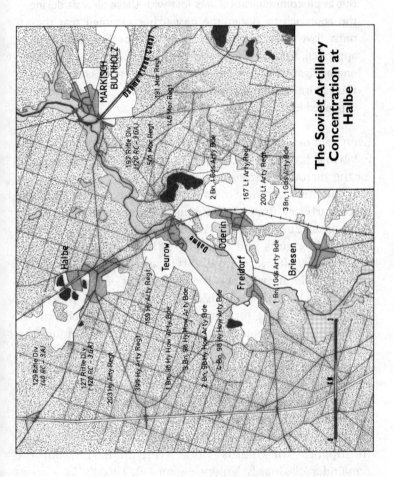

The Soviet Artillery Concentration at Halbe

The despatcher sent off five aircraft, the first at 2215 hours, the second at 2350 hours and the third to the fifth at about 0200 hours, and they should have reached their destination. But as all communication was lost with these aircraft during the approach to Berlin, the despatcher assumed that they must have been shot down by fighters or flak during the approach. One aircraft reported being shot down by an enemy fighter. As a result of the loss of radio contact and the failure of the first aircraft to return, the despatcher cancelled further operations at 0200 hours.[11]

Even if one or another air drop had succeeded in the following days, it would hardly have been of much account for the surrounded troops.

In addition to the Soviet forces already deployed, some special artillery units were brought in, and a total of six air corps from 2nd and 16th Air Armies. In all some 280,000 men, 7,400 guns and mortars, 280 tanks and SPGs, and 1,500 aircraft were now pitted against 9th Army. Of particular significance was the deployment of the 1st Guards Breakthrough Artillery Division on 25 April. This was one of the Stavka reserve formations normally allocated only to support specific break-through battles at the beginning of a major operation. However, after the successful breach of the Oder–Neisse defences in Operation Berlin, it was realised that there would be no further requirement in this particular role and these divisions were reallocated to the fronts with which they had fought the opening battle.

Koniev had already detached 19th Guards Mortar Brigade to support 3rd Guards Tank Army in Berlin, but the remainder of Guards Major-General V.B. Husid's 1st Guards Breakthrough Artillery Division was now sent to support 3rd Guards Army against the 9th Army pocket opposite Halbe and Märkisch Buchholz. Divisional headquarters was established at Briesen and the subordinate formations and units allocated in direct support of the infantry formations in Army Artillery Groups (AAGs) and Divisional Artillery Groups (DAGs) as follows:

AAG 3rd Guards Army	98th Heavy Howitzer Artillery Brigade
AAG att. 120th Rifle Corps	1st Guards Cannon Artillery Brigade
DAG, 197th Rifle Div (120th Rifle Corps)	3rd Light Artillery Brigade 167th & 200th Regiments 16th Heavy Mortar Brigade
DAG, 329th Rifle Div (21st Rifle Corps)	2nd Guards Howitzer Brigade 169th, 203rd & 359th Regiments 30th Mortar Brigade 146th, 191st & 501st Regiments

This system greatly increased the firepower of the existing divisional artillery groups in dealing with local incidents, while enabling coordination to provide a massive artillery concentration when necessary. All artillery units were allocated standing barrage, concentrated fire and moving defensive fire target areas. The batteries were protected by anti-tank barriers and given sectors for firing over open sights should German tanks break through to them, and special provision was made for fighting at night. The heaviest guns of the 98th Heavy Howitzer Artillery Brigade were located immediately behind the 21st Rifle Corps facing Halbe.[12]

The troops of 1st Ukrainian Front built defences along the anticipated breakthrough route from Märkisch Buchholz to Luckenwalde, three engineer brigades laying some 40,000 mines between them and erecting numerous barricades reinforced with explosives along a 12-kilometre strip.

The 3rd Guards Army was ordered:

- to concentrate a division in the Teupitz area as a reserve.
- to occupy all woodland tracks.
- to establish strongpoints along the Berlin–Cottbus autobahn and to reinforce this area with artillery units.
- to place strong anti-tank defences in the Tornow–Neuendorf sector, concentrating two anti-tank artillery regiments there.
- to concentrate one division in the Brand–Staakow–Wolzow [Waldow?] sector and another in the area Neuendorf–Schönwalde.
- to concentrate 2nd Tank Corps as a mobile reserve in the same area, and a regiment or brigade for the same purpose in the Teupitz area.
- to erect strong barriers in the Lübben–Teupitz sector.[13]

This concentration of several divisions in the rear of 3rd Guards and 28th Armies provided sufficient resources to establish a second cordon backed by reserves, with 28th Army's 38th Guards Rifle Corps deployed with its 96th Guards Rifle Division near Golssen, its 50th near Baruth and its 54th by Lindenbrück. Meanwhile 3rd Guards Army's 76th Rifle Corps was detailed to attack in the general direction of Straupitz–Schlepzig and to cooperate closely with 1st Byelorussian Front's 33rd Army on its right.[14]

A major factor that might have helped the break-out to succeed was the element of surprise, but this was denied by the Red Army's complete air superiority. The Red Air Force had identified the German movement towards Märkisch Buchholz, Löpten and Halbe, as well as the concentration of troops and materiel on the western edge of the pocket on the day before. This resulted in attacks from 4th Air Bomber Corps, mainly from 70 twin-engined Pe-2s, on the identified target.[15] Artillery fire met the marching columns mixed with the refugee treks and hit their assembly and camping areas. Chaos reigned as shot-up tanks, burning SPGs, abandoned vehicles and wrecked

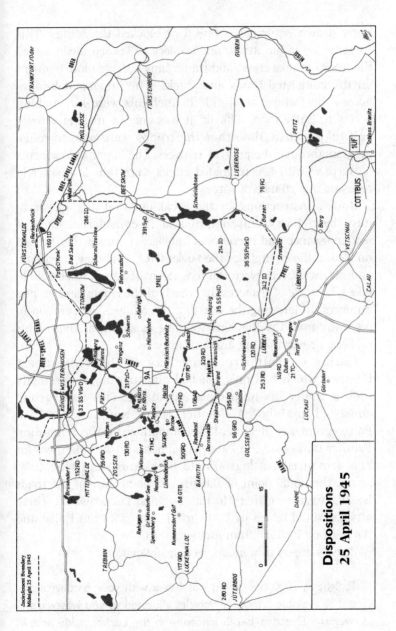

**Dispositions
25 April 1945**

Zeiss/element Boundary
Midnight 25 April 1945

horse-drawn equipages strewed or blocked the routes. This combination of air attacks and artillery strikes repeatedly forced the troops to take cover, and traffic jams became more frequent on the congested roads and tracks. The important bridges across the Dahme at Märkisch Buchholz were hit, making access to Halbe more difficult. It was only by making detours and taking their time that the troops were able to make progress through the press of refugees. The important elements of surprise with a coordinated attack were thus lost, severely reducing any chance of success.

Busse's instructions for the break-out that day appear to have been hasty, impromptu and ill-considered. Lack of reconnaissance and operational intelligence meant that he had no idea of the strength of the Soviet forces that now faced him, and his own forces were still too widely dispersed to be able to take advantage of a successful breach of the enemy lines in any numbers. In ignoring the fact that the refugees' desperation to get away from the Russians was just as strong as that of his soldiers, he was making a serious mistake.

Seizing on Battlegroup *von Luck* of the 21st Panzer Division, which had only reached him that day, he promptly took it under his immediate command. This battlegroup consisted mainly of Colonel Hans *von Luck*'s 125th Panzergrenadier Regiment, accompanied by the remaining Panther tanks of 22nd Panzer Regiment. Busse's plan was for two armoured battlegroups to break out simultaneously, secure the nodal point of Baruth and obtain use of the roads leading west from there to Jüterbog and Luckenwalde. These attacks would be led by Battlegroup *von Luck* from Halbe and Battlegroup Pipkorn from further south.

Busse's orders to *von Luck* were as follows:

Tonight at 2000 hours you will attack with your battlegroup and all available armoured vehicles allocated to you westward over the Dresden–Berlin autobahn in the Luckenwalde area in the rear of the 1st Ukrainian Front attacking Berlin. The break-out point is to be kept open to enable the following elements of the 9th Army to reach the west on foot. This is not open to the civilian population: thousands of refugees would hamper the operation.[16]

Similarly, Battlegroup *Pipkorn*, led by SS-Colonel Rüdiger *Pipkorn*, and consisting of the remains of his 35th SS Police Grenadier Division and the remaining tanks of the 10th SS Panzer Division *Frundsberg*, was to strike out westward from Schlepzig, north of Lübben. *Pipkorn* happened to be an old friend of *von Luck*'s from their recruit days, but had more recently been compulsorily transferred as a General Staff officer to the Waffen-SS.

By 1900 hours several tanks had arrived to join *von Luck*'s battlegroup, including some small, fast Hetzer tank-hunters. Ammunition was loaded and fuel shared out, but as no supply trucks were to accompany them, their capacity for fighting and movement was limited to what they were now carrying. These preparations could not go unnoticed and by nightfall some hundreds of women and children with their primitive carts and baggage had gathered round, and *von Luck* did not have the heart to turn them away.

They set off at 2000 hours, their first objective being Baruth, the important traffic junction astride the swampy bottom of the Nuthe glacial valley. When they reached the Berlin–Dresden autobahn, they found individual Soviet supply trucks on it, heading for the capital, so road blocks were established north and south of the crossing point.

There were then (no longer) two bridges across the autobahn south of the Teupitz–Halbe exit, the southernmost of which had been blown. From there one of the original tracks connecting the villages before the forestry grids were imposed led in a shallow S to Baruth. *von Luck*'s force made good progress, despite having to traverse these woodland

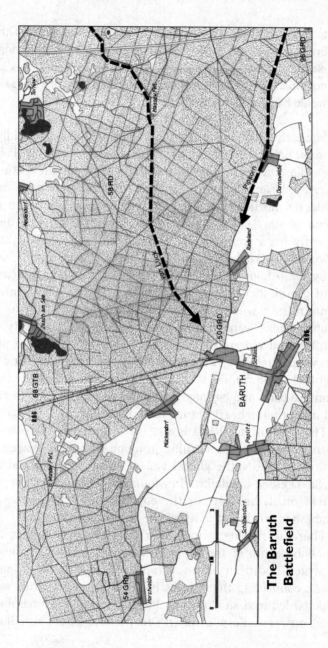

The Baruth Battlefield

tracks and fire breaks in the dark. Whenever the tanks stopped the civilians would close up behind and wait for the next move.

In order to reach the Juterbog road, *von Luck* would have to seize, pass through and hold Baruth, as the valley bottom that the town straddles is otherwise virtually impassable to tanks because of the network of irrigation ditches running through the water meadows.

They reached the outskirts of Baruth at about midnight but, as they emerged cautiously from the woods, they suddenly came under heavy anti-tank and machine-gun fire. Clearly the Soviets had anticipated a break-out attempt at this point. The defences here included some Josef Stalin heavy tanks which had been dug in so that only their turrets were exposed. The Stalin tank was superior in armour to anything the Germans had, its only known weakness being the time it took to reload its formidable 122mm gun. These tanks effectively blocked the line of advance, so Colonel *von Luck* decided to wheel his battlegroup round to the right and then send in his Panzergrenadiers to take the town from the north, this appearing to be the easiest break-out route, providing he did not get involved in lengthy fighting that would give the Soviets time to reinforce their positions.

Just then some Panthers of Battlegroup *Pipkorn* appeared from the east. The southern group's attack from its positions near Schlepzig in the Upper Spreewald had also begun at about 2000 hours, but proved unsuccessful. When the leading elements reached the defensive positions of 329th Rifle Division, they had encountered heavy fire and come under repeated flank attacks, which gave them a severe mauling and caused the leading elements to scatter. Only a few individual groups actually got as far as the autobahn near Staakow, where the bridge crossed the autobahn south of Halbe, and then pushed on via Dornswalde for Baruth.

Despite these welcome reinforcements for the Germans, the

Soviets were able to do better and towards dawn it became clear that, with ammunition and fuel rapidly running out, the German troops would be unable to break through. *von Luck* therefore radioed General Busse informing him of the hopelessness of the situation, together with his decision to continue the attack while the cover of darkness lasted, but that he feared more counterattacks and air attacks with the coming of daylight. Busse ordered the battlegroup to stay where it was, avoid direct attacks and wait for the remainder of 9th Army to catch up.

Instead von Luck summoned his subordinate unit commanders and told them that he had decided to disband his force and give them the opportunity of breaking out in small groups. He himself would return to the pocket with his adjutant, Captain Liebeskind, a liaison officer and a runner to explain his actions. However, as it turned out, Pipkorn was killed during this action and von Luck captured early on 27 April on his way back. Some of his men actually reached the Elbe, but most were either killed or captured.[17]

From Radeland, the nearest village east of Baruth, schoolboy Erwin Hilldebrands reported:

> During the fighting Soviet soldiers hid under the roofs, in the sheds and barns, facing north-east, and many foxholes were dug along the eastern edge of the village. In addition, there were some 122-mm artillery pieces also aimed towards the woods. One gun was destroyed and lay on the roadside for weeks. There were over fifty SS dead lying just inside the woods on the right-hand side of the track leading to Neuendorf.
>
> The crew of an unknown type of tank heading towards Baruth from Dornswalde were shot at the entrance to Radeland by the Soviets, their bodies being put into the mass grave with the others mentioned above, the tank crews in their black uniforms being treated as SS.

The northern part of Baruth was attacked by Soviet aircraft on 25 or 26 April, as we could see clearly from the west side of Radeland.[18]

One of the last messages from 9th Army reported at 2230 hours:

... continual air attacks over the whole of the army's area, heavy losses of men and equipment, as well as considerable changes of route ... V Corps attacked towards Baruth with the southern group from the Schlepzig area at 2000 hours. Strong enemy attacks at the moment at Teupitz and Märkisch Buchholz. Following defensive action, northern group attacking from Teupitz and Märkisch Buchholz at about 2400 hours. The southern group has had partial success south of Krausnick. Two bridges under construction over the Dahme. First impressions: the enemy is constantly reinforcing. The army is engaged in heavy defensive fighting along the whole front Schwielochsee– Königs Wusterhausen, with main points at Beeskow and north of Neugolm, Storkow, Zernsdorf.[19]

Army Group *Weichsel* commented on these battles:

The enemy has mounted strong attacks supported by tanks and ground-attack aircraft against the encircled 9th Army from the east and north. The virtually total failure of air supply has so weakened this bravely fighting army that the successful execution of its task has become questionable should re-supply tonight fail. V Corps has connected with the right-hand attacking group at Mückendorf in its attempt to break out. The left-hand group has thrust through the woods north-east of Baruth. With a view to preventing a breakthrough to the west, the Soviets have also made some strong counterattacks here. They were able to break through the left-hand thrust from the south near Massow forest warden's lodge and at the autobahn and to penetrate the right-hand thrust at Teupitz from the north. General Busse reports: 'Holding on and fighting to the last goes without saying for the 9th Army.'[20]

Nevertheless, Busse's words, like other similar bombastic messages in the Nazi vein by senior German officers during the course of the war, could not disguise the failure of his first attempt at a break-out.

During the night of 25/26 April, Hitler repeated his efforts to get both armies to come to the relief of Berlin. In an order to the 12th Army he demanded: 'Disregarding your flanks and rear, your attack groups are to act with firmness and determination to form keenly coordinated thrusts.' To achieve this, it was ordered:

1. The 12th Army with its southern group, abandoning the security of the Wittenberg area, is to reach the line Beelitz–Ferch, thus cutting off the rear communications of the Soviet 4th Tank Army advancing on Brandenburg, and at the same time to pursue the attack eastwards to unite with 9th Army.

2. 9th Army, while holding on to its present eastern front between the Spreewald and Fürstenwalde, is to attack by the shortest route to the west and link up with 12th Army.

3. Once both armies have combined, they are to push northwards and destroy the enemy formations in the southern part of Berlin and establish a solid link with Berlin.[21]

NOTES

1. GPW, p. 382; Koniev, *Year of Victory*, p. 172; Toland, *The Last Hundred Days*, p. 451.
2. Koniev, *Year of Victory*, pp. 171–2.
3. Gellermann, *Die Armee Wenck*, p. 79.

4. Kreisleitung Jüterbog booklet, pp. 23–4.
5. Förster/Lakowski, 1945 – Das Jahr der endgültigen Niederlage der faschistischen Wehrmacht, p. 337.
6. Lakowski/Stich, Der Kessel von Halbe 1945, pp. 80, 82 [citing Refior Berlin Diaries, p. 141].
7. Busse, 'Die letzte Schlacht der 9. Armee', p. 167.
8. Fleischer, 'Der Kessel von Halbe'.
   The Il-2 was named Ilyusha after its designer, Sergei V. Ilyushin, and was a ground-attack aircraft armoured with up to 13-mm plate, making it virtually impervious to infantry fire. At this stage of the war it was armed with two 37-mm wing-mounted cannon and two 7.62-mm machine guns in the engine cowling, and could also carry four 82-mm rockets or 100-kg bombs as an external load.
9. Lakowski/Stich, Der Kessel von Halbe 1945, pp. 72–9.
10. Gädtke, Von der Oder zur Elbe, pp. 30–2.
11. Lakowski/Stich, Der Kessel von halbe 1945, pp. 95–6 [citing Federal Military Archives RH 19 XV/10, Sheet 296].
12. Domank, 'The 1st Guards Breakthrough Artillery Division at Halbe'.
13. Lakowski/Stich, Der Kessel von Halbe 1945, pp. 65–6.
14. Ibid., pp. 63–6.
15. The Pe-2 was named Peshka after its designer, Vladimir M. Petlyakov, and was a dive-bomber with a three-man crew, armed with six machine guns and 1,000 kg of bombs.
16. Von Luck, Gefangener meiner Zeit, pp. 272–3.
17. Koniev, Year of Victory, p. 168; Lakowski/Stich, Der Kessel von Halbe 1945, pp. 72–96; von Luck, Gefangener meiner Zeit, pp. 272–6.
18. Schulze, Der Kessel Halbe–Baruth–Radeland, pp. 54–5.
19. Lakowski/Stich, Der Kessel von Halbe 1945, pp. 91–2 [citing Federal Military Archives RH 19 XV/10, Sheet 334].
20. Ibid., p. 96 [citing Federal Military Archives RH RH 19 XV/10, Sheet 413].
21. Förster/Lakowski, 1945 – Das Jahr der endgültigen Niederlage der faschistischen Wehrmacht, p. 338.

EIGHT

PREPARING THE BREAK-OUT
26 APRIL 1945

lements of the *von Luck* and *Pipkorn* battlegroups continued fighting around Baruth during the early hours of 26 April, and some of the dug-in Stalin tanks were blown up by specially detailed units, but there was still no follow-up by other units coming from the pocket. Some groups occupied Mückendorf and the woods around it, but concentrated artillery fire prevented any further progress against the 395th Rifle Division, which had moved up from the Golssen area. Shells bursting in the treetops caused many casualties among the German troops and accompanying civilians.

Hans Lehmann described events in Baruth that day:

The Baruth Schloss was occupied by Waffen-SS and Wehrmacht troops of units mainly made up from stragglers on 25/26 April 1945. Heavy fighting broke out, most of the damage coming from Soviet mortars, artillery and tanks. Aircraft were also active over the northern part of the town and the woods. German supply canisters were even dropped on 26 April, and a Ju 52 carrying ammunition and Panzerfausts crashed on the Mühlenberg [hill] that night, having apparently been shot down.

Two temporary cemeteries were established for the

fallen Soviet soldiers, one at the crossroads outside the town cemetery and one in front of the Schloss. The remains from both were transferred to the Soviet War Cemetery on the B96 in 1947. There were about 400 Soviet soldiers in the cemetery at the Schloss.[1]

Counterattacks by two other Soviet divisions into the left flank of the German forces caused the latter to split and threw them back into the woods north-east of Baruth, while an attack by 4th Bomber Air Corps with 55 machines at midday had a catastrophic effect. Repeated strikes on the approach routes by 1st and 2nd Air Assault Corps, using between eight and ten aircraft at a time and flying some 500 missions, brought further heavy casualties and chaos to the break-out traffic. In the end these troops were cut off, surrounded and mainly destroyed, although some of the tanks are said to have reached as far as Sperenberg.[2] According to Soviet accounts, this break-out attempt resulted in 5,000 prisoners, 40 tanks and SPGs destroyed and the capture of nearly 200 guns and mortars.

Apparently surprised by the strength and aggressiveness of this attack, Marshal Koniev took further measures to cope with all eventualities. One of these was an attack towards Münchehofe, aiming to penetrate the pocket from the south. More troops were fed in to strengthen the blockade along the Luckenwalde–Märkisch Buchholz front, especially north of the Hammerfliess stream and along the autobahn. The 149th and 253rd Rifle Divisions took up positions along the autobahn from Teupitz to Terpt (due west of Lübbenau), thus also covering the road west to Luckau, and the three divisions of 28th Army's 3rd Guards Rifle Corps occupied the Lindenbrück–Baruth–Dornswalde stretch of woods immediately west of the autobahn. Elements of 3rd and 4th Guards Tank Armies were also deployed, the 3rd Guards Tank Army contributing 71st Mechanized Brigade, an SPG regiment and a mortar battalion to the Rehagen–Neuhof sector around the Gross Wünsdorfer See facing south, while 68th Independent Guards Tank Brigade deployed along the Kummersdorf Gut–Baruth front facing north-east.

In this way three defensive cordons were established to a depth of 15–20 kilometres. The concentration of armour on the Zossen–Baruth road also included a mobile reserve. Every break-out attempt from now on would be even more difficult and complicated for the German troops.[3]

Busse's article on 9th Army's last battle was written in Soviet captivity and published ten years after the event. Of 23 pages, only three are devoted to the pocket and break-out phase and contain chronological errors, dating the main break-out as 26 April instead of 28 April, and what he wrote of 24 April clearly, and totally unfairly, refers to the *von Luck/Pipkorn* attempt of 25 April:

> The first attempt on 24 April to slip away from the constrictions of the pocket to the west failed. The armoured troops committed to the gap near Halbe did not wait for the arrival of the infantry, as they had been strictly ordered to, but drove on for their own safety. So the Russians closed the breach before the infantry could prop it open and get through. The author has unfortunately forgotten the names of the commanders and units who left their comrades in the lurch on this occasion.[4]

It seems that Busse was trying to cover up his own inadequacy here, for he himself was responsible for issuing the relevant orders, and for organising the follow-up by the infantry that failed to materialise. He was also to blame for not allowing the armoured troops to take ammunition and fuel reserves with them to sustain their action. His failure to have a proper grip on the situation may have been partly due to his headquarters being on the move from the

Scharmützelsee railway station to the Hammer forestry office during the night, but still does not excuse him.[5]

SS-Second Lieutenant Porsch of Tank-Hunting Company *Dora II* continued his account:

> I knocked out two anti-tank guns near Märkisch Buchholz that stood in our way. A few hours previously I had been awarded the Knight's Cross. A staff officer brought it to me, as I could not leave my men.
>
> Things were happening as never before in this war. We sat in a pocket and the Ivans hammered us with weapons of all calibres and massive air attacks. Soldiers of all branches of the service and ranks up to general were fighting with rifles or machine-pistols in their hands, men, women and children swarming around us. Afraid that we would break out of the pocket and leave them behind, they clustered around us and fell in heaps from Ivan's explosive shells. As often as we tried, as often as we attacked, we still came up against a fresh barrier that cost death and suffering.[6]

However, 9th Army was not Koniev's only major problem that day, for General Wenck launched his rescue operation with XX Corps from the line Brandenburg–Belzig at dawn, not heading towards Jüterbog as the OKW expected but towards Potsdam, where the Soviet forces did not appear to be quite so strong. The roads were blocked with refugees, so the troops had to move across country on either side of the railway line leading to Berlin. Wenck's aims were given as saving: the wounded from the field hospitals within the army's operational area, the remains of 9th Army, the Potsdam garrison, and the refugees. Consequently, General Carl-Erik Koehler, commanding XX Corps, was instructed to secure his flanks on the Elbe to ensure an open passage to the west.

The 12th Army hoped to achieve surprise with this attack, but Hitler had issued the following Führer-Order on 23 April,

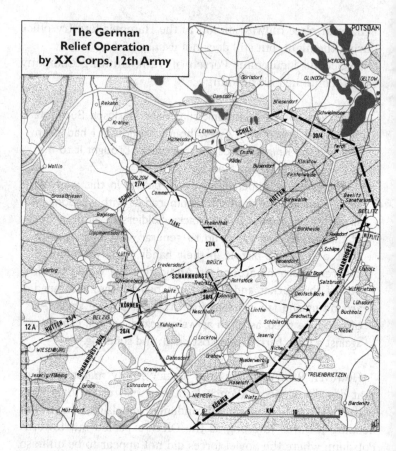

which was distributed in Berlin in leaflet form to boost the morale of the garrison and inhabitants:

To the Soldiers of Wenck's Army!

An order of immense importance has removed you from your combat zone facing the enemy in the west and set you marching eastward. Your task is clear. Berlin must remain German. The objectives given to you must be achieved whatever the circumstances, for operations are in progress

108

elsewhere to inflict a decisive defeat on the Bolsheviks fighting for the capital and from this the situation in Germany will change completely. Berlin will never capitulate to Bolshevism!

The defenders of the capital have found renewed courage with the news of your rapid progress, and are fighting with bravery and determination in the certainty of soon hearing your guns. The Führer has summoned you, and you have gone forward into the attack as in the days of conquest. Berlin awaits you! Berlin encourages you with all the warmth of her heart.[7]

Having redeployed during the previous night, XX Corps launched its attack on either side of the railway leading north-east to Berlin. As there had been no time for a formal reconnaissance, the *Ulrich von Hutten* Infantry Division in the lead was preceded by a reconnaissance team in eight-wheeled armoured cars with 75-mm guns, motorcyclists and an infantry company in APCs, followed by a vanguard of motorized infantry with some 50-mm anti-tank guns. On its right was the *Scharnhorst* Infantry Division, and on the far right the *Theodor Körner*, which was tasked with securing the extending right flank.

At first all went well. The angle of attack avoided the prepared line of defence held by 5th Guards Mechanized Corps and 13th Army along the Wittenberg–Potsdam road (Reichsstrasse 2), and caught 6th Guards Mechanized Corps on an exposed flank. A number of Soviet units were captured intact, including some supply columns and a tank workshop. The young trainees of XX Corps fought with all the elan of the German Army during the first years of the war under their experienced instructors.

During the night the *Ferdinand Schill* Division came in on the left flank with orders to head for Potsdam.[8]

Marshal Koniev badly wanted 4th Guards Tank Army's 10th Guards Tank Corps to meet the threat posed by the advance of 12th Army on Berlin but, much to his annoyance, it remained fully committed in bottling up General Reymann's Army Detachment *Spree* on the Wannsee and Potsdam 'islands'. As Koniev himself admitted, a force of 20,000 men could not simply be ignored.[9] However, he says remarkably little about this day in his memoirs, presumably preferring to forget what must have been in fact a serious rebuff.

Meanwhile 13th Army's 24th Rifle Corps had been detached and, since its 395th Rifle Division was already in the Golssen–Baruth sector, 117th Rifle Division (102nd Rifle Corps) assumed the all-round defence of Luckenwalde, and 280th Rifle Division (27th Rifle Corps) was stationed as corps reserve in the Jüterbog area. This deployment was so arranged that the Soviet units could engage either the 9th or the 12th German Armies.[10]

There appears to have been a major break-out attempt that night. Whether or not it was authorized by General Busse remains unclear, but it seems that elements of V, V SS Mountain and XI SS Panzer Corps were involved.[11] One group of infantry with artillery pieces and transport in train reached as far as the western outskirts of Freidorf, the village in which the headquarters of 1st Guards Breakthrough Artillery and 389th Rifle Divisions were located, before they were stopped by 5th Battery, 203rd Guards Howitzer Artillery Regiment, at a range of 150 metres. Some of the gunners had to resort to their carbines and sub-machine guns to defend themselves. The battery later claimed to have killed 90 Germans as well as destroying a 150-mm gun, a four-barrelled rapid-firing anti-aircraft gun, and six trucks. The rest of the regiment engaged more German infantry 300 metres north of Freidorf. The Germans retreated with heavy losses but then counterattacked and re-entered the village before being finally beaten off in this bitter encounter.[12]

The 1st Byelorussian Front's 3rd Army was instructed to have its 40th Rifle Corps attack in the direction Mittenwalde–

Motzen that day, occupy the the sector Brusendorf–Motzen–Pätz and establish contact with the troops of 1st Ukrainian Front. Its 35th Rifle Corps was to advance towards Pätz and its 41st towards Prieros, and they were then to occupy the Gross Köris–Prieros sector. The 2nd Guards Cavalry Corps was to thrust towards Märkisch Buchholz and, with 69th Army operating in the centre with its right flank against Görsdorf–Streganz, was to occupy the sector Prieros–Schwerin–Behrensdorf. Finally, 33rd Army had to deliver the main blow in the Beeskow–Kehrigk direction, with a subsidiary blow on the left flank towards Gröditsch.

Meanwhile some 1,500 Soviet bombers, ground-attack aircraft and fighters were tasked with supporting their own troops, preventing 9th Army from manoeuvring, smashing German concentrations in the woods and at the Spree and Dahme crossing points, preventing resupply by air, and conducting aerial reconnaissance.[13]

Both fronts used pamphlets and loudspeakers to try to persuade the German troops to give up the fight and surrender, thus saving themselves casualties, but these efforts proved mainly ineffective, the determination of the Germans to escape Soviet captivity and break out to the west being far too strong, even among stragglers from shattered units, whether still armed or not.[14]

An SS-second lieutenant with Battlegroup *Becker* reported:

We reached Prieros at 1000 hours on 26 April and took up positions in front of the town, then set off again that afternoon for Hermsdorf. Supplies were already short but there was enough ammunition available. There were often unpleasant incidents. Wounded and civilians all wanted to be taken along with us even when they could hardly move themselves.

The night was cold and the sentries were often unable to distinguish friend from foe. The Prieros–Streganz road was blocked during the night. It began to rain as we lay without cover in the necessary positions, Russian mortaring being very heavy. We often had the feeling that Ivan knew exactly where we were. The men were completely exhausted, and I and an Army second lieutenant spent the night checking the sentries, coming across sentries who had fallen asleep. We had a cursory roll call: there were still 74 men of the old company, 43 from the 2nd Battalion/ 88[th Grenadier Regiment], and over 30 men from other units. Some were already wounded, but everyone knew that we would only get out if we stayed together.

An SS-captain from Wagner's staff [Division *Nederland*] found us, bringing an urgent request for us to hold out at all costs! There were not only us soldiers but, above all, women and children in the pocket.[15]

Ernst-Christian Gädtke continues his account:

We were alerted early on 26 April. The Russians were attacking from the west and north-east. We quickly broke out and withdrew to a wood south of Neubrück, north of Märkisch Buchholz. We got a bit of a rest in the Hammer Forest, disturbed only by occasional attacks from Russian ground-attack aircraft. We lay camouflaged under the trees, so they didn't bother us much.

With us and around us were gathering the pitiful remnants of 9th Army. The field kitchens, such as there were, formed assembly points for the shattered or simply scattered units, and food was doled out only to members of their own units, thus serving to get the troops together again.

What we didn't know, and only discovered much later, was that Zhukov's armies had long since thrust through to Berlin on the direct route via Seelow–Müncheberg–Rüdersdorf, and that our fighting since 17 April had amounted only to pathetic pinpricks in the southern flank of the Russian troops, who had long since gone past us. The Russian formations had certainly not taken this seriously, otherwise, in view of the comparison of strengths, there would have been nothing of us left.

While a large part of 9th Army had remained in its positions on the Oder on Hitler's express orders, Koniev's armies had broken through north-westwards from the Lausitz and had reached the southern outskirts of Berlin ahead of Zhukov's troops. The 9th Army had been encircled.

There was no more talk now of a relief attack on Berlin, for it had become a question of breaking out to the west. The efforts of the units to assemble, and get themselves into order in the Hammer Forest, served only as preparations for the march and break-out from encirclement.

After all the chaotic events of the past days since we had left our positions in the woods near Fürstenberg, we were astonished how everything came together: field kitchens and supply wagons, a handful of trucks with all sorts of supplies and ammunition, finally two guns and fifty or so men, in effect stragglers – that was all that was left of the 32nd SS Tank-Hunting Battalion.

Fuel was scarce, so all the supply vehicles had to remain behind here, only the assault guns and the field kitchen were to drive on, as were the fuel truck as long as it had a few full cans of petrol. We crammed our packs from the supply vehicles and sorted out what seemed to be the most important, and what we could carry, the rest being thrown carelessly into the undergrowth. The field kitchen's vat steamed and there was no lack of food. Only the essentials would be taken on the march, so our messtins were filled to the brim and we could have as much as we liked. The remaining supplies, especially arms and ammunition, were loaded on to the few vehicles coming with us, the last tanks and assault guns, a few self-propelled anti-tank and anti-aircraft guns, and some towing vehicles. I was lucky to be assigned as relief gunner to one of the remaining assault guns, and so had the prospect of riding at least part of the way.

Once it was dark, we rolled ourselves up in our blankets and tent-halves and tried to sleep on the forest floor next to the gun.[16]

NOTES

1. Schulze, *Der Kessel Halbe–Baruth–Radeland*, p. 30.
2. Kortenhaus, *Der Einsatz der 21. Panzer-Division*, pp. 139–40.
3. Lakowsky/Stich, *Der Kessel von Halbe 1945*, pp. 92–3.
4. Busse, 'Die letzte Schlacht der 9. Armee', p. 167.
5. Tieke, *Das Ende zwischen Oder und Elbe*, p. 192.
6. Wilke archives.
7. Wenck, 'Berlin war nicht mehr zu retten', p. 64 f.
8. Wenck, 'Berlin war nicht mehr zu retten', pp. 65–6; Gellermann, *Die Armee Wenck*, pp. 83–7; Tieke, *Das Ende zwischen Oder und Elbe*, p. 331.
9. Koniev, *Year of Victory*, pp. 179–80.
10. Lakowski/Stich, *Der Kessel von Halbe 1945*, p. 66.
11. Wilke, *Am Rande der Strassen*, p. 54.
12. Domank, 'The 1st Guards Breakthrough Artillery Division at Halbe'.
13. Lakowski/Stich, *Der Kessel von Halbe 1945*, pp. 66–8.
14. *Ibid.*, p. 68.
15..Wilke, *Am Rande der Strassen*, p. 83.
16. Gädtke, *Von der Oder zur Elbe*, pp. 32–3. German soldiers were issued with waterproof tent-halves that could be worn as capes or fastened together to form simple pup-tents.

NINE

THE POCKET SHRINKS

27 APRIL 1945

Fragmentary break-out attempts from Halbe continued from the night before, and 1st Guards Breakthrough Artillery Division claimed to have destroyed four infantry companies, eight machine guns, neutralized a howitzer battery, killed 130 Germans and captured a further 35, plus an artillery piece.[1]

However, one break-out group took the village of Zesch and reached as far as the Soviet third cordon at Neuhof on the Zossen–Baruth road (Reichsstrasse 96) in the north, while a few small groups managed to get through the third cordon on the Zossen–Baruth road and reached as far as Paplitz in the south. The 13th Army's 395th Rifle Division in its fire-brigade role and 4th Guards Tank Army's 68th Guards Tank Brigade counterattacked, leading to some heavy fighting around Zesch. Further south another group was driven out of Dornswalde by 96th Guards Rifle Division of 28th Army's 3rd Guards Rifle Corps. The soldiers breaking out of the encirclement fought as their predecessors had done of old, but their attacks were checked and their combat teams shattered. Partly surrounded once more, they suffered heavy casualties, and only a very few were able to flee unnoticed into the surrounding woods and hide. Soviet claims for the day amounted to 6,200 prisoners, 47 tanks and APCs, 180 guns and mortars, and 1,132 vehicles captured.[2]

Extracts from the diary of a soldier from Hamburg, later killed, describe events that day:

> After I had made a few notes in my diary, we had to move on again. Our transport and everything was left behind — even though the vehicle was carrying several wounded — and we moved off to the right from the road into a wood. There we came across a large group of stragglers and were told that in the last pocket everything had had to be left for Ivan — vehicles, supplies, ammunition, wounded — and those who had had enough had surrendered to the enemy.
>
> We then came to some marshes that deprived us of the last of our strength. The second lieutenant from the previous day and a captain lay down on the saturated ground, their strength at an end. The captain pulled himself up, propped himself against a tree trunk and said: 'Comrades, I am disbanding our group. Whoever thinks he has to, push through to Berlin.'
>
> I had lost Helmut in the confusion again. It was not long before I came to a barn that stood alone in the meadows. I crept inside and slept until the sun went down. The sleep had strengthened me, and when I opened my eyes, there was a captain and nine comrades lying beside me. They were all southern Germans who wanted to go home. They had a map and a compass, and I was invited to join them. They wanted to cross the Elbe near Wittenberg, and so I was happy to have at last found people wanting to get away from the Russians.[3]

This unknown soldier probably belonged to one of the many groups of men from the shattered 9th Army who had become separated from their units and were wandering around the woods afraid of capture by the Russians.[4]

Generals Busse and Wenck received a further order from Colonel-General Jodl that day demanding:

> Concerted attacks by 9th and 12th Armies should serve not only to rescue 9th Army, but especially to save Berlin . . . XX Corps, after reaching the line Beelitz–Ferch, is to attack [north-east to] Löwenbruch–Stahnsdorf; 9th Army to thrust north via Trebbin, establish contact with 12th Army and cover the rear on the line Luckenwalde–Baruth.[5]

Major Brand of 21st Armoured Reconnaissance Battalion wrote about the situation within 21st Panzer Division:

> Orders from above obviously still inevitably mean higher casualties on our side. Attempt on 27 April to convince General Marcks to break away from the Army and break through to the west unilaterally. Marcks puts off the decision until later.[6]

General Marcks was a disciple of the fanatical Field Marshal Ferdinand Schörner, who had set up flying courts martial to deal with any unauthorized troops found behind the lines or away from their units, and Colonel *von Luck* had previously lost a senior NCO escorting tanks sent back for repair as a result of this. From the comments of *von Luck* and Brand, there can be little doubt that Marcks was distinctly unpopular with his officers.[7]

Within the pocket communications continued to deteriorate. One German soldier noted that day: 'The rumour is going around that we are breaking out.'[8] In fact attempts were made to break out at several points of the encirclement, but there is no evidence as to who planned or ordered them. From the Soviet point of view, these were seen as important attempts to force a breakthrough by means of waves of attacks, but could in fact have been the efforts of individual

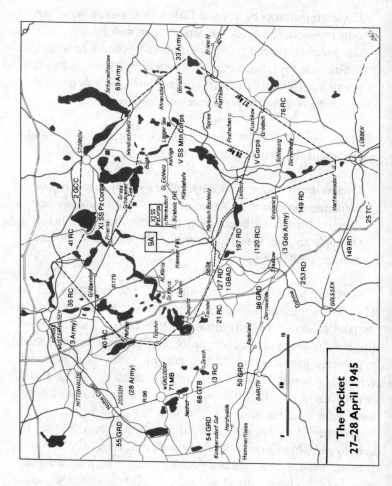

The Pocket
27–28 April 1945

units acting on their own initiative, or simply local counterattacks.

Marshal Koniev commented:

The stronger the pressure was exerted against them and the harder the blows they received from behind, the more vigorously they tried to break through to our rear. Each thrust from behind seemed to pass through them to us, in front. The enemy concentrated their battle formations and attacked us more and more actively. This was only to be expected, for there was no alternative but surrender.[9]

The pressure on the northern, eastern and southern parts of the perimeter were hard for 9th Army to take. Nowhere was it able to stop the advance of the overwhelming Soviet forces, the German troops having to give up more and more territory and villages.

The Gross Köris sector could no more be held than the gaps between the lakes near Prieros, Storkow and Wendisch Rietz, where the positions of 32nd SS Division and Panzergrenadier Division *Kurmark* had to be abandoned, their lines of retreat being strewn with vehicles, either shot-up or destroyed because of lack of fuel, and heavy weapons blown up for lack of towing vehicles or ammunition. SS-Captain Paul Krauss described the scene:

It was now just a matter of getting out of the ever-narrowing pocket to the west intact. More and more motor vehicles mixed with the horse-drawn carts of the refugees in column after column winding their way through the forest tracks to Halbe, where the break-out was to take place. All the time there were enemy ground-attack aircraft overhead shooting at the throngs of people and vehicles, causing casualty after casualty. Bodies were flying through the air; here and there vehicles were beginning to burn and falling apart; ammunition trucks were exploding. Chaos had begun and everyone pressed in from behind, no one wanting to leave the column or lose contact.

It was not until late afternoon on 27 April that the stream of vehicles ceased with only the odd column coming up behind. It appeared that the main body had reached Halbe.[10]

On the southern edge of the encirclement near Märkisch Buchholz, one of the important traffic junctions, fierce fighting took place, the village itself changing hands several times that day. Soviet armour finally reached the line Kuschkow–Schlepzig–Halbe–Löpten, and both Teupitz and Halbe were re-occupied by Soviet infantry, thus blocking off the whole break-out sector.[11]

During the course of the day the size of the pocket was not only considerably reduced, it was also split as a result of a thrust by troops of 1st Byelorussian Front's 3rd Army from the Gräbendorf area west of Prieros as far as Gross Köris and Prieros, a move that the remains of 32nd SS Division and its tank-hunting battalion were unable to prevent. SS-Captain Krauss wrote of this many years later:

The 9th Army in the area south of Berlin was already in a big pocket that had become split into several small ones at Müllrose, Prieros and elsewhere. The Prieros pocket was about 21 kilometres across. In it were about 10,000–14,000 German soldiers of all arms of service and also about 20,000 civilians with their herds of cattle, individual animals, household articles; there were families, women with children, some on foot, some with horse-drawn carts, handcarts. All this under continuous artillery and mortar fire and air attack from the Russians, which could not fail to hit something each time. Conditions in the pocket were horrendous. Soldiers, civilians, children, women and vehicles moved round in a circle, trying to avoid the fire like a giant, thousand-legged worm biting itself in the tail. Officers, soldiers, civilians with their families, whole groups of German people were shooting themselves. I looked across at this spectacle shattered, stunned and helpless.[12]

Apart from Krauss' report, little of this particular pocket is known, nor is anything to be found about it among Soviet sources.

However, the Army and Waffen-SS units taking the brunt of the fighting on the northern and eastern sectors of the perimeter had had enough, and at 1400 hours that day their commanders convened at the command post of XI SS Panzer Corps, which was located at the Birkbusch forest warden's lodge, and told SS-General Mathias Kleinheisterkamp that, if he did not conduct an immediate break-out on his own initiative, they would do so themselves. (If this was the attitude of subordinate formation commanders, then confidence in General Busse and his headquarters was clearly lacking.) A break-out was then agreed for early next morning, providing the combat teams of 32nd SS Division could first disengage on the eastern sector of the perimeter along the line Eichholz forest warden's lodge–Kehrigk–Bugk. As a preliminary measure, SS-Colonel Hans Kempin resumed command of the combat teams of V SS Mountain Corps that had meantime been detached to various commands over the past few days while securing this part of the perimeter.[13]

Meanwhile 9th Army reported by radio to Army Group *Weichsel* as follows:

V Corps: enemy penetrations near Märkisch Buchholz forced back. Enemy in Teupitz and Teurow. The redeployment of V SS Mountain Corps on the line Hartmannsdorf [near Lübben] Dürrenhofe–Kuschkow– Pretschen–Plattkow–Ahrensdorf–

southern edge Scharmützelsee strongly pressed by the enemy.
XI SS Panzer Corps: breach between Gross Schauener See and Langer See.

The seriousness of the situation is reflected in this signal from Army Group *Weichsel* to 12th Army: '9th Army's attacking spearheads at Mückendorf (NE of Baruth). Strong counterattacks. Help from the west urgently desired.'[14] This was a request that 12th Army was no longer in a position to meet. Wenck's troops were fully engaged all along the whole line of advance. The 9th Army would have to make its own way.[15]

The 1st *Scharnhorst* Grenadier Regiment took Reesdorf and was then ordered to stop and consolidate there, while the 3rd *Scharnhorst* on the right flank reached and held the line Schlalach–Brachwitz–Buchholz, dug in and repelled Soviet counterattacks. The *Scharnhorst* Infantry Division was supported in these operations by the 1170th SPG Brigade, which suffered heavy casualties in the process.[16]

Wenck's attack had thus isolated 6th Guards Mechanized Corps from the rest of 4th Guards Tank Army at a time when this corps was extended over a distance of some 28 kilometres. The 5th Guards Mechanized Corps and 13th Army were having to form a double front, expecting Busse's 9th Army to try and break out to the west at any moment from behind them, while the rest of 4th Guards Tank Army was still heavily engaged in the containment of the Potsdam and Wannsee 'islands'.[17]

Next morning the Army Group's situation report on the events of the 27th to the OKH contained the following:

Breakthrough attempt failed. Armoured spearheads with the most valuable elements have broken out to the west contrary to specific orders, or been destroyed. Other attacking groups have been stopped or in part thrown back with considerable loss. The physical and mental condition of officers and men, as well as the ammunition and fuel situation, allows neither a renewal of the planned break-out attack nor long holding out. Especially hard is the shattering misery of the civilian population concentrated in the cauldron. Only through the measures taken by all generals has it been possible to keep the troops going until now.[18]

By evening the remains of 9th Army had withdrawn back into the core of the remaining pocket, where the forests of Halbe and Märkisch Buchholz formed the assembly areas, resembling vast military encampments. Tanks and SPGs were to be used to provide the decisive thrust at the head of the breakthrough next morning. This time the attack would be along the line Halbe–Kummersdorf Gut. What nobody knew was that this led directly into the Soviets' best prepared defences in depth.

Conditions for the remaining inhabitants of Halbe were described in various accounts. One of these came from Ingrid Feilsch, who was then 15 years old:

Hans, my eldest brother, was watching a wounded man being bandaged in the yard when the first shell hit the house. He was killed instantly. A French prisoner of war, who was living with us, brought him down into the cellar.

Next day another shell struck, killing my youngest brother, the three-year-old, in his cot, as well as a playmate and his grandmother. My mother lost both her feet. That was the most terrible thing. We looked for a medical orderly for hours, but where was the help? Mother cried until the next day, then she was dead. My five-year-old brother Ernst and myself were now alone. Father came back late from the war.[19]

Herr G. Fonrobert also described his experiences:

I myself experienced the horrific inferno of the bloody encirclement battle as a war-wounded civilian in a house in the Halbe settlement that changed hands three times in bitter, close-quarter fighting. The experience remains vividly in front of my eyes even today.

After the railway tracks at Halbe had been blown up by the engineers, there was a stream of hurrying people flowing through the streets of Halbe all day long. A chaotic confusion of wounded soldiers on different kinds of military vehicles, as well as refugee groups of mainly women and children, all seeking to escape from the Russians as a result of Goebbels' lying propaganda.

Meanwhile our village had been occupied by SS and military police units, and soon afterwards we clearly heard the sounds of artillery and infantry fire. The civilians took shelter in their cellars.

And then at dawn on 25 April began the fearful slaughter of the Halbe pocket that was to last six days and six nights.

The air shuddered with the din of heavy weapons of all sizes, of tank battles, the roar of mortars, rockets and the rattle of machine guns, interrupted at times by strafing from Soviet ground-attack aircraft. There were seven of us in the cellar of our house, including a nine-year-old child, finally sitting quite apathetic and numbed by the ear-deafening explosions – sleep was out of the question – pressed close to the cellar walls and waiting for the end with horror after the neighbouring house had been torn in half by a shell and our own house had suffered considerable damage.

Following the bloody rounds of man against man around our house, in which there were dead and wounded, the soldiers of the Red Army finally occupied it and set up a command post in the living room upstairs and in the cellar, showing themselves to be very humane, giving us cigarettes and chocolate.

Later, eight male inhabitants of the settlement, including myself, were tasked by the Soviet military with seeing to the severely injured lying on the sports ground, but soon had to withdraw again and take cover, despite our white armbands, when we were fired on recklessly by the SS unit lying on either side of the sports ground and started taking casualties as civilians in the auxiliary medical service!

In seeking cover, we saw a frightful scene at a crossroads at the edge of the village. An anti-tank barrier had been attacked shortly before, and piles of bodies lay there, some in a cramped position and squashed by the tanks that had rolled over them, wounded crying out for help, dying horses trying to struggle up again, puddles of blood everywhere, burning and destroyed houses, collapsing ruins, abandoned guns and scattered equipment – a picture of horror and devastation, truly a face of war that could not be worse depicted.[20]

Notes

1. Domank, 'The 1st Guards Breakthrough Artillery Division at Halbe'.
2. Wilke, *Am Rande der Strassen*, p. 54.
3. Lakowski/Stich, *Der Kessel von Halbe 1945*, pp. 101–2.
4. *Ibid.*
5. Förster/Lakowski, *1945 – Das Jahr der endgültigen Niederlage der faschistischen Wehrmacht*, p. 342 [citing Federal Military Archives RH W.30.10./6, Sheet 842].
6. Brand in the author's *Death Was Our Companion*.
7. Von Luck, *Gefangener meiner Zeit*, pp. 259, 264–5, 270–1.
8. Lakowski/Stich, *Der Kessel von Halbe 1945*, p. 97.
9. Koniev, *Year of Victory*, p. 180.
10. Spaether, *Die Geschichte des Panzerkorps 'Großdeutschland'*, pp. 637–8.

11. Kortenhaus, *Der Einsatz der 21. Panzer-Division*, p. 140.
12. Lakowski/Stich, *Der Kessel von Halbe 1945*, pp. 104–5, citing Krauß Report, 1997.
13. Wilke, *Am Rande der Strassen*, pp. 123–4.
14. Lakowski/Stich, *Der Kessel von Halbe 1945*, pp. 97–8.
15. Wenck, 'Berlin war nicht mehr zu retten', p. 66.
16. Gellermann, *Die Armee Wenck*, p. 84.
17. Tieke, *Das Ende zwischen Oder und Elbe*, p. 238.
18. Lakowski/Stich, *Der Kessel von Halbe 1945*, p. 105 [citing Federal Military Archives RH 19 XV/10, Sheet 393f.].
19. *Halbe mahnt...!* 1963 pamphlet, pp. 15–16.
20. *Ibid.*, p. 17.

TEN

THE EYE OF THE NEEDLE

28 APRIL 1945

According to Soviet sources, the fighting on 28 April began with an attack along a five-kilometre front by a divisional-sized battlegroup supported by 20 tanks. This occurred in the Löpten–Teurow sector astride Halbe on the inter-front boundary between 40th Rifle Corps of 3rd Army and 21st Rifle Corps of 3rd Guards Army. The battle raged for hours, but ferocious close-quarter fighting and heavy covering fire failed to secure a decisive breach for the Germans. There was no question of a breakthrough to the autobahn. The German forces, commanded by SS-General Kleinheisterkamp, came from the remains of 712th Infantry Division of XI SS Panzer Corps, 286th Infantry Division of V SS Mountain Corps, and 275th and 342nd Infantry and 35th SS Police Divisions of V Corps, plus a number of independent units. Unfortunately for Kleinheisterkamp's plan, 32nd SS Division had come under increased Soviet pressure and had been unable to disengage from the perimeter to reinforce the breach as had been intended. Consequently, the units on the northern perimeter were also forced to hold on. It is possible that some small groups managed to break out of the encirclement, but the majority were thrown back with heavy losses.[1]

Corporal Harry Zvi Glaser, a Lithuanian-born Jew, had been forced out of his country by the German invasion of

1941 and enlisted in the Red Army as soon as he was old enough in 1944. Now leading a rifle section in 2nd Battalion of 438th Rifle Regiment, 129th *Orel* Rifle Division of 3rd Army, he wrote of his experience at Halbe:

On 28 April our unit was ordered to pull out of Berlin and make a forced march overnight down the 35 kilometres of autobahn to Halbe. At dawn I deployed my section on the eastern edge of the village overlooking a vast neglected pasture, and a Maxim machine gun was brought up to reinforce us, which I placed on our right flank. After I had briefed my men, I went off to check the farmhouse behind us. I found some frightened civilians in the cellar and told them in German: 'Stay indoors, don't leave the house under any circumstances until you get fresh instructions!'

'Ja, jawohl, Herr Offizier!' came the reply. I spotted some cans of meat on a shelf. 'Please take them!' said an old man, the only male in the family, so I took two cans to feed my hungry men and went back to the trenches, having to step over the bodies of several dead German soldiers.

The pasture in front of us remained empty until suddenly a woman appeared with a baby in her arms running across the field towards the village and just as suddenly disappeared again. Then I was summoned to battalion headquarters.

The battalion commander and his staff were on the south side of the street dividing Halbe in two and were looking south across the pasture to the woods, where white flags were waving among the trees. The battalion commander turned to me and said: 'Corporal, you speak German, don't you? You see the white flags? It's less than a kilometre. If you want to earn the "Red Banner",[2] go and clarify the situation and bring back some delegates for their surrender with you.'

I started across the pasture but had gone only about 200 metres when the flags disappeared and several gunshots

128

sounded from the woods. There was no one to be seen, and my battalion commander and his staff had also disappeared, so I returned to my section.

Then a runner appeared: 'German tanks are moving towards the village with infantry following them!' The pasture immediately became alive with attacking German infantry. We held our fire until 200 metres then started mowing them down, forcing them to retreat. But it was bad behind us, where the German tanks were rolling forward with machine guns firing from their turrets and followed by infantry assault teams. The supporting 45-mm gun sited on the pavement was unable to stop them and was hit by a shell from a Tiger that wrecked it and killed the crew. We were taking casualties and tried to withdraw but were pinned down until dusk, which came suddenly and enabled us to crawl out of Halbe with our wounded. The battalion commander had been killed and the whole battalion was in retreat.[3]

An SS-sergeant-major of the 32nd SS Motorized Signals Battalion reported:

At 0200 hours on 28 April our unit ceased to exist. We were split up into infantry combat teams. Our team was led by the unit administrative officer, our commander having already said his goodbyes and wished us good luck in the break-out. During the break-out attempt we were separated and I only had my runner with me. It was chaotic.

I had never been so astonished during the whole of the war as I was that morning of 28 April. What I saw in the column left me speechless, changing to blind rage, anger and aggressiveness. There were officers and their drivers sleeping peacefully in their vehicles with their legs over the folded-down windscreens. Others were eating breakfast with appetite, even small fires could be seen for heating coffee. A peacetime scene, while several hundred metres away death was reaping a rich harvest. While mini combat teams were trying to effect a breakthrough, thousands of men here of all ranks from the Army, Waffen-SS, Luftwaffe and Flak were lying around and waiting for the others to smash through the encirclement so that they could drive out in peace and quiet. No officer made any attempt to form a combat team out of this lot. A flak captain was having a shave by his vehicle with his field tunic hanging neatly from a coathanger on the vehicle. A large number of these 'comrades' had to pay for this attitude with their lives or long years of imprisonment under the Soviets . . . it was just a leaderless horde.[4]

The troops began to desert, flee and panic. Command and control were lost and many soldiers decided to strike out on their own. That morning 9th Army lost some 3,000 prisoners, 15 tanks and over 60 guns, and an unknown number of dead and wounded.

Once more the 1st Guards Artillery Breakthrough Division, with its 300 guns deployed south of Halbe, played a decisive role in the Soviet success. There was no way for the encircled troops to match this mass of artillery, as an inhabitant of Teupitz recalled:

I had experienced the bombardments in Champagne during the First World War, taken part in the Battle of the Somme and been in the bitter ring at Verdun, but what occurred in the Halbe cauldron during these days put all that I had seen before into the shade. With clockwork precision, all day long until dusk one bomber squadron after another brought its deadly loads to the big woods around Halbe, Teupitz and Märkisch Buchholz and dropped them on the fully congested country roads. Without a pause the rockets hissed in and the guns hammered at the makeshift positions the German troops had dug.[5]

That morning, in accordance with orders issued by Marshal Koniev the night before, 3rd Guards Tank Army in Berlin launched a concerted attack on the extreme right wing of its area of operations in Schöneberg with the aim of crossing the Landwehr Canal by nightfall. The main attack got under way as planned and it was not until sometime later in the morning that it was suddenly realised that virtually the whole of the eastern half of their proposed line of advance was already occupied by Chuikov's troops, for whom the weight of Koniev's artillery preparations could hardly have been welcome. The emotions that this event raised can well be imagined.[6]

Koniev, however, barely mentioned this incident in his memoirs:

> Meanwhile, during the morning, Chuikov's 8th Guards Army, Rybalko's neighbour on the right, resolutely advanced west, all the way to the southern bank of the Landwehr Canal, and reached the Anhalter Railway Terminal, Lützowplatz and the intersection of Plauener Strasse and Maassenstrasse.
>
> In view of the rapid westward advance of Chuikov's troops and in order to prevent Rybalko's 9th Mechanized Corps from getting mixed up with Chuikov's 8th Guards Army, I ordered Rybalko that, after he had reached the Landwehr Canal, he should turn his most advanced units west and continue his advance in the zone of operations newly established by that time for the 1st Ukrainian Front.[7]

One assumes that General Chuikov's thrust westwards across the inter-front boundary could only have been effected with Marshal Zhukov's connivance, and there was no way that 3rd Guards Tank Army was going to be allowed to close up to the Landwehr Canal. However, at midnight Moscow time GHQ issued orders for a new inter-front boundary, which diverted 3rd Guards Tank Army in a north-westerly direction, well away from the city centre.

With his Berlin ambitions thus thwarted, Koniev left General Rybalko to complete 1st Ukrainian Front's role in the city as best he might. Koniev had taken a tremendous gamble in concentrating all his available resources in a single powerful thrust on the Reichstag, but had been defeated by factors arising out of the rivalry between himself and Marshal Zhukov – which had been skilfully exploited by Stalin without regard for the military implications.[8]

The Halbe pocket had now been reduced to a sixth of its original size, the steadily growing threat by the four Soviet armies surrounding them giving the encircled concentration of troops and refugees no peace. Constant fighting was taking place on the perimeter while bombers and ground-attack aircraft struck from above whenever the weather allowed, and the fire from artillery, mortars and rockets continued to take a steady toll.

From Prieros, now the northernmost tip of the pocket, the company-sized combat team of 1st Battalion, 86th SS Regiment *Schill*, conducted an unsuccessful counterattack against the Soviets occupying Kolberg, but was able to hold its ground on the necks of land between the lakes in that area. Its left-hand neighbour, the combat team of 87th SS Regiment *Kurmark*, covering the line Neubrück–Prieros, was decimated by an attack, backed by aerial bombardment, by Soviet armour coming from Klein Köris. Behind it along the line Schwerin–Hammer–Hermsdorf–Gross Eichholz were combat teams formed from elements of Panzergrenadier Division *Kurmark* and 32nd SS Field Training and Replacement Battalion of 32nd SS Division under the overall command of SS-Colonel Kempin of the latter formation.[9] They were attacked by Soviet forces and *Seydlitz-Troops*.

SS-Lieutenant Bärmann, who was wounded in the attack, gave an account of this engagement:

> Shortly before midday on 28 April we reached the place that we had been ordered to, about three kilometres north-

Marshal Georgi Konstantinovitch Zhukov, C-in-C 1st Byelorussian Front.

Marshal Ivan Stepanovitch Koniev, C-in-C 1st Ukrainian Front.

General of Infantry Theodor Busse, GOC 9th Army.

General of Armoured Troops Walter Wenck, GOC 12th Army.

Baruth. The Soviet cemetery on Bundestrasse 96 north of the town.

Baruth. The Soviet cemetery monument.

Baruth. The Soviet cemetery monument, detail.

Märkisch Buchholz. The road bridge on the Halbe road with the weir of the Dahme Flood Canal beyond.

Märkisch Buchholz. The junction of the Dahme River and Flood Canal north of the town.

Märkisch Buchholz. The town centre.

Halbe. The road junction north of the level crossing with the dominating village church tower showing rear centre.

Halbe. The road junction north of the level crossing seen from the village centre.

Halbe. The railway station seen from the level crossing.

Halbe. The high street looking west with the site of the main anti-tank barricade in line with the balcony on the left.

Halbe. The high street looking east from the site of the main anti-tank barricade.

Hennickendorf. A Soviet T-34/85 destroyed by a Panzerfaust, which also killed the German firing it. *Lothar Schulze*

Kummersdorf Gut. The recently erected memorial to 830 persons killed in the vicinity in 1945, 304 of whom are unidentified.

Dobbrikow. Abandoned German command vehicles. *Lothar Schulze*

Schönefeld. The entrance to the radio station where SS-Sergeant Bertold Fink tanked up his Königstiger with diesel. *Lothar Schulze*

Elsholz. The spot where the last Königstiger of the 502nd SS Heavy Panzer Battalion crossed Reichsstrasse 2 into 12th Army territory. *Lothar Schulze*

SS-Sergeant Bertold Fink of the 502nd SS Heavy Panzer Battalion. *Lothar Schulze*

SS-Corporal Waldemar Ott, driver of SS-Sergeant-Major Streng's Königstiger. *Lothar Schulze*

SS-Sergeant-Major Ernst Streng of 502nd SS Heavy Panzer Battalion. *Lothar Schulze*

Corporal Harry Zvi Glaser of the 129th Orel Rifle Division, who fought in Halbe. *Glaser*

Above: Rudi Lindner as a police captain in the Soviet Zone later in 1945. *Lindner*

Right: Königstiger No. 231 of the 502nd SS Heavy Panzer Battalion abandoned in a swamp near Beelitz. *Fleischer*

Left: A Panther command tank of a Waffen-SS unit abandoned near Beelitz. *Lothar Schulze*

Right: Erwin Bartmann in 1944 as an NCO in the Leibstandarte-SS Adolf Hitler. *Bartmann*

A dead horse team in the aftermath of the Halbe break-out. *Chronos-Film*

Soldiers and civilians killed during the Halbe break-out. *Chronos-Film*

Soviet infantry under fire in a forest. *Evgeni Bessonov*

Soviet infantry attempting to advance despite German artillery fire. *Evgeni Bessonov*

Above: Marshal Koniev and his staff in the woods south of Berlin. *Lothar Schulze*

Left: Soviet T-34/85s carrying escorting infantry. *Evgeni Bessonov*

Soviet T-34/76s forcing their way into a forest. *Evgeni Bessonov*

Harry Zvi Glaser with President Clinton at the White House during a ceremony in which he was presented with the Order of Glory by President Yeltsin.
Harry Zvi Glaser

Halbe Cemetery holds the remains of over 20,000 German civilian and military casualties of the fighting in the area, only 8,000 of whom have been identified
William Durie

west of Hermsdorf. SS-Sergeant Althaus took up a defensive position with his recovery tank armed with twin machine guns, and soon afterwards the Russians attacked out of the woods from the north-east. While Althaus and other combat capable men of the battalion conducted the defence, some comrades threw me into a Volkswagen jeep and drove deeper into the woods. Most of the vehicles were damaged in the fighting and had to be left behind. A rocket launcher unit fired without pause and gave us some space.

We were then ordered to regroup at the Hammer forestry office ...

Low cloud kept the Russian aircraft off us, although some individual, unaimed bombs fell that could not fail to find victims in the closely packed pocket. According to the staff, the pocket now measured three by five kilometres and contained about 30,000 troops and 10,000–15,000 civilians, men women and children.[10]

The Hammer forestry office area was covered by a combat team from Panzergrenadier Division *Kurmark* that afternoon. On the eastern and southern parts of the perimeter, where the terrain prevented the use of armour, penetrations by Soviet infantry often split the defence, creating small pockets that were inevitably reduced in due course.

For the encircled, the situation in the pocket became ever more chaotic with constant movement, lack of sleep, scarcely enough to eat, contaminated drinking water, unbelievably high casualties and inadequate attention and facilities for the wounded. The 9th Army had no choice but to act or go under. There was now only sufficient ammunition left for another two days and there was absolutely no hope of resupply by air. Although a few of the soldiers were prepared to surrender, the majority were strongly against it. Leaflets, loudspeakers and attempts at negotiation under flags of truce and by civilians organized by the Soviets yielded no significant results.

General Busse belatedly realized that 9th Army had been betrayed and sent a radio message with the content: 'It seems that the 9th Army is already written off.'[11] Kleinheisterkamp's independent break-out attempt of that morning must also have come as a form of betrayal to him, but at last seems to have spurred him into taking action himself. However, when one examines his actions, the tardy transfer of his headquarters into the Spreewald indicates an indecisiveness and reluctance to assume responsibility for the break-out to the west, even though he had Hitler's authority and orders to do so. By the time he reached Hammer on 26 April, the congestion in the area was such that he had little chance of exercising effective control over his subordinates. He had failed to support Battlegroup *von Luck*'s attempt on 25 April. This, and the apparently independent attempts by subordinate formations stemming from pressure from below, had cost him dearly in armour and fighting troops, severely weakening his chances of a successful mass penetration of the Soviet forces facing him. And then, as we shall see, he placed himself and his headquarters staff immediately behind the strongest armoured spearhead for 9th Army's break-out, in which his exercise of control became purely local as contact was lost with other units, and the rearguard was abandoned to its fate.

The 9th Army's very last conference took place at 1500 hours that afternoon, when all available generals and divisional commanders met in a sandpit close to the forestry office at Hammer on Reichsstrasse 179. Following an appraisal of the situation, the decision was made to risk a last break-out attempt and break through to 12th Army. Contact had been lost with the commanders of V Corps and V SS Mountain Corps, so what remained of XI SS Panzer Corps would have to take the lead. The plan was for them to break out to the west in three groups that evening. Those tanks still remaining would pave the way, and General Busse would go with them.

The desperate situation in which the encircled troops found themselves left little choice of action. The officers present at General Busse's conference were unanimous that the break-out should take place immediately, and that it could only be achieved with the concentrated action of the remaining armoured forces and the whole of the available artillery. There was little enough left; in essence only the reduced *Kurmark* Division, 502nd SS Heavy Panzer Battalion and the few remaining guns and mortars. No participant at the conference could identify any worthwhile break-out route other than through Halbe, which was known to be occupied by strong Soviet units. This almost unknown village would become the eye of the needle through which everyone would have to pass. It was not difficult for the Soviet commanders to work out where the next attack would come, as the German preparations could hardly be concealed from aerial observation, so any possibility of surprise could be ruled out.

There was no information about the Soviet forces. The 9th Army no longer had any facilities for aerial reconnaissance, so knew nothing of what lay outside its perimeter. No one knew anything about the Russian positions, the organization or strength of the opposing troops, nor of the possibility of counterattacks in the depths of the 60-kilometre stretch of wooded country, bounded by the lakes around Zossen and Teupitz in the north and the Hammerfliess stream in the south, through which the already exhausted troops would have to march. It could take days for them to reach 12th Army's positions near Beelitz.

Meanwhile command and control within the pocket had virtually collapsed. Even the basic military requirement of reliable communications for the conduct of the forthcoming action was lacking. There was now only sporadic radio communication with Army Group *Weichsel*, and Headquarters 9th Army had only occasional contact with its subordinate formations, none of which was able to establish a stable network. Finally, the lack of maps made it difficult to command the troops in action.

The planning and execution of the breakthrough demanded immediate decisions that had to be made almost blind, contrary to all operational experience. The orders were thus kept correspondingly brief and went directly to the commander of XI SS Panzer Corps: 'XI SS Panzer Corps will strike the breakthrough breaches. 1800 hours assemble for break-out.'

At this point the command post of this corps was at the Klein Hammer forest warden's lodge near Hermsdorf. In order to fulfil the task allotted him, SS-General Kleinheisterkamp summoned those of his subordinate commanders who could be contacted to his command post. He decided that the spearhead would be formed by the remains of the *Kurmark* Division and the 502nd SS Heavy Panzer Battalion, split into two wedges. The more northerly one would consist of the remaining Panther tanks of the *Kurmark*'s Panzer Regiment Brandenburg, now down to less than battalion strength, and other elements of the division. Behind the 502nd in the southern wedge would come HQ 9th Army, HQ XI SS Panzer Corps and HQ Panzergrenadier Division *Kurmark*. The remaining forces still under command would then follow on behind. What remained of 21st Panzer Division would cover the breakthrough from the north-west, with the remnants of 32nd SS Panzergrenadier Division *30. Januar* guarding the east. This formation would provide the rearguard under the divisional chief engineer, SS-Major May, with orders to disengage from the enemy at 0500 hours on 29 April.[12]

As SS-Lieutenant Bärmann of the 32nd SS Tank-Hunting Battalion recorded:

The order to break out came towards evening. The remains of the 32nd SS Tank-Hunting Battalion were to form the rearguard. As our guns could only fire forwards, that meant us driving backwards for over 60 kilometres.[13]

SS-Colonel Hans Kempin, commander of the 32nd SS Division, also described the position:

> My last contact with General Busse was by radio, during which he informed me that he was trying to find a gap in the encirclement near Potsdam through which he could take headquarters 9th Army out of the pocket. He instructed me to take over command of the individual reachable units as a rearguard and to decide myself whether to break out to Berlin or towards the Elbe [12th Army]. On receipt of these orders, I saw myself having to stop the last counterattack by [omission in original] and his battalion, disengage and arrange the handover of the main dressing station with about 2,000 wounded to the Russians . . .
>
> When I and my staff reached a clearing in the woods before Halbe, I found several thousand soldiers there who had given up, lots of burnt-out tanks, buses, trucks and so on. The general view was that going any further was impossible. I therefore had another row with Jeckeln, the then commanding general of V [SS Mountain] Corps.
>
> I ordered the commander of my headquarters' security company, Fahland, to stay there and went on with my staff to Halbe during an air raid, and got through. There was no one to be seen, but plenty of corpses. Braun then went back to fetch the company. From your description, I take it that we had come from the Hammer forestry office.
>
> I can still recall a shot-up truck behind Halbe that must have been carrying pay, for the notes were lying around on the ground and no one had seen to them.[14]

Artillery Regiment *Kurmark* and the remaining heavy weapons were ordered to fire a barrage on Halbe with the last of their ammunition at 1800 hours. After that their equipment was to be destroyed. All units were to take only the most essential vehicles, all the remainder having to be

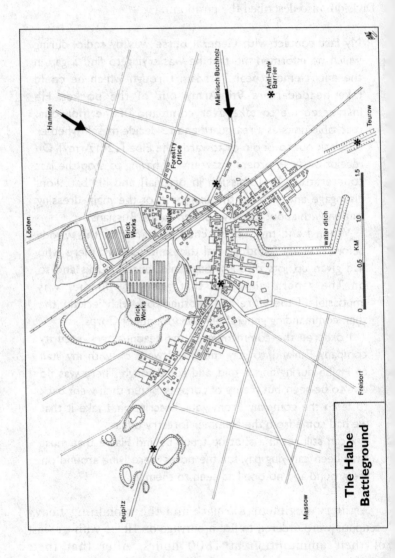

The Halbe Battleground

destroyed after their fuel tanks had been emptied for the use of the armour.

The materiel strength of these spearheads was relatively weak. The 502nd SS Heavy Panzer Battalion had probably only 14 of its formidable Tiger II (Königstiger) tanks left.[15] The fighting troops available for the spearheads were also greatly outnumbered by those unprepared to fight who were following them, as tens of thousands of armed and unarmed soldiers, civilians, wounded and sick pressed hard on their heels. For most of the refugees opting to break out with the troops, although they must have realised how slim their chances of survival were, the conditions and prospects were now so bad that the break-out, however slender a chance it offered of getting safely across the Elbe, presented a worthwhile gamble. This time Busse did not try to stop them. Fortunately, the weather was bad that day, low-hanging clouds continuing to prevent Soviet aircraft from attacking the German concentrations with any precision.[16]

The 9th Army's remaining artillery, firing from positions east of Halbe, opened fire as planned at 1800 hours on targets in and around the village. Once the ammunition had been used up, the guns and mortars were destroyed as ordered, and the gunners then joined in the break-out as infantry.

Grenadier Tag of the 2nd Company of Panzergrenadier Division *Kurmark*'s APC battalion was in the thick of it:

We had to keep open a woodland track that the Russians kept under threat by worming their way forward. Towards evening we received the order to mount up and move off. Our company still had at least six APCs and some troop transporters which were packed full. After a few hundred metres we came under infantry and anti-tank gunfire from the left. With the help of some tanks, these enemy positions were overcome and we moved on.

As night began to fall our column turned on to a track leading to Halbe. Once more we came under short-range anti-tank gunfire. Jumping off and engaging came automatically. I stuck a hand grenade down the barrel of an abandoned anti-tank gun and moved away. As a protection against ambush, we then advanced on either side of the woodland track with our vehicles following at some distance behind.[17]

However, the southern wedge was unable to take advantage of the brief artillery preparation, the vast numbers of disorganized troops delaying the departure until 1830 hours, by which time the Soviets were ready for them. It was only then that the tanks and SPGs moved off with their escorting infantry along the roads leading to Halbe, followed by the other vehicles, such as tank-hunters, APCs, trucks, cars and ambulances. On either side of the road and between the vehicles moved soldiers, Volkssturm men and civilians, the flotsam and jetsam of this closing war.

At first this human flood was able to approach the town without hindrance but, as the spearhead reached the outskirts of the town at dusk, it came under heavy fire. After a short exchange, the tanks rolled into the village at about 2100 hours. It soon became apparent that the artillery preparation had failed to reduce the fighting capacity of the Soviet units there to any significant extent, and casualties began mounting rapidly.

Beyond the junction of the road to Teupitz, near the village church, the leading tank came up against a barrier, originally erected against Soviet tanks, that consisted of two rows of pine logs rammed into the earth with the space in between filled with sand. This barrier extended right across the road, forming a formidable obstacle to further progress. The pressure from behind immediately formed a blockage at this point. A witness, the driver of one of the leading tanks, described what happened next:

> At once, all broke loose! Shells were exploding all around, not only high explosive, but phosphor shells too. It seemed that the Russians had long since identified 9th Army's break-out point through air reconnaissance and prepared a trap for us in Halbe. All the buildings around us were hit and caught fire, illuminating the scene in ghostly fashion. I then spotted two Russian tanks behind the anti-tank barrier. The Russian fire was becoming increasingly strong and driving over the barricade looked suicidal to me.[18]

The Soviet fire hindered every manoeuvre, and the two leading tanks were lost, as will be described shortly. Eventually the tanks managed to bypass Halbe and reached the autobahn at daybreak.

The town itself, into which ever more people and vehicles were pushing, was surrounded on three sides and had the fire of 1st Guards Artillery Breakthrough Division directed on it. A massive barrage using five artillery brigades had been planned against this breakthrough sector, starting with a five-minute all-out bombardment and going on to ten minutes of methodical fire, for which the firing of 1,000 shells per minute had been planned.[19]

A second anti-tank barrier, several hundred metres beyond the church on the road to Teurow, blocked the progress of another group for hours. This road, which had been shot up by German rocket launchers, presented the same horrific picture as the other breakthrough sectors with the dead lying on top of each other, people crushed to death by the tanks, and wounded crying out for help. There was no differentiation between civilians and soldiers in this mêlée.[20]

In and around Halbe, the various groups, no longer under proper control, sought to break through the Soviet positions and reach the shelter of the woods. Many units tried to bypass Halbe rather than go through it. SS-Captain Paul *Krauss* of 32nd SS Tank-Hunting Battalion was with the remains of his unit in the woods north-east of the village, where they destroyed all the remaining wheeled vehicles. He then went forward with his liaison officer, SS-Second Lieutenant van Hogen, to reconnoitre the route, leaving SS-Lieutenant Schnur to follow with the main body twenty minutes later. Krauss recorded:

Van Hogen and I came to a copse that was full of German soldiers and civilians. In front of us was Halbe railway station, which was occupied by the Russians, who were firing at our copse with machine guns and mortars. The cries of the wounded and dying were coming from all around, and something had to be done as quickly as possible. While van Hogen went back to fetch our men, I gathered some officers and NCOs around me, explained the situation and told them that I was taking command and that, as soon as my men arrived, we would break through. Whoever wanted to could join us.

We waited for van Hogen and the rest of the Supply Company in vain. Instead we heard the sounds of fighting coming from their direction. Now 9th Army's general break-out appeared to be in full swing. We could not wait any longer, so I charged the red-brick buildings of the station shouting: 'Forward, grenadiers, forward!'

Some 300 followed me, soldiers and civilians, including women and children. Our fearful cries and firing hit the Russians like an apocalypse, and they fled from the station buildings. We charged right across the railway embankment and reached a copse on the far side. Those who fell, or were wounded, were left behind.

We came to a sunken track that was about two metres deep and two hundred metres long. The whole wood was under constant fire from the Russian artillery and mortars. There were dead and wounded lying everywhere, soldiers and civilians. My mob scattered here, with individuals and small groups all heading west. Cohesion had collapsed, the mass refusing to be led any longer. All discipline had disappeared.[21]

SS-Colonel Kempin reported that many officers and NCOs had removed the epaulettes bearing their rank insignia in rejection of any further disciplinary responsibility.[22]

The progress of the southern wedge was described in some detail by Rudi Lindner, then an officer cadet with the 1241st Grenadier Regiment, which by then had been reduced to company strength:

We paraded with the 9th Army's southern armoured spearhead, which consisted of 14 Tiger tanks, assault guns, APCs and motor vehicles, arranged as follows:
• The vanguard, consisting of 2nd Company, 502nd SS Heavy Panzer Battalion;
• The remains of 1241st Grenadier Regiment as close infantry escort for the tanks;
• Part of an APC company of the Kurmark;
• The Reconnaissance and Pioneer Platoon of the 502nd;
• 1st Company, 502nd, with the battalion commander and signals officers, and a mortar battery;
• The remainder of the 502nd with a self-propelled four-barrelled anti-aircraft gun, motorcycles, ambulance and medical officer.

This day, 28 April, which began so calmly as we were detailed off as tank escorts to the armoured columns, and ended so tragically, will always remain in my memory. We did not know then that we were preparing for a journey into hell and that for most of us it would be our death. Our platoon, now made up of one officer and 15 grenadiers, was assigned to the leading Tiger tanks of the spearhead, whose platoon commander was SS-Second Lieutenant Kuhnke.

I found myself on the second tank, commanded by SS-Sergeant-Major Ernst Streng, and with SS-Sergeant Ott as the driver. We fastened ourselves on to the tank mountings with our belts and equipment straps, so that we would have our hands free for firing our rifles and Panzerfausts, and for throwing grenades.

At about 1800 hours on 28 April, the heavy weapons fired a barrage on Halbe, after which the guns were blown up. Then at about 1830 hours our armoured column moved out of the assembly area towards Märkisch Buchholz and Halbe. We thrust through Märkisch Buchholz without encountering any significant resistance, then moved along a woodland track towards Halbe. The northern armoured spearhead of the Panzergrenadier Division *Kurmark* was also rolling along another woodland track towards Halbe. Short halts for observation and reconnaissance delayed our advance.

A Russian anti-tank barrier in front of Halbe caused the first big delay. A mortar battery went into action and fired a salvo on the resistance nests on the eastern edge of Halbe, while our leading tank platoon engaged the barrier. The Russian security forces then pulled back into Halbe village. Our armoured vanguard was then ordered to push on into Halbe, and our Tiger tanks set off again. We drove into the village south of the railway station, reaching a straight street lined with trees, where the back gardens of the first houses lay.

We thought that here, too, we would encounter only minor resistance, but with a blast all hell broke loose. We had driven into an ambush.

At this point I should mention that following us in the woods to the right and left of our armoured column, if a little further back, was a stream of soldiers and refugees, who kept closing up to us whenever we stopped. In their fear of losing contact and becoming prisoners of the Russians, but also because of non-existent or insufficient combat experience, most of the soldiers were conducting themselves in a totally unmilitary fashion, so that unfortunately very many of them had to pay with their lives for it. For instance, behind each tank in Halbe there was a cluster of some forty to sixty people seeking shelter, and every time we stopped the numbers increased. In addition, many soldiers were unarmed, and most of the soldiers who were armed did not or were unable to use their weapons. In practice, only the leading tank could fire forward, while we grenadiers sitting on top fired obliquely into the roofs and windows.

It was now about 2000 hours as we drove into Halbe and another anti-tank barrier appeared before us, but this time open. The leading tank had got to within about seventy metres when it fired a shot to clear the way, drove on and stopped about thirty metres from the barrier.

Suddenly the inferno broke out with concentrated anti-tank-gun fire coming from ahead, artillery and mortar fire from above, and rifle fire from the roofs and windows of the houses right and left of the street. The artillery fire, with explosive shrapnel and phosphorous shells, and the mortar bombs, caused especially frightful casualties among the numerous, exposed and crammed together groups of people. The street was immediately filled with dead and wounded. Panic, confusion and deadly fear could be seen in the faces of the living, as cries for help came from the wounded and dying.

Our leading tank received a direct hit and started burning. Our second tank tried to turn, got stuck and was hit by a phosphorous shell, and also caught fire. The phosphorous shells burst with glowing white splashes on the tank, and there was phosphor everywhere on our steel helmets and tent-halves. Stinking smoke erupted as the tank began to burn. The crew bailed out and we also jumped off and ran to the third tank. (I later learnt that the crew managed to put the fire out and get the tank going again.)[23]

SS-Sergeant-Major Ernst Streng, the commander of the second tank (No. 223) on which Lindner was riding, also gave his account of this action:

We asked for an infantry storm troop. We were standing thirty metres from the anti-tank barrier and could neither turn nor shoot in the narrow space within this tree-lined street. Only the lead tank could fire. A bitter fight had broken out on a narrow frontage from house to house, yard to yard, and ditch to ditch. The street was choked with dead and wounded, and trucks loaded with wounded were wedged between the tanks. The houses began to burn, flaming red flickered over the roofs and from the windows, loud explosions came through the darkness. The Russian defensive fire increased by the minute, especially the dreadful mortar fire. Wild screams of pain came from the wounded calling for help from the mowed-down ranks covering the road surface and pavements.

Phosphor shells exploded with glowing white sparks. We were under enemy tank fire. Now it was getting serious. While the flashes of the enemy guns were difficult to identify, our tank stood out like a dark mass between the blazing fires. There was no way out either to the right or rear. The general's jeep that had been in front of us before had driven off. The tanks were standing one behind the other, and in this situation we suddenly received a direct hit. A blinding whiteness sprayed out. Within seconds the vehicle was on fire and gleaming with light. Ott shouted: 'Tank on fire!' on the intercom. Everyone wrenched open their hatches in fright and we tumbled out of the turret head first and hit the road surface hard. Ott hit the side panel as he fell and hurt his ribs. We jumped down from the tank to the street, but turned around and looked at the dark mass of our tank covered in flames in the middle of a mess of fallen telegraph poles, roof tiles and tree branches.

Then we realised that it must have been an incendiary shell. We jumped back aboard, one after another, clattering into the fighting space. The driver groaned as he got behind his steering wheel. He did not think that he could drive any more, and this in the midst of all the confusion around us. But he had to drive, he had to! We cursed and swore at him – he couldn't leave us now – the tank and crew were depending on him. Our rapid exchange of words was full of swearing.

Kuhnke was not answering any more. What had happened? The commander ordered our tank to reverse immediately into the side street. It was high time. There was no question of getting through, we simply had to get out of this narrow trap if we were to avoid casualties.

In turning, Kuhnke's tank was set on fire by a tank shell as it tried to escape from the narrow street as quickly as possible. A Tiger that had forced its way forward near us (we couldn't tell in the dark whether it was from our platoon) was trying to reverse on the pavement, and in doing so caught its tracks on the front of a heavy truck, crushing the cab and engine under the tank's rear. As a result of this, the flaming gases from the tank's exhaust set fire to the crushed fuel pipes. The flames suddenly shot up enveloping the truck and tank in a sea of fire. The badly wounded riding on the back and turret of the tank and the crew fell like flaming torches to the street with wild screams of pain. Who would see to them? Everyone had to look after themselves. We drove on immediately, as the burning tank threatened to engulf us. Kuhnke's tank burst apart with a bright flash of flame. The subsequent explosions sprayed the ammunition over the glowing tank sides into the dark of the surrounding night. The street behind us was already clear.

Blinded by the fire, we got the vehicle moving slowly in reverse in the darkness under the trees. The tracks caught on the crushed dead on the street, who were perhaps being run over for the tenth time. The centre of the street had been under tank fire from behind the anti-tank barrier for several minutes.

Our tank did a 180-degree turn on the spot and rolled away, back along the street. In these uneasy seconds, the crew had an fatalistic feeling, for at any moment an enemy tank shell could hit the rear of the vehicle and, at that range, we knew full well that it would come straight through our relatively weak armour. When at last we could turn into the side street, we were deeply grateful to have survived the hard, costly encounter. Our way led right over a main street on which Kuhnke awaited us.[24]

SS-Second Lieutenant Kuhnke had dismounted in order to consult with his company commander, SS-Captain Neu and his battalion commander SS-Major Kurt Hartrampf, whom he found together in the former's tank. It was decided to pull back under cover of the leading tanks and bypass Halbe to the north. Kuhnke then returned to his leading tank, which tried to turn left behind a row of trees but got stuck on a tree stump exposing its glowing exhaust to the Soviet gunners in the darkness. The tank was hit in the rear by a shell that set it alight, and the crew had to bail out. Kuhnke was then given a lift by SS-Second Lieutenant Justus of the Reconnaissance Platoon in his armoured personnel carrier.[25]

Meanwhile Second Lieutenant Dahlinger, commanding 11th Company of Panzergrenadier Regiment *Kurmark*, was leading his men in house-to-house fighting along the main street under murderous anti-tank, artillery and mortar fire. When they regrouped in a copse to the west of the village, he found that he had only 40 men left of the original 160 of his company on the Seelow Heights.[26]

Rudi Lindner, with the escorting infantry, continued:

Houses were on fire everywhere. We wanted to climb on to the third tank, but gave up and tried to establish some order behind it, which, however, did not fully work out. Together with some other soldiers, we tended to the wounded and also persuaded the majority of the people not to seek cover behind the tanks but in and between the houses, so that the tanks could manoeuvre, but we also had to witness the dead and wounded being crushed under the tanks. The street was full of dead and wounded and every minute there were more. Meanwhile fighting had begun in the houses.

With this we got enough air and space to be able to direct our fire at the roofs and windows in the direction of the anti-tank barrier. Slowly the paralysis of the first shock began to wear off especially among the combat-experienced soldiers, and more and more joined in, halfway restoring order out of chaos in helping the wounded and getting them off the street into houses and gardens, and in using their weapons.

We, the soldiers on the tanks and those behind them, found, as so often during the war, that in situations like this one's ability to think becomes blocked and trained reflexes take over. It was only much later that we became fully conscious of what a suicide mission we had been committed to as cannon fodder, and what enormous luck we had in coming out of this inferno alive. I still marvel that I came through Halbe hit by neither a bullet nor a splinter and only got some splashes of phosphorous on my steel helmet and tent-half.

Although during the war I had very often, as an infantryman, been bombarded with weapons of all kinds, especially on the Eastern Front in Russia, I had never experienced such concentrated fire on such a small area and on so many people.

Meanwhile the tanks had turned round and we sat on

them with the remainder of the comrades of our platoon. Only eight men of our platoon were still alive, the others having been either killed or wounded.[27]

SS-Lieutenant Klust of 502nd SS Heavy Panzer Battalion was in his Tiger a few hundred metres behind the lead tanks:

We drove into Halbe between 2000 and 2100 hours. The village was a confused mass of vehicles, soldiers and civilians, and Russian shells were exploding literally on people's bodies. We could not possibly get through this in our tank. In this chaos, SS-Major Hartrampf came up to me and said: 'Klust, the lead troop is stuck fast. We have to get round Halbe to the left. Take over the lead and drive on. This way we will get some space and get on.'

I gave my driver, Bert Fink, the new direction and we drove about 400 metres out of Halbe to the south and then turned back west again. We came under heavy anti-tank gunfire from a patch of woods some hundred metres off and were hit without too much damage. My gunner, Ferdinand Lasser, a typical imperturbable Bavarian, fired even before I had completed the order. We could no longer aim precisely, as it was already quite dark, but Lasser silenced the anti-tank guns with five shots. Then we drove on again, and when we reached the woods we wheeled left for the Massow forest warden's lodge.[28]

Rudi Lindner, with the escorting infantry, continued his account:

We were glad as our armoured column moved back slowly, taking us away from this frightful bit of street. From the railway station we then went south a little and then later drove westward through the woods once more.

During the manoeuvring of these Tigers of the leading

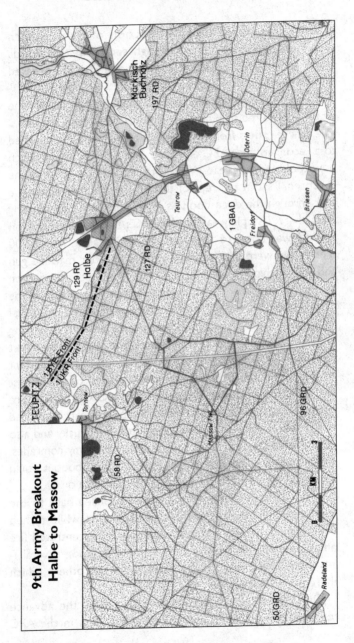

9th Army Breakout
Halbe to Massow

platoon, and the change of direction of the southern spearhead to a new breakthrough sector in the woods south of Halbe, even more soldiers and civilians pressed into 9th Army's break-out point at Halbe.

Before turning west we made a short halt to unload the wounded and redistribute the officer cadets among the tanks. The officer cadets from the two shot-up tanks were assigned to a reconnaissance APC equipped with a machine gun, which now took over the lead. We had to reconnoitre towards the autobahn. I sat in the rear of the APC and had to cover the rear through the open door. As I was unable to see properly from there, I stupidly sat on the APC's rear towing hook, an error I was soon to regret. After having gone about 100 metres, we were shot at from in front and our machine gun and sub-machine gunners opened fire. I had not reckoned on the driver suddenly reversing at full speed. I slipped off the towing hook and fell on the road, turning in such a way that I lay in the direction of travel and on my stomach, pressing myself close to the ground. The tracks of the APC rattled past right and left of my body. Fortunately the APC had sufficient ground clearance. Once the vehicle had gone over and past me, the driver noticed and stopped the APC. Covered by fire from our machine guns, I rolled aside and ran back uninjured to the rear of the APC. Once more I had been lucky and also didn't have to worry about being laughed at by my comrades. Although there was nothing for me to laugh about, it could have been far worse, and I had to put a good face on it.

With all our weapons firing, the APC pulled back to the armoured column, where the tanks had meanwhile turned their turrets to two o'clock and opened concentrated fire on an assembly of T-34s and other vehicles. Soon several T-34s were alight, making good targets of the others, which therefore withdrew.

Our Tigers received the order to resume the advance towards the autobahn and the officer cadets in the APC were reallocated to the tanks. I was assigned to the tank commanded by Harlander with four other comrades. We climbed aboard and the armoured column set off once more. After a few hundred metres we came under fire again and our tank was hit in the tracks, but kept on firing.

We had driven into a concentration of Russian troops, but under the covering fire of our Tiger's crew, the armoured column was able to fight its way through towards the autobahn, and with them also went the rest of the officer cadets of our platoon. I heard nothing more of these comrades, either in the days to follow or later on.

Now it became uncomfortable for us on our immobilized tank. We came under heavy fire from Panzerfausts, which fortunately were all fired too high and exploded above us in the trees, showering us with splinters and branches. From the illumination of a flare we saw that we were in the assembly area of some heavy Stalin tanks, and one of these colossi was already turning its turret in our direction as the light went out. A lightning bang, a frightful howling and then a crash shook our tank, which had received a direct hit. The crew bailed out, shouting: 'Harland is dead!'

We also jumped off and ran instinctively in the direction of the least noise of combat to the next woodland track, where we dug in. This was the time to keep our nerve. We were completely on our own, our tanks had gone over the hill, there were Russian troops in the woods, where exactly no one knew, and our tank crew had run off in another direction.

The most important questions for us were to establish whether the track was free of the enemy and whether it led to the autobahn. I therefore went along the track in a westerly direction to find out. The track was free of the enemy for about 1,000 metres and led, as we luckily later discovered, to the autobahn.

I was glad to get back to my comrades and to get a little sleep before we marched on again.[29]

Now leading the break-out by 502nd SS Heavy Panzer Battalion, SS-Lieutenant Klust continued:

We drove westwards along a forest track. Many soldiers were marching around our tank, or trying to climb aboard. Some were riding on top and even blocked the air intake for the engine, causing it to overheat. My order to get off the tank and give us some close security was only partially successful.

After another few hundred metres, I had us stop. Orientation was nil. I only had a completely inadequate map showing neither woodland tracks nor precise landmarks. Several vehicles, including a Tiger, closed up behind.

After a brief consultation, we drove on and suddenly found ourselves on top of a Russian bivouac with the odd small campfire. Apparently a Russian supply convoy had bedded down here for the night. Both sides were taken by surprise. We had to get on. Just as I was setting off, a lieutenant-colonel wearing a leather coat jumped on my tank and shouted that we were heading in the wrong direction, but I replied that I was in charge and closed the hatch on him.

We drove on with firing going on all over the woods, friend and foe being indistinguishable in the dark. After another few hundred metres, I stopped again for the others to catch up.[30]

SS-Lieutenant Bärmann described the composition of this column:

Without orders, we formed up in a new column west of Halbe: two Königstigers, three Panthers, two Hetzers, several APCs, a self-propelled 20mm Flak, and vehicles of all kinds. In addition, infantry, most of whom had no weapons.[31]

After they had waited all the previous day, the orders for 32nd SS Tank-Hunting Battalion to move did not arrive until the evening of the 28th. Ernst-Christian Gädtke explained what followed:

> Once more we cut down on what we would carry, once more we had some hot food and were then issued with cold rations. Finally, in the evening as dusk fell, we moved off to the south-west towards the village of Halbe. The Russian lines followed the Lübben–Gross Köris railway line and we were to breach them at Halbe.
>
> It was dark by the time we reached Halbe, the fighting vehicles following close behind each other along the woodland tracks, those who could sitting aboard, and those on foot keeping close on either side of the track. Everyone was trying to keep as close as possible to the vehicles.
>
> From up in front, from Halbe, came the sounds of battle: infantry fire, the barking of anti-tank guns, the hammering of machine guns. Slowly, with interruptions and delays, the advance continued. Firing was going on in all directions and from all directions, and no one knew who was firing, who was friend and who was foe, who was firing at whom. In Halbe, barns and the roofs of houses were burning. We rolled on through the village, firing on both sides. Dead were lying in the street and between the houses, Russians and Germans all mixed up together. Shots, hits, explosions. Nobody was taking care of those lying there. Somehow we got through.[32]

We have another descriptive account from Eberhard Baumgart, originally of the Security Company of 32nd SS Division and now with a combat team guarding the headquarters staff:

> Late in the afternoon we found ourselves in the wood north-east of Märkisch Buchholz again. Soldiers were

camping everywhere and standing around vehicles, including quite a lot of trucks, staff cars and command vehicles. The most senior bigwigs collected around them with their red stripes and gold on their collar patches and caps. These gentlemen were studying maps and conferring, while NCOs were searching among the pines for members of Waffen-SS units. We were really glad not to have been forgotten. The *30. Januar* Security Company had come together again and was apparently complete.

Night descended and movement was discernible in the wood around us, but we were not allowed to ride on the tanks. We waited in hope, but had to return to the ranks. The places on the tanks were to be taken by the gentlemen of the staff. Some moonlight came through the pines revealing sandy tracks. The tanks rolled past us and apparently took another direction. The sound of their motors faded away.

We crossed a road and I read 'Märkisch Buchholz' and 'Halbe' ahead on a signpost. The wood on either side of the road was swarming with soldiers. In front of us Russian artillery fire was coming from the direction of Halbe. The enemy fire increased and shells of all calibres burst among the treetops, breaking tree trunks and ripping holes in them as splinters whistled through the air and branches showered down. That was quite some bombardment. We were expected. I jumped from cover to cover and dived behind pine trees with only one thought: 'not me!' In the bright flashes of the explosions I saw some silhouettes flitting about, but only a few. I came through all right myself and saw to left and right of me motionless, waiting soldiers. I wanted to get them to move along with us, but they wouldn't move. They remained lying there under fire, waiting for others to open the way for them.

We came across some despondent wounded men and some dead ones. I reached the roadway just short of the village. The artillery fire was going over us, so now the mortars took us on as their target. Ducking down, we hastened towards the station, having to avoid or jump over corpses. On the left-hand side was a railwaymen's hut. It had really been hailing down hard here! I had seldom seen such a mass of dead in a small area in all the war, and then only on the Russian side, but these were Germans. The wood was now getting less dense and I could see the hut more clearly. Men were pressed tightly together along its length like a swarm of bees to a post. What we saw there looking like frozen grains of salt turned out to be totally terrified soldiers. They thought that they were in dead ground, safe from enemy fire, but what a mistake that was. They just turned round when shouted at. This was only a few metres from the railway level crossing barriers, which stuck up into the grey skies. On the crossing was a carpet of corpses, grey-green corpses. I could see only German soldiers. I had to get away from here. But where to? I could see nothing but corpses, corpses in front of us, on and beyond the crossing. And whoever hesitated here would soon be lying among them.

At first I tried to avoid the dead, for there were some wounded among them, but the dead were lying on top of each other in the middle of the crossing, and one couldn't make out where one was treading. I had to grit my teeth and get on. The storage sheds near the station were beginning to burn and I could read 'Halbe' on the station sign. I will never be able to forget this place. I had to get away. We hastened along the street, which opened out in the grey of the pinewood only a few metres away [the road to Teurow and Freidorf]. There was some cover in the roadside ditches and many soldiers gathered here. Some vehicles also appeared, driving in both directions. Confusion and uncertainty clearly reigned here.[33]

Second Lieutenant Kurt Schwarz, of the 1st Battalion of Panzer Regiment *Brandenburg*, came through Halbe that evening in a group of four Panthers. They turned south towards Teurow and then west again for the autobahn:

> Suddenly I was whirled round in the turret by a hard blow, a hit by a mortar bomb. The gunner and loader bandaged me up in the turret. Shortly afterwards we were hit in the side of the engine space and our Panther burst into flames. I screamed: 'Out!' We found cover together in a hollow close to the burning tank. Suddenly there was a big explosion and the pressure blew the turret off the turret ring. We pressed ourselves down in the hollow, and the seven-metre long gun barrel hit the ground right in front of us.[34]

Second Lieutenant Ernst Habermann of the same unit was leading a group of tanks in his APC and witnessed the destruction of two of the German tanks as they approached the autobahn:

> A ferocious fight broke out here. Lieutenant Petersen's tank was shot up and he was killed. Our APC was rammed by a Königstiger when it reversed while engaged by an anti-tank gun, and we had to continue on foot behind our tanks. I was about to get on to a passing tank when it was hit and I was wounded in the thigh. After a second hit, only the wounded driver and the radio operator bailed out. We lay down under the shot-up Panther and were tending our wounds, when it suddenly burst into flames, and we had to move away. Near the autobahn we found six dead soldiers who had been shot in the back of the neck.[35]

Günter Führling and Heiner Lüdermann, two officer cadets with orders to report to their parent 303rd Infantry Division still in their pockets, decided to leave the rearguard on the banks of the Dahme and make their own break-out to the west that evening. After passing endless, jammed, stationary columns of transport through Märkisch Buchholz and the woods leading to Halbe they came to the town. Führling depicted the scene in Halbe:

The noise of battle grew louder as we approached the railway embankment, which had to be crossed even though it was being swept by machine-gun fire. We had the impression that the firing was coming from both sides, but especially from the south. We did not have to crawl over the embankment, we could creep over, as there were so many dead soldiers that they protected us like a wide and high bulletproof screen on either side. We could hear no signs of life coming from these bodies; they had been riddled with bullets.

The station was on our right. The road forked and we came across some notices indicating that the troops should turn down the road to Teurow and that the general had already gone down that way with a Tiger in the lead and broken through.

I can still recall the details of the break-out, but I was astonished that information like this could be passed on so quickly in such chaos, when the sounds of battle were deafening. Standing on this street in Halbe, I did not yet realise that the break-out had become hopeless. We imagined that the leaders would be up ahead. The troops in the street should not have been leaderless, going like sheep to the slaughter, but that was exactly what was happening. Obviously the signs pointing the way down Kirchstrasse had been put up by *Seydlitz-Troops* in German uniform. They had taken up a position that would not be fired on by the Russians, and the Germans were being directed straight on to the Russian machine guns. The Russians had occupied the church on the right-hand side of the street and were firing from the church tower.

Although it was dark, the images remain fixed in my memory — but not the ear-deafening noise. The street was several hundred metres long and had most of its buildings on the right-hand side. The left-hand side was full of dead that had been dragged aside to clear the street. In the darkness it seemed that only the right-hand side of the street was inhabited. Like on the railway embankment, there was a wall of several thousand dead along the street that had fallen within these few hundred yards. I saw nothing of the trampled and mangled bodies, but I could hear the whimpering, groaning and cries for help. But everyone was concerned only for themselves, looking out for Russian snipers in the windows of the buildings, or from where the most fire was coming. Tanks and supply trucks stood still on the street as the attack faltered.

There were some Hetzers right in front. They did not have movable turrets, so the whole vehicle had to turn in order to aim the gun. Soldiers were using them as cover, running behind the three or four Hetzers, thinking that most firing was coming from ahead. We, however, had the impression that the fire was coming mainly from the right out of the gaps between the buildings, or the windows, so we passed along the left-hand side of the tanks, and were correct. There was no panic, just dull routine procedure. Each told the other what to look out for. No one smoked, for matches and cigarettes would betray you in the dark. A motorcycle sidecar wheel was stuck so close to one of the tanks that the passenger would be crushed if it moved. We could only alert the crew to this after some agonising minutes, as our knocking sounded just like infantry fire to the crew inside. All were hoping that the column would break free, as there was supposed to be only slight Russian resistance to be overcome up ahead.

We suspected that the spearhead would be immediately ahead of us around the slight bend in the road, not knowing that the road had been blocked off by the Russians in Teurow. As nothing was moving forward, we decided to take a break, and climbed through the window of a building on the right-hand side of the street. In the dark we noticed and sensed that the room was completely full of soldiers. There were only two places still free on the floor right next to the window opposite, the most dangerous place in the room. A soldier was sitting on a chair, which I had not noticed when I tried to sit down. Shortly afterwards the building was hit by a shell and the room filled with dust. 'Is anyone hurt?' somebody called out. From the floor, where 15 to 20 men were sitting tightly packed together, came the answer, 'No.' I felt some crumbly moisture on my helmet and struck a match. Then I saw that the soldier on the chair had been decapitated. It was the soldier sitting on the chair, where I had wanted to sit. I extinguished the match to loud cries of protest. Heiner and I did not linger any longer. We did not feel any safer in the street, but hoped to make some progress. Since the attack was still being held in check, we went back to the railway and crept back over the embankment to the edge of the woods. As we could get no idea what was happening, we went back into the chaos on the street with its many dead and wounded, and no movement either forward or back, although everyone wanted to move on.

Where the village ended and the street became the main road again, there was a pinewood on the right, which we reached safely. We then checked every foxhole and the like, in this manner covering several hundred metres until we came to a house on the main road, whose steps led down to a wash cellar.

What we could not know was that the breakthrough was taking place only 3,000 to 4,000 metres away, where troops were crossing the autobahn with all the available heavy tanks and almost all the SPGs, but with heavy losses.

According to General Busse there were some 30,000 to 40,000 of them.

Totally exhausted, we crept into the house's wash cellar, thinking that we had found a safe shelter. The threat of being taken prisoner was with us every moment, and we wondered how the Russians would react. As officer cadets we had no NCO lace sewn on our uniforms and only had to unbutton our epaulettes to remove our rank insignia.

It was already becoming light when we went down the steps. Although we expected to be taken prisoner, it happened sooner than we had expected. After about twenty minutes the demand came in German: 'Come out, Ivan is here, leave your weapons!' *Seydlitz-Troops?*

As I emerged, I saw only Russian uniforms and Mongolian faces, several of the soldiers having only a cord instead of a belt around them. One of them took my Finnish dagger with its beautifully decorated leather sheath that I wore on my belt and had forgotten to remove, and thumped me with his rifle butt because of it. In the background I saw Russian soldiers advancing in line abreast through the woods on Halbe.

We had not noticed this dawn counterattack. We prisoners – about ten men – now marched off in the direction we had wanted to take, but under an escort that we would certainly have avoided. We went a few hundred metres through a wood past some dead German soldiers, and were surprised how far they had come.[36]

Günter Führling's encounter with *Seydlitz-Troops* in Halbe is corroborated by SS-Major Hartrampf, commanding the vanguard of the northern wedge, who visited a police post on the edge of the village and was told that it was clear of the enemy, but when he went forward to find out why his tanks were not moving, the policeman accompanying him disappeared, and he suspected that he and his men must have been *Seydlitz-Troops* posing as policemen.[37]

The remains of the SS Panzergrenadier Division *Nederland*, down to about 300 men, also broke out near the village. SS-Major-General Jürgen Wagner divided his men into three groups for the break-out, the first under SS-Captain Tröger of 1st Battalion, 48th SS Panzergrenadier Regiment *General Seyffarth*, the second under SS-Second Lieutenant Reischütz, and the third under SS-Second Lieutenant Bender.[38]

Since movement within the pocket could not be concealed from the Soviets, they pressed hard upon the weak securing units from east of the Dahme. As there were no longer any heavy weapons available, the German troops had to resort to their own resources and counterattacked in classic style, using hand grenades, spades and sub-machine guns. Among them was the *Mathiebe* Combat Team from 1st Battalion, 86th Grenadier Regiment *Schill*, which retook the area around the Streganz brickworks and held on to it. This defensive battle, which also included the retaking of Hermsdorf by the combat team, went on all day.

SS-Lieutenant Bärmann of the 32nd SS Tank-Hunting Battalion wrote:

Our divisional staff were in Hermsdorf, where a general was directing traffic with a pistol in his hand. Only in this way could panic be prevented, and the streams of traffic flow in orderly fashion.

The headquarters moved on to the Hammer forestry office, which first had to be cleared of its Russian occupants, but they had to leave 2,000 wounded behind in Hermsdorf in the care of their last two medical officers and some medical orderlies.[39]

The outward flow of troops and refugees remained sluggish, being constantly interrupted by attacking aircraft and heavy artillery fire. Nothing was known of developments at the break-out point. Stragglers and soldiers who had distanced themselves from their units mingled with endless streams of refugees moving this way and that all day long through the narrow pocket, attracting the Russian aircraft like moths to a flame. The dead and wounded could no longer be tended to or made safe. Apart from the lack of ammunition, there was also a lack of bandages and medical supplies. Doctors and medical orderlies were scarcely to be seen.[40]

The SS-second lieutenant of Battlegroup *Becker*, which was still within the main pocket, continued his account:

On 28 April we moved as the last unit and, after a few kilometres, occupied a new position on a small height near a village. The Russians came across the open ground and attacked us with loud cries. Aircraft pinned us down and it became a bitter fight. We had to repel their attacks four times, mainly in close combat with some indescribable scenes.

Our ammunition ran out in the afternoon, but a runner appeared at the last moment carrying several boxes of ammunition, and we made a counterattack with 50 men, the rest being incapable of taking part. Wounded Russians were screaming, and some of the barns and houses had caught fire. We could not have withstood another Russian attack.

Soldiers who rejoined our unit later reported that a so-called Seydlitz officer had said to them: 'Just tell them that their positions are about to be attacked by two battalions to force a way into the pocket and split up the remaining units.'

We received the order to abandon our positions at 2100 hours on this terrible day. We were to proceed towards Halbe via Hermsdorf. Unfortunately, the sounds of fighting in front of us had become even stronger. Suddenly we were unable to go on. A wounded soldier came back and said that Halbe was seven kilometres away and that there had already been two days of bitter fighting there with a frightful number of dead.[41]

That afternoon the *Schill* and *Hutten* Infantry Divisions of General Wenck's 12th Army continued their advance towards Potsdam. Lieutenant-General Engel of the *Schill* Division deployed two regiments of infantry, the SPGs and two platoons of tanks in his spearhead, using APCs and armoured cars to cover the flanks.

The *Scharnhorst* and *Körner* Infantry Divisions were equally heavily engaged around Beelitz, where an attack on the sanatorium located in the woods outside the town met bitter resistance. The approach to the sanatorium was blocked by a strongly defended transformer building which had first to be reduced by anti-tank gunfire before fighting for the hospital buildings could begin. There the Soviets conducted their defence from the underground corridors connecting the individual buildings – even though the corridors were filled with 3,000 sick and wounded. As soon as the Germans had taken the first building, the evacuation of the patients with their medical attendants was begun. With them were some representatives of the International Red Cross who later negotiated their acceptance by the American forces on the Elbe.[42]

The area now held, extending along the line Nichel–Reesdorf– railway junction north of Beelitz-Ferch, and including Elsholz, Buchholz and Brachwitz, provided a suitable catchment area for receiving break-out groups from either Berlin, Potsdam or Halbe. A situation report by 12th Army read:

> The enemy has been able to penetrate Potsdam from the north. Our own attack thrust forward with the right wing farther to the east, taking Salzbronn and Elsholz. Hard fighting around Beelitz. North of there leading elements of the *Scharnhorst* Division have reached the railway crossing six kilometres north of Beelitz. Spearheads of the *Hutten* Division have taken Ferch. Striking along the Schwielowsee during the night.[43]

The suggestion was then sent to 9th Army to concentrate its efforts towards the Beelitz area, where the Soviet forces were relatively weak and scattered over a wide area, providing the only reasonable chance of success. The 12th Army would try to hold its ground as long as possible against the already increasing pressure. A signal received from the OKW ordering 12th Army to close up to the line of the Havel between the Schwielowsee and Brandenburg was ignored.[44]

Meanwhile, acting on orders received the day before, 4th Guards Tank Army's 5th Guards Mechanized Corps took up the offensive from its positions along the line Buchholz–Treuenbrietzen and seized the villages of Brachwitz and Schlalach in the swampy terrain beyond the railway line to the west in some bitter fighting. The Soviets claimed to have destroyed six SPGs in this engagement.[45]

NOTES

1. Wilke, *Am Rande der Strassen*, p. 124.
2. The second highest Soviet decoration after the Order of Lenin.
3. Adapted from Harry Zvi Glaser's account in the author's *With Our Backs to Berlin*.
4. Wilke, *Am Rande der Strassen*, p. 63.
5. Domank, The 1st Guards Breakthrough Artillery Division at Halbe'; Lakowski/Stich, *Der Kessel von Halbe 1945*, p. 108.
6. Koniev, *Year of Victory*, p. 184; Erickson, *The Road to Berlin*, p. 600. Koniev was still aiming for the Reichstag.
7. Koniev, *Year of Victory*, p. 184. The only Plauener Strasse then and now is in Hohenschönhausen in north-east Berlin. Koniev probably meant Pallasstrasse.
8. Koniev, *Year of Victory*, p. 187.
9. Wilke, *Am Rande der Strassen*, p. 48.
10. Tieke, *Das Ende zwischen Oder und Elbe*, p. 312.
11. Lakowski/Stich, *Der Kessel von Halbe 1945*, p. 111.
12. Lakowski/Stich, *Der Kessel von Halbe 1945*, pp. 111–18.
13. Tieke, *Das Ende zwischen Oder und Elbe*, p. 315.
14. Letter to Dr Lakowski, cited in Lakowski/Stich, *Der Kessel von Halbe 1945*, pp 182–3.

THE EYE OF THE NEEDLE

15. These tanks are referred to indiscriminately by witnesses as either Tigers or Königstigers. Schulze, *Der Kessel Halbe–Baruth–Radeland*, p. 83 supplies the following information:
'The exact number of Tiger IIs available near and in Halbe cannot be established due to the varied and conflicting accounts. The strength return for the 502nd at Klein Hammer gives seven each for the 1st and 2nd Companies, but already here the figure of seven for the 1st Company is doubtful. Tieke, *Das Ende zwischen Oder und Elbe*, gives 14 in Halbe, Scholz counted 12 in Halbe at night. Führling, *Endkampf an der Oderfront*, says 13 and Streng/Ott seven. Even the standard works have doubts, so that one must enquire about each tank: was it really a Tiger, or in fact a Panther? Thus three Tigers were listed as casualties in or near Halbe, Kuhnke (211), Harlander (213) and Münster (214). Apparently a further two Tigers were lost between Halbe and Löpten. Steng/Ott's account of seven refers to Massow, where Schneider gives five, two having become stuck crossing the autobahn and having to be blown up. Thus two tanks were lost, one of them Kämp's (123).

Of the six Tigers of the 502nd in Massow early on 29 April 1945, we have the following fates:

Hellwig's 222 was ordered by Streng to secure the Reichsstrasse 96 crossing to the north towards Wünsdorf. Hellwig came back without it, the Tiger having had to be blown up by Neuhof.

Pott's Tiger was shot up on the R 96 and none of the crew was able to bail out.

Stehmann's 111 was blown up between Fernneuendorf and Sperenberg.

Neu's Tiger stopped near Märtinsmühle (or Hennickendorf?) with water in the fuel.

Streng/Ott's penultimate Tiger 223 was shot up at about 0500 hours on 1 May between Schönefeld and Zauchwitz, about 300 metres south-east of the footbridge over the Nieplitz stream. After the wounded crew had bailed out, now under the command of Neu, the tank blew up and the 18-ton turret was blown off. Ott ended in Soviet captivity.

Klust/Fink's last Tiger, finally under the command of SS-Lieutenant Egger, reached the radio towers between Schönefeld and Elshoz, where they tanked up with diesel. The vehicle drove on for a further three or four kilometres before giving up the ghost. Driver Fink had discovered, without realising it, the later much cited multi-fuel engine. The tank was blown up in 1946/47.

According to an eyewitness, Erwin Schade, who was then 14 years old, bits flew up to fifty metres away.'

16. Tieke, *Das Ende zwischen Oder und Elbe*, pp. 332–3; Ziemke, *Battle for Berlin*, p. 119; Komornicki, *Polnische Soldaten stürmten Berlin*, p. 143.

17. Tieke, *Das Ende zwischen Oder und Elbe*, p. 315.

18. Lakowski/Stich, *Der Kessel von Halbe 1945*, p. 119.

19. Domank, The 1st Guards Breakthrough Artillery Division at Halbe'.

20. Lakowski/Stich, *Der Kessel von Halbe 1945*, pp. 108–18.

21. Tieke, *Das Ende zwischen Oder und Elbe*, pp. 319, 321.

22. *Ibid.*

23. Lindner in the author's *Death Was Our Companion*.

24. Fey, *Panzer im Brennpunkt der Fronten*, pp. 198–9.

25. Tieke, *Das Ende zwischen Oder und Elbe*, p. 317.

26. *Ibid.*

27. Lindner in the author's *Death Was Our Companion*.

28. Tieke, *Das Ende zwischen Oder und Elbe*, p. 320.

29. Lindner in the author's *Death Was Our Companion*.

30. Tieke, *Das Ende zwischen Oder und Elbe*, p. 320.

31. *Ibid.*

32. Gädtke, *Von der Oder zur Elbe*, p. 34.

33. Wilke, *Am Rande der Strassen*, pp. 58–9.

34. Helmut Jurisch in corresondence with the author.

35. *Ibid.*

36. Führling, *Endkampf an der Oderfront*, pp. 123–8.

37. Tieke, *Das Ende zwischen Oder und Elbe*, p. 316.

38. Tieke, *Das Ende zwischen Oder und Elbe*, p. 319.

39. Tieke, *Das Ende zwischen Oder und Elbe*, pp. 310–11.

40. Wilke, *Am Rande der Strassen*, p. 55.

41. *Ibid.*, pp. 83–4.

42. Wenck, 'Berlin war nicht mehr zu retten', pp. 65–6; Gellermann, *Die Armee Wenck*, pp. 85–6. Patients from the main civilian and military hospitals in Berlin and Potsdam had been evacuated here to a lung clinic and adjacent barracks (Ramm, *Gott Mit Uns*, p. 228). General Koehler, in a letter written to the commander of the 83rd US Infantry Division on 26 April appealing for the acceptance of the sick and wounded, anticipated finding 6,000 in his operational area, so it is possible that there were something like this figure recovered overall.

43. Lakowski/Stich, *Der Kessel von Halbe 1945*, p. 113.

44. Gellermann, *Die Armee Wenck*, pp. 87–9.

45. Kreisleitung Jüterbog booklet, p. 26.

ELEVEN

BREACHING KONIEV'S LINES

29 APRIL 1945

The repeated attacks by the German armour finally succeeded. The Soviet cordon was breached and their positions overrun. The Red Army troops at Halbe were unable to close the gap fast enough, their artillery and tank fire failing to smash the desperate German assault.

Before it was full light on 29 April the German commanders had to get their people flooding through this breach. It was a hectic scramble, but XI SS Panzer Corps and V Corps managed to get through and away. For the rearguard, as will be recounted later, it was not so easy. It seems that the Soviets also managed to block the gap before V SS Mountain Corps could get through, and that this formation then had to bear the brunt of the Soviet artillery fire in its own struggle to break through an area already strewn with the casualties of the earlier fighting.[1]

SS-Major Hartrampf, commanding 502nd SS Heavy Panzer Battalion, maintained a good grip on his lead tanks and any resistance encountered was soon overcome. Whenever there was a hold-up, Hartrampf would appear in his APC and get his tanks moving again, though he later recalled that XI SS Panzer Corps, more often than he would have liked, sent the radioed question: 'Where are the leading tanks?'[2]

SS Lieutenant Bärmann, driving along in an SPG, reported:

As it became light on 29 April, we drove on cautiously and soon came to a barrier with two T-34s behind it. They were immediately engaged by the Tigers driving behind us. I called down below: 'Two o'clock right – aim!' Together, we overcame the anti-tank guns and tanks.

Spirits improved. At the autobahn west of Halbe, we came up against another anti-tank barrier that we also overcame. With daylight, the Russian ground-attack aircraft began attacking, but our self-propelled Flak fired flat out so that they were unable to aim their bombs.[3]

The lead tanks of 502nd SS Heavy Panzer Battalion reached the Cottbus–Berlin autobahn at dawn and came under fire. One or two well concealed Russian tanks engaged the German vehicles as soon as they approached the autobahn, but SS-Major Hartrampf was on the spot and gave orders for an attack by a Tiger and a hastily assembled infantry storm troop, which soon put them out of action. The lead tanks then crossed the autobahn and waited in the woods opposite for the others to catch up. However, although the first group of opposing tanks had been dealt with, others firing from further off along the autobahn opened up as soon as a German vehicle approached. Even so General Busse managed to get across in his command APC and drove on to the rendezvous at the Massow forest warden's lodge.[4]

Rudi Lindner's account of this period continued:

It slowly became light as we slipped along the track under cover of the wood. As this led to the west, it had to lead to the autobahn. Suddenly in front of us was the nose of an armoured vehicle. 'Take cover! One man forward to reconnoitre!'

After ten minutes came the report that it was an assault gun. Its crew, who had their dead commander aboard, were about to cross the autobahn under cover of the morning haze, but did not know if the woods opposite were occupied by the enemy or not, and were also afraid that there might be flanking anti-tank gun fire along the autobahn, so they were happy to see us and for us to find out for them. A brief order: 'Under simultaneous covering fire, over the autobahn in bounds.' We were soon on the other side. All we found on the other side were empty foxholes and dead bodies. We welcomed the chance to drive our assault gun several kilometres in the westerly direction ordered for the break-out to the assembly point at the forest warden's lodge at Massow. We found ourselves on a woodland track on which soldiers were moving along in groups of all sizes.

We soon arrived at 9th Army's assembly point, reported in and received 16 men's worth of rations and ammunition to divide among the remaining five of us, sufficient to eat ourselves full once more, for we did not know when we would get any more.

Here the extent of the tragedy at Halbe quickly became apparent. Many comrades were missing from our unit, the majority of our company of Panzergrenadiers having been killed or wounded; there was no accurate account.

We were again allocated as tank escorts for the coming march. We were to advance on foot with the task of screening ahead and on the flanks. The men of our little unit could now keep together and keep an eye on each other, as we were now independent and no longer bound to the tanks.

However, we soon noticed that there was no longer a strong overall command. A leaderless mass of soldiers and refugees was wandering through the woods. Military discipline and comradeship had fallen by the wayside. The majority of soldiers of all ranks moved like sheep around and behind the tanks, trying to get aboard whenever they stopped. Just as in Halbe, hits from anti-tank, artillery and

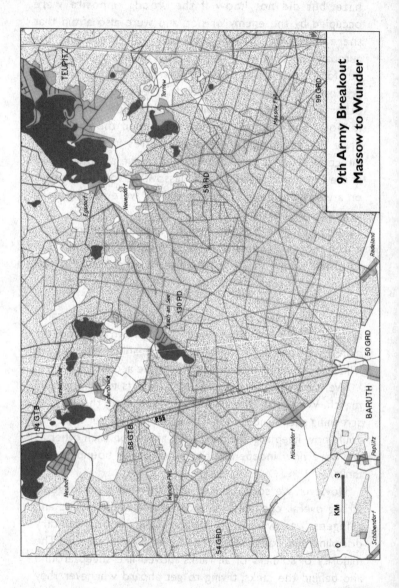

9th Army Breakout
Massow to Wunder

mortar fire, as well as the many air attacks, had had a catastrophic effect on soldiers and civilians alike. Each impact cost ten to twenty times the number of dead and wounded as it would have done under normal combat conditions. At first the wounded were tended to and the dead laid aside in the woods, but later, especially at night, this ceased. People became more and more numbed. Hunger and fatigue added to this, and only the fear of becoming prisoners of the Russians drove the soldiers on, regardless of casualties.

This stream of humanity moved not only along the woodland tracks but also left and right through the woods, so that our task of securing the tanks against enemy close-quarter engagement was no longer necessary.

Not from overwhelming bravery, but out of old combat experience, our practice was to use every halt to get further ahead. We knew: 'He who does not get through the enemy cordon within five to ten minutes once it is breached and uses the gap will get the concentrated fire of the Russian weapons on the breakthrough point.'

This was the motto we kept to, and whenever the call was given: 'Infantry forward! Tanks forward!' that was how we acted, whereas, in such a situation, the majority of soldiers of all ranks would often press back into the woods.

The advantage for us was that the way forward was free for the unfortunately few remaining soldiers and ever fewer tank crews. Each tank crew in 9th Army's breakthrough to the west was putting its life on the line with the danger of being shot up time and time again, and each time had to face up to this and not pull back into the woods.[5]

The survivors of the main break-out group began gathering at dawn around the Massow forest warden's lodge and continued to arrive in an endless stream of soldiers and civilians. Some soldiers were able to rejoin the units they had become separated from during the break-out. Major-General Hölz, chief of staff of 9th Army, and SS-General Klein-heisterkamp, commander of XI SS Panzer Corps, failed to appear.[6] General Willy Langkeit's liaison officer from the Panzergrenadier Division *Kurmark* also turned up and reported that the general's command APC had been hit, but that the general had got out and gone off in another direction. He had reportedly been captured. Some 4,000– 5,000 people had lost their lives during the night and countless numbers were wounded.[7]

The assembly area was made secure while General Busse consulted with the unit commanders over their next move. SS-Major Hartrampf proposed the Wunder forest warden's lodge, west of the Wünsdorf– Baruth road as their next rendezvous, and that was accepted. Fresh orders were issued and the group set off again.

SS-Lieutenant Bärmann continued his account:

> While we were securing the assembly area at Massow, General Busse drove up in his APC. In reply to my question how far we had to go to get to Wenck's Army, he replied sixty kilometres. Our fuel would not last sixty kilometres, as was the case with just about all the armoured vehicles. He said that when necessary we would have to obtain fuel by force, as the armour had to stay in the lead if 9th Army was to get through.[8]

The usual order of march was armoured vehicles with combat-ready and willing soldiers in the lead, followed by various vehicles carrying wounded, but many reports also say that staff officers with their luggage were near the front. Last of all came the once vast but now rapidly declining number of stragglers and civilians.[9]

Several Soviet attacks of divisional size then caused the German groups to split into two pockets; the first contained those still trapped east of Halbe, and a second, large one was in the Staakow Forest between Zesch, Dornswalde and Radeland. Contact had been lost with V SS Mountain Corps' rearguard, which was fighting desperately to break out of the reinforced Soviet cordon and in so doing not only inflicted heavy casualties on the Soviets but also served to distract attention from the remainder of the escaping 9th Army. Although the rearguard units managed to break out of the Halbe position, they were unable to break through the Soviet cordon and remained under a hail of shell and mortar fire.[10]

Late in the afternoon the main group reached the Wünsdorf–Baruth road (Reichsstrasse 96) and railway, coming up against another Russian anti-tank barrier on the same line on which Battlegroups *Pipkorn* and *von Luck* had foundered three days previously. SS-Major Hartrampf, who knew the area well from his time at the Wünsdorf Tank School, gave SS-Lieutenant Ulan and his platoon of Tigers precise instructions to block the road from the north at a certain point until 1800 hours.

The troops moved off again across the railway and parallel road, but were fired on from their right flank, where they should have been protected by Ulan's tanks. What they discovered next day, when Ulan rejoined them, was that he had taken up position at the designated point but had then been ordered further north by a colonel, who had appeared out of nowhere and then threatened him with a court martial when he objected, another *Seydlitz* ploy.

The main break-out group had closed up to the road and railway, where Russian tanks and anti-tank guns now dominated the crossing point from both north and south. SS-Major Hartrampf, who had meanwhile lost his APC, again took over and organized an assault. Some Tigers were deployed to tackle the opposition coming from the flanks, while others plunged across and took cover in the woods beyond before going on to form a bridgehead around the

Wunder forest warden's lodge. Hartrampf got his unit across intact but other units were broken up in their attempts, the survivors crossing individually or in small groups.[11]

Rudi Lindner continued his account:

On the afternoon of 29 April we drew near to a Russian cordon with strong defensive positions on the line of the railway and road between Zossen and Baruth.

Our little combat team worked its way forward with other soldiers under cover of the woods to the edge, where happily the equivalent of the strength of a battalion of infantry gradually accumulated. Our spearhead had been brought to a halt by tank and anti-tank gun fire from the flanks. As our tanks spread out right and left along the edge of the woods and engaged the enemy tanks and anti-tank guns with their guns, we attacked on a broad front. We crossed the railway line and road in bounds and forced our way to the other side under cover of the concentrated fire from our rifles, Panzerfausts and hand grenades into the woods opposite. Once we had broken through and overcome the cordon, we thrust through with our tanks to the forest warden's lodge at Wunder.[12]

Helmut Jurisch, a radio operator in the *Kurmark* Panzergrenadier Division's *Brandenburg* Panzer Regiment, also reported his experience here:

Of the 14 Panthers surrounded in the Halbe pocket, only nine survived 28 April, including the one in which I served as radio operator. With three other Panthers we crossed the autobahn unscathed in the night, guided by our guardian angel, and that morning reached the railway running alongside Reichsstrasse 96 between Wünsdorf and Baruth. While we were crossing the railway embankment there was an explosion inside the tank and stabbing flames and spraying sparks forced us to bail out. As the Panther rolled back down again it burst into flames; we picked ourselves up, slightly singed. The other Panthers were engaging the anti-tank barrier that had knocked us out. A trick of fate had spared our lives, for, as the tank climbed the embankment, the shell aimed centrally at the front of the tank had passed underneath and exploded against the gearbox located between the driver's and radio operator's seats.[13]

SS-Lieutenant Bärmann also fought here:

We were still stuck on the Zossen–Baruth road. The situation was obscure. Some infantry overtook us and we drove on to the south after the infantry. After a few hundred metres we realised that we had fallen into a trap set up by the *Seydlitz* people. We were met by a belt of anti-tank guns, several T-34s and trees full of snipers, so we drove back to the start point.[14]

SS-Grenadier Muhs had a similar experience:

An army officer took over command and tried to establish some sort of order in our mob. We followed him, thinking that it would soon be over, home, no more bloodshed. Then I saw some badly camouflaged Russian trucks and tanks in the background, and I realised what the game was. We were in a trap set by *Seydlitz-Troops*. During a general palaver, I and a few others disappeared into the undergrowth. One has to be prepared for anything![15]

The lead tanks reached the Wunder forest warden's lodge and SS-Lieutenant Klust reported:

We drove up to the Wunder forest warden's lodge. A few shells from my Tiger at some T-34s ensured that the

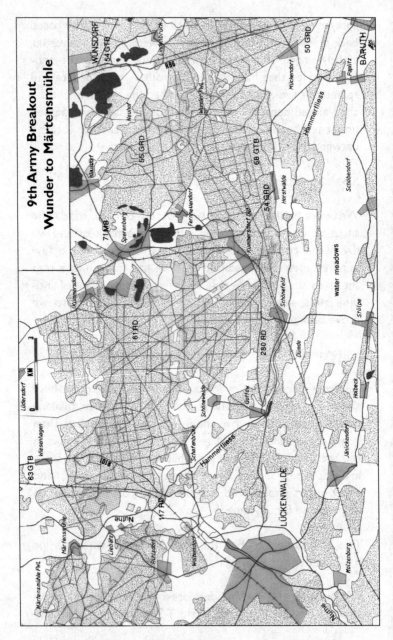

Russians left. German soldiers approached from all directions and a heated discussion started.[16]

SS-Lieutenant Bärmann continued:

About eighty men and seven SPGs of my battalion reached the Wunder forest warden's lodge. SS-Lieutenant Hörl took over the command. SS-Second Lieutenant Stachon appeared with his APC, which was filled with our wounded, who were being tended to by SS-Sergeant-Majors Everding and Wahl. I went with Hörl as his gunner. Our radios were all unserviceable, so we had no long-range communication. We set off again at about 1930 hours. Shortly before dark there was an attack by Russian bombers, which fortunately failed to hit us.[17]

SS-Grenadier Tag also reached the rendezvous:

Another big group assembled at the Wunder forest warden's lodge, including Waffen-SS Tigers, members of the Luftwaffe, elements of the Panzergrenadier Division *Kurmark* with the remains of Second Lieutenant Dahlinger's 11th Company. During the conference an unidentified colonel appeared and broke into the conversation, imploring those standing around to follow him as he knew a safe way out. And the talking continued. Then came the word *Seydlitzmann* and some catch questions were asked. There were some shots and the colonel collapsed. Similar incidents occurred elsewhere, where an NCO and a sergeant were identified as *Seydlitz* people and shot. We now paid more attention to the uniform; good, clean uniforms were a clue to *Seydlitz* people.[18]

SS-Lieutenant Klust was still with the leaders in his Tiger:

As the gathering was quite large and Russian aircraft were crossing over us, bombs could be expected to fall at any moment. Without waiting for orders, I had my Tiger drive off, knowing the rest would follow.

The column moved off towards Kummersdorf.[19] We were ashamed to see more civilians carrying weapons than soldiers. A large meadow-plain was enclosed by the edge of the woods opposite. Three Tigers and a few SPGs shot up some identified T-34s and anti-tank guns. Some soldiers and civilians charged across on a wide front, and the Russians fled.[20]

SS-Lieutenant Bärmann resumed:

We passed the village of Horstwalde. After a broad meadow valley, the land began to rise. Suddenly everything stopped. Of all things, the leading Jagdpanzer had run out of fuel at a tree barrier. Then, in this situation, the cry went up: 'Ivan is attacking!' Meanwhile it had become dark, so who on earth could tell where and who Ivan was? Firing everywhere. We towed the Jagdpanzer back out of the barrier with our SPG and syphoned off the last drops of fuel before blowing it up.[21]

Several wheeled vehicles had their fuel tanks emptied at Wunder before being destroyed, enabling the armoured vehicles to continue to lead the break-out. The march resumed through the woods in various-sized groups to Kummersdorf Gut, where the artillery ranges were reached during the night and the railway station, farm and military installations taken by storm. However, an advance by 71st Mechanized Brigade on Kummersdorf Gut with attacks on the flanks of the leading elements by the 50th and 54th Guards Rifle Divisions resulted in the formation of a third pocket near Klausdorf–Kummersdorf Gut–Horstwalde. This remained connected to the second pocket by a narrow corridor, but a certain number of soldiers became separated from the main party, were forced to the south, surrounded and taken prisoner.[22]

Willi Klär described events at Kummersdorf Gut:

On 26 and 27 April the Red Army deployed artillery pieces facing today's demolition area from the forest warden's lodge as far as the blown bridge where the road forks off to Fernneuendorf, as well as along the edge of the woods as far as Mönninghausen. Then, on the evening of Sunday, 29 April, Russian soldiers entered our homes and ordered the inhabitants to go to the cellar of the old folks' home: the 'Germanskis' were coming.

The din started at about 2200 hours with bangs and flashes. There were screams and suddenly there were wounded German soldiers in the cellar. They belonged to General Busse's 9th Army, which had been surrounded in the Spreewald, and were now trying to reach the west via Halbe, Zesch, Mückendorf, the forest warden's lodge at Wunder and the Kummersdorf Ranges towards Trebbin. Those troops who survived the encirclement intact would join up with General Wenck's 12th Army.

There were several wounded from explosive bullets among the civilian population, including a ten-year-old, Fritz Feldner, who received a splinter in his thigh that hit the artery. He died from loss of blood within a short time, as there were no doctors available.[23]

Erwin Bartmann, a sergeant from the SS Grenadier Regiment *Falke*, recounted his experiences on this day:

Once more we were without an officer and we set off again to the west. We then met a long column of soldiers and refugees trying to save their skins, and followed them. We

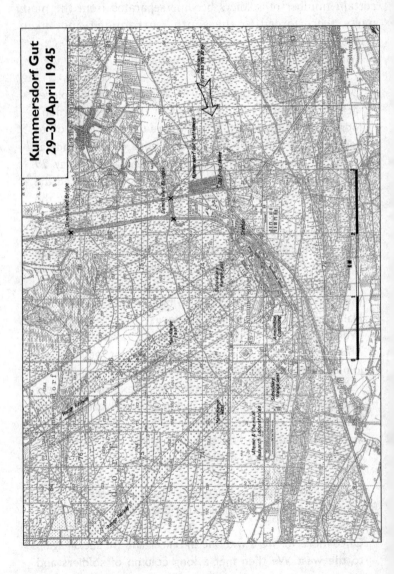

Kummersdorf Gut
29–30 April 1945

came to the weapon-proving ranges at Kummersdorf, where we had to fight the Russians yet again. Beyond Kummersdorf, I and a few Waffen-SS comrades found ourselves in an unending column of soldiers of all arms of the Wehrmacht, generals and senior officers with their staffs. Again we came up against *Seydlitz-Troops* as we went through the woods. As was later discovered, the *Seydlitz-Troops* were under the command of Russian commissars. We were attacked in the woods by Russian infantry and *Seydlitz-Troops*. As we went along a firebreak they moved parallel to us and then attacked us from the flank. The *Seydlitz-Troops* wore German uniforms but were armed with Russian sub-machine guns. They kept on attacking us, mixing in with the column. When one appeared with an armband in his pocket with the words *Komitee Freies Deutschland*, one of the officers came up shouting: 'Where are the SS? This man must be executed.' I personally would have nothing to do with this big shot. We told them to do it themselves if they wanted someone killed. (I disliked these gentlemen of the senior staff intensely. At that time all they were doing was thinking of saving their own skins.) We moved from place to place, from south to north, and back to the south. The long procession of human beings went from one road junction to another, meeting up with other units.[24]

The *Seydlitz-Troops* were particularly active during this phase, as in this account by an unidentified soldier:

Near Sperenberg a second lieutenant suddenly appeared near me and wanted me to go and speak to his general. We were just about to make an attack, and some T-34s had been reported, when the second lieutenant said to me that we should stop the attack and fire three red flares. He had a flare pistol with him. The general was wearing camouflage uniform without badges of rank. When I went up to him and enquired his name and where he came from, he said that he was General Eckert and that he came from Führer Headquarters. I told him that we were continuing our attack and would fire no red signal rockets. He ordered the attack broken off, but then a Russian shell exploded nearby and he was killed. I checked him over: grey trousers, camouflage jacket, no medals or badges, no papers. I took the flare pistol from the second lieutenant and told him to bury his 'general'. He was a *Seydlitz* man.[25]

Despite the additional commitment by the Soviets of 71st Mechanized Brigade from the Wünsdorf area, 68th Independent Guards Tank Brigade from the Horstwalde area, and 117th Guards Rifle Division from Luckenwalde, the main German group was only checked briefly between Sperenberg and Kummersdorf Gut. By this time any formal command structure in the break-out groups had ceased to exist, but these desperate German troops maintained their successful efforts until nightfall that day, having overcome three Soviet cordons and covered about 25 kilometres, nearly half the way to Beelitz.[26]

Some, like Major Brand's 21st Armoured Reconnaissance Battalion of 21st Panzer Division, were less fortunate, as he reported:

About 2,000 leaderless officers and soldiers had tagged on to the battalion, together with the same number of civilians of all ages and both sexes. Renewed break-out attempt early on 29 April. Success near Halbe at first, with the Russians withdrawing with heavy losses, but at the bridge where the road crosses the autobahn west of Halbe, the whole unit fell into a Russian trap. Hundreds of dead, semi-demented civilians, frightful state of affairs. Three fatal casualties in my own command vehicle. Control was lost. Women raped to death by Russians from a nearby camp lying in the woods and on the roads.[27]

But the horror was not yet over at Halbe. Erika Menze from Märkisch Buchholz, then seventeen, was one of the refugees who tried to get through Halbe that day:

On 29 April there was nothing to remind us that, according to the calendar, this was a Sunday. We hardly thought at all. Climb up on the truck, down from the truck, take cover. One was just moving and acting automatically. Sometimes I thought to myself: 'Don't get wounded.' There were already many wounded soldiers sitting and lying on the trucks. We reached just short of Halbe on this terrible Sunday morning of 29 April.

Again and again we had to take cover in the shallow ditches on the edge of the woods. The mud splashed so! Then things quietened down a bit. We looked up and saw clearly where we were. Off to the right the tall buildings of the post office and railway station. On the left the wood, where the Poliklinik stands today. In front of us the road that leads to Märkisch Buchholz on the left and goes straight ahead across the railway lines into the village.

I don't know by what miracle we had remained unscathed until then. I don't know now how I got across the railway lines at Halbe station. What I saw was horrible. The tanks rolled down Lindenstrasse covered all over with wounded soldiers. One fell off and the next tank rolled right over him, squashing him flat, so that the next tank rolled through a pool of blood. There was nothing of this soldier left. It happened in seconds.

I had to take care where I lay. The pavement near the Drassdo Bakery was covered in corpses, all German soldiers. Many more dead were lying alongside the houses, stacked up at an angle, leaving no cobblestone or piece of pavement uncovered. I had to pass over these dead soldiers, their heads yellow, grey, crushed flat, their hands yellow, grey or greyish-black, only the wedding rings glimmering gold or silver. A horrific scene.

At last I reached the home of the cobbler Luban. This far and no further. It must have been about noon, for some women had cooked some cabbage soup and we each got a large cupful. But that was the end of our longed-for respite.

Two Russians came to the cellar entrance and explained to the inhabitants that the Germans were attacking again and that we all had to leave the cellar. I grabbed my food bag and we left the cellar one after the other. I saw the Russian soldiers for the first time at the house door.

We all ran across the yard and behind through the garden into the open field, where there was a stack of logs several metres long. I lay down there on my back, not moving an inch. Then all hell broke loose.

There was firing over us, behind us and beside us, all kinds of small arms fire, the bigger stuff not so close. One got used to the sound of firing and explosions from the bigger weapons.

But what came next was not possible to make out. Heavy weapons were roaring and Stalin-Organs were mentioned. Heavy and light machine guns were rattling and tracer bullets whistled over us. 'Don't move! They're firing at anything that moves', a woman near me cried out. This lasted from early afternoon until dusk. The barrage must have lasted six hours. The woman next to me was wounded twice, her brother-in-law too. They comforted each other as best as they could.

After hours of bombardment, it became quieter. During the bombardment we had seen many shot-up ruins collapse.

Night began to fall. A Russian took a large glass of what looked like sugar or semolina from a handcart standing not far from us. I thought, so he comes and helps himself and we have to stay still. But he only looked very shyly towards us. He needed it as much as we did. As we looked back there was no horizon to be seen. Everything was covered in smoke. We all tried to stand up, then noticed how cold we had become.

German soldiers came and hurried us up. The Russians had been driven off and we should get away quickly towards the autobahn. But going on again with them was nonsense, carrying on in the hell of the pocket. We had long been encircled, as we discovered months later.

We reached the woodland track on which soldiers were emerging from Halbe. I went along under cover of the tanks hand in hand with a soldier, who gave me a lump of sugar, saying that it would calm me.

Meanwhile it had become pitch dark. There was the glow of a fire here and there, so that we could make out the tanks. Before long we came under fire again. The soldier showed me a place, somewhere between uneven ground and a heap of brushwood. The fire-fight intensified. I despaired and began crying for the first time in days. Suddenly the soldiers started running with a loud 'Hurrah!' The Russians had to think they were outnumbered. Later came the many wounded, suffering, groaning, calling for the medical orderlies. We were completely incapable of helping them.

The wood came to an end in front of us. Over there in the darkness the soldiers thought was the autobahn. We could hear tanks moving, but no one knew whether they were German or Russian.

So the column wheeled left. You couldn't see your hand in front of your face. We could hear some soldiers placing two wounded on a motorcycle combination, but it was no longer serviceable. The stream of humanity would stop from time to time, then move on again.[28]

Another officer cadet from the same regiment as Rudi Lindner reported on events in Halbe that day:

On 29 April 1945 at about midday (the day of the abortive break-out attempt of several units west of us) three four-wheeled scout cars and about the same number of

Volkswagen jeeps suddenly appeared before our positions [the sparse screen formed by the 1st Battalion, 86th SS Volunteer Grenadier Regiment *Schill*] from a westerly direction. Their commander was a young second lieutenant, a Hitler Youth leader type. At first we took them for *Seydlitz-Troops* and wanted them to disarm immediately, but they identified themselves as a reconnaissance unit of the *Friedrich Ludwig Jahn* Division of 12th Army coming from the area west of Teupitz. Their unit had become badly disorientated in the last few days and had contact neither to the west nor to the east. By the sounds of battle coming from the east, there must still be strong elements of our own troops around. Their commander wanted to know for sure and so had sent out this reconnaissance unit. Any stragglers were to be brought back with them. The officer had radio contact, so we sent him on to the XI SS Panzer Corps battlegroup, but what happened then remains unknown. During a short cigarette break we learned something about the other divisions [of 12th Army] for the first time. This encounter took place in the woods three kilometres north-east of Halbe, north of the track to the Klein Hammer forest warden's lodge on the Dahme Flood Canal.

We only hoped that our armoured vehicles would keep on driving west and that at last we would not have to march any more. We came to another road, crossed a railway line and were able to read the name 'Halbe' on a road sign. We were making a gentle turn with our tank into the village, when we were suddenly fired on from all sides. Within a few minutes our first three tanks had been blown up. The crews squeezed themselves out of the narrow hatches completely wrapped in flames, like human torches. Everything happened quickly. Flares shot into the air and rifle fire whipped through the dark. Our remaining tanks turned round and as rapidly as it had started everything became quiet. Then suddenly someone shouted: 'Don't shoot, they're our comrades.'

Everyone wanted to move on and pressed into the village street, but heavy rifle whipped into our ranks from the buildings as we formed a perfect target in front of the bright background of burning tanks. Only the trees on the street provided minimum cover from one side. Then shots from Russian anti-tank guns and tanks started coming from the western end of the village street.

There were no officers to give orders in these chaotic circumstances. We had no maps and no plan how to get out of this Halbe mousetrap. At last a sergeant-major shouted: 'Machine guns and Panzerfausts up front.'

We fired at the windows of the buildings from which we were being fired at and, under cover of our fire, a few grenadiers stormed the buildings. Some dull hand-grenade explosions came from the buildings and we had found our cover. We immediately started moving the wounded off the street into the cellars.

The blazing night was filled with the horrible cries of the wounded, the bangs of exploding ammunition from the burning tanks, bursts of machine-gun fire, rifle shots and Russian gunfire.

We saw a wounded comrade who had had a leg shot off and were trying to pull him to safety by his arms as enemy rifle bullets whistled past. Then one of our tanks caught him with its tracks when it was turning and squashed him flat.

A medical orderly appeared to take over the care of the wounded whom we had carried in and said to us: 'Make sure that you get through. I'll stay with the wounded and hand them over to the Russians.' We silently shook his hand and made our way out of the back of the building, feeling safer when we reached the edge of the woods.

We soon reached the Lübben–Königs Wusterhausen autobahn, which we crossed at about midnight on 29 April.

At last we reached the edge of the woods, where we found foxholes that had only been abandoned a few hours before. A small building stood on the far side of the woods – I don't know whether it was a forest warden's lodge – from which a white flag was waving. It was the first white flag that we had seen. This apparently idyllic scene was abruptly disturbed when about 30 Russians rushed out of the building to seek cover in the adjacent woods. We engaged them with machine-gun fire at a range of about 150 metres, but what stunned and left us shattered, was a naked and raped girl with a head wound lying about 100 metres left of the building and a soldier in German uniform hanging from a pine tree next to her. We were struck dumb, staring silently at the two dead persons, at the raped girl and the hanging soldier, who looked at us with glazed eyes. We cut down the dead man and went on slowly, each with the firm resolve that it was better to die than to be taken prisoner. We carried on under the cover of the woods as Russian planes crossed over above searching for us.[29]

Horst Wilke confirmed this last incident:

This building in the woods must have been the Massow forest warden's lodge, which had been burnt out during the fighting. I myself went past there at about 0530 hours on 1 May, and several timbers were still glowing. The track going past it was being used by the Russians as a supply route to the autobahn. The positions were full of dead soldiers and civilians. A bit aside from the track lay a naked girl of about 12–15 years old, and next to her a dead German soldier who still had some rope around his neck. We had a good view of the terrain with the rising sun.[30]

Other units had yet to pass through Halbe. The SS-second lieutenant of Battlegroup *Becker* continued his account:

We only took up temporary positions on 29 April, but the Russians kept approaching hesitantly. We had captured two machine guns with a quantity of ammunition the previous day, and were amazed that the Russians had mainly German weapons. We went on in the afternoon and reached the outskirts of Halbe. It really was frightful. I have never seen so many dead, though unfortunately most were German. The Russians had dug in their T-34s to try and prevent the cauldron being breached, but we still had some Königstigers on our side, so it was possible to break through their positions. Later, in Russian captivity, we were told that 55,000 Germans and 5,000 Russians fell at Halbe on 29 April.

We were under constant attack from low-flying aircraft, but by 1700 hours Halbe was behind us as we followed an avenue to the west. I was wounded in the left thigh by a low-flying attack, which was no pleasant birthday present, but I carried on with an emergency dressing. We marched on all night towards Beelitz. We came to an artillery range, where there were Russian snipers in the trees. By this time we had been sharply reduced to about seventy men.

We were suddenly fired on again that afternoon from behind and everyone started running. I could only get at most thirty men into position. Heavy mortar fire drove both friend and foe under cover. I was wounded again by a mortar splinter in my lower left leg; a splinter went in above the ankle between the shin and fibula. We also came under fire from Stalin-Organs during the night of 30 April–1 May.[31]

And an armourer with V SS Mountain Corps reported:

We reached the village of Halbe at about 1300 hours on 29 April. On the through road towards Baruth we came up against a Russian anti-tank barrier, where hundreds of German dead lay, sometimes two or three on top of each other, including some police in their green uniforms. It was horrible. The anti-tank barrier was blown up. We had a few tanks with us, including Tigers, which formed our spearhead, drawing many civilians, including some French prisoners of war, along with the big crowd.[32]

The chaos in the original pocket had now become even worse, with continuous attacks from Soviet aircraft, mortars and rockets. That evening several composite groups tried to break out once more, together with countless refugees and uniformed marauders. This time the route was to be via the forest warden's lodge at Massow, where only weak Soviet forces were thought to be, but this was a fallacy, and all these groups were wiped out.[33]

Those elements of the Panzergrenadier Division *Kurmark* which had formed the northern wedge, and covered the main breach from the north, fought hard to get through north of Halbe, then followed the Halbe–Teupitz road to the autobahn. With them were some elements of the 10th SS Armoured Reconnaissance Battalion *Frundsberg* which had been holding the perimeter in the Köris area, but this battalion's 3rd Company had been cut off during the break-out by the Russian forces filling the woods and only very few of them were to survive.

Further north, near Töpchin, SS-Second Lieutenant Porsch's Tank-Hunting Company *Dora II* met its fate, as he later recorded:

Our little gang was getting smaller and smaller, again and again a few good comrades were being left lying. The dead had to be buried quickly, as we had to keep on fighting and pushing forward without rest.

Then we were trapped in a clearing between Märkisch Buchholz and Töpchin, an enemy battalion having caught us in its clutches and surrounded us. We held out against all attacks for two days with our 42 men and then mounted a final counterattack. Without a round in the chamber, the last eleven climbed out of their holes and followed me with my Wolchow club raised high against the attacking Soviets. We were then overcome in close-quarter fighting, my Wolchow club breaking on a Russian helmet, and the fight was over.

At my request, the Russian regimental commander, who had personally led the last attack against our little gang, granted me three hours in which to bury our dead. We dug a long pit and laid them down, one after another, with their faces to the east towards the rising sun, as all the dead of my company were put to rest. When we went to lay their weapons beside them, as was the custom in our unit, some officers protested, but with a wave of his hand their commander, an elderly colonel, silenced them and let us continue. Once we had smoothed over the grave, we formed a half-circle in front of it and sang our farewell tribute with hoarse voices.

The Soviets stood there silently, side by side, and listened. Then we had to make our way into captivity. I was soon separated from my men and never saw any of them again.[34]

However, XI SS Panzer Corps' greatly reduced rearguard, under SS-Major May, managed to get through the same area and pushed through westwards north of the main group, meeting up with it in the Trebbin Forest the following night.[35]

The condition of the troops in his break-out group was now such that General Busse signalled General Wenck:

The physical state and morale of the officers and men, as well as the states of ammunition and supplies, permit neither a new attack nor long resistance. The misery of the civilians who have fled out of the pocket is particularly bad. Only the measures taken by all the generals have enabled the troops to stick together. The fighting capacity of 9th Army is obviously at an end.[36]

This bitter struggle continued for two days. The Soviets then claimed to have killed 60,000 and captured 120,000 prisoners, 300 tanks and self-propelled guns and 1,500 pieces of artillery. In the obscurity of the woods the Soviets may well have been misled, at least temporarily, into thinking that they had caught the bulk of 9th Army and later, having realized their error, were happy to prolong the myth.

Marshal Koniev then reinforced his defence sectors and ordered attacks on the various German groups, in all deploying 15 infantry regiments or armoured brigades with about 150 tanks and SPGs, and 1,000 artillery pieces, mortars and anti-tank guns. He had 13th Army's 395th Rifle Division redeploy from the Golssen–Baruth sector to the Mückendorf area, while 117th Guards Rifle Division of the same army was ordered to attack towards Kummersdorf Gut to prevent a breakthrough to Luckenwalde, which 68th Independent Guards Tank Brigade was ordered to block off. Then, to block the route to Beelitz, he had 63rd Guards Tank Brigade and 7th Motorcycle Regiment of 10th Guards Tank Corps of 4th Guards Tank Army deploy from the Michendorf area to Trebbin, where these forces were to control the traffic junctions. The 71st Mechanized Brigade, which was deployed along the Zossen–Kummersdorf Gut railway line in the Sperenberg area, was reinforced by two regiments of 61st Rifle Division of 28th Army. 3rd Guards Rifle Corps, also of 28th Army, was given the task of destroying the German troops in the Mückendorf woods with a double thrust from the Lindenbrück–Zesch sector to the south and from the Radeland–Baruth sector to the north.[37]

Meanwhile Zhukov's armies narrowed down the remaining pockets of resistance east of Halbe during the day, their advance reaching the line Halbe–Löpten–Hammer–east bank of the Dahme, while 1st Ukrainian Front's 3rd Guards Army maintained pressure along the line Teurow–Märkisch Buchholz.

From the Prieros area we have the following account:

On 29 April 1945 at about 0400 hours I was wounded while manning a forward position near Prieros, apparently by *Seydlitz-Troops*. My sleeping comrade was not hit by their fire, and I had to wake him from his exhausted sleep to bandage me. Neither had our company, 200 metres back, noticed, although I had thrown two hand grenades. The mill that I was told was our main dressing station turned out to have been vacated and I had to fight for a place on the trucks heading back, eventually finding a place on a mudguard. Ever more wounded had to be taken aboard and any combat-capable soldiers were obliged to get off, most of them being unarmed.

Even when the trucks were more than overloaded with wounded, there were still more waiting on the roadside. A young army doctor had to decide who among the wounded being transported had to get off. I watched him closely and noted that the decision over life and death was not an easy one for him.

As I was travelling on the mudguard, I was told, since I was fit enough, to look out for enemy aircraft as we drove along. Many times we had to take cover on the side of the road, for which the many foxholes dug there provided a good service. As yet again more ground-attack aircraft approached, I could only see one such foxhole some distance away. I ran to it and dived in at the same time as another soldier, who had the same intention as myself. It turned out to be a happy surprise, for the other soldier was a chap I had known from Stralsund who had been in the same company, and from then on we stayed together.[38]

General Wenck's attack had made good progress that day and by the evening the leading elements of Lieutenant-General Engel's *Ulrich von Hutten* Infantry Division had reached the village of Ferch at the southern tip of the Schwielowsee, some ten kilometres south of Potsdam, but in so doing reached their operational limit. The 12th Army could only improve its newly won positions a little, while holding on against increasing Soviet pressure, as it awaited the arrival of the others to break through to them. There was some particularly severe armoured fighting around the autobahn fork.

Lieutenant-Colonel Alfred Müller led his *Schill* Division through the Lehniner Forest on the left flank, and a Major Nebel pushed forward with some SPGs along the firebreaks to the very end of the forest, where the Russian armour was waiting and engaged them. However, Nebel's guns outflanked the danger points to hit the Soviets in their flanks and rear. The sounds of battle carried right through the Lehniner Forest to the lakes and the Potsdam garrison beyond.

Wenck contacted General Reymann of the Potsdam garrison and ordered an immediate break-out to his lines, which was begun that evening and completed the following night, the garrison making its way by boat across the Schwielowsee, or along the shore by foot. Reymann broke through with the leading groups and met up with Lieutenant-Colonel Müller. They silently shook hands before Reymann moved on to report to Wenck's headquarters. When they arrived, the troops of the Potsdam garrison were then shared out among the Schill and Hutten Divisions as reinforcements.[39]

Wenck then signalled an invitation to General Weidling in Berlin: 'Counterattacks by 12th Army stalled south of Potsdam. Troops engaged in very heavy defensive fighting. Suggest you break out to us.' This signal was not acknowledged and it is doubtful if Weidling even received it.[40]

Wenck passed Busse's message on the state of his troops on to the OKW, which in the meantime had put an end to any chances of relief from this direction by disclosing 12th

Army's dispositions and intentions in the afternoon radio communiqué. This made it even more difficult for 12th Army to hold on to its positions. The army's situation was already precarious enough in any case with 5th Guards Mechanized Corps and 13th Army trying to cut off its line of retreat to the Elbe. That same evening Wenck's position was further imperilled by a sudden attack northward towards Wittenberg by American troops bursting out of their bridgeheads in his rear. Fortunately this attack was not pursued, presumably because of the policy imposed from above of not intervening in the Soviet area of operations.[41]

Wenck signalled the OKW again that evening:

> The 12th Army, and in particular XX Corps which has temporarily succeed in establishing contact with the Potsdam Garrison, is obliged to turn to the defensive along the whole front. This means that an attack on Berlin is now impossible, since we have also ascertained that we can no longer rely on the fighting capacity of the 9th Army.[42]

During the night Wenck received the following reluctant acknowledgement of the situation by signal from Field Marshal Keitel:

> If the Commanding General 12th Army, in full knowledge of the current situation at XX Corps, and despite the high historical and moral responsibility that he carries, considers continuing the attack towards Berlin impossible . . .

Wenck now had a free hand to pursue his own plans.[43]

Hitler himself must have realised that the end was near. Having rejected General Weidling's desperate break-out plan for the Berlin garrison, he sent the following signal to Colonel-General Jodl that evening:

1. Where are Wenck's spearheads?
2. When will they resume the attack?
3. Where is the 9th Army?
4. Where is it breaking through?
5. Where are Holste's XXXXI Panzer Corps' spearheads?[44]

NOTES

1. Lakowski/Stich, *Der Kessel von Halbe 1945*, p. 121.
2. Tieke, *Das Ende zwischen Oder und Elbe*, p. 320.
3. *Ibid.*, p. 323.
4. *Ibid.*, p. 322.
5. Lindner in the author's *Death Was Our Companion*.
6. Hölz had been promoted from colonel to major-general on 23 April.
7. Lakowski/Stich, *Der Kessel von Halbe 1945*, pp. 121–2; Tieke, *Das Ende zwischen Oder und Elbe*, p. 323. According to his family, Langkeit surrendered to the British on 22 May, so it seems he may have either avoided capture by the Soviets, or managed to escape. (Letter to the author).
8. Tieke, *Das Ende zwischen Oder und Elbe*, p. 323.
9. Lakowski/Stich, *Der Kessel von Halbe 1945*, p. 122.
10. *Ibid.*, pp. 123–4.
11. Tieke, *Das Ende zwischen Oder und Elbe*, p. 324.
12. Lindner in the author's *Death Was Our Companion*.
13. Helmut Jurisch in correspondence with the author.
14. Tieke, *Das Ende zwischen Oder und Elbe*, p. 325.
15. *Ibid.*
16. *Ibid.*
17. *Ibid.*, p. 326.
18. *Ibid.*, p. 325.
19. A distinction has to be drawn between the village of Kummersdorf and the artillery proving ranges at Kummersdorf Gut with their own railway station six kilometres to the south. In all the soldiers' accounts 'Kummersdorf' means the artillery ranges complex, not the village proper.
20. Tieke, *Das Ende zwischen Oder und Elbe*, pp. 325–6.
21. *Ibid.*, p. 326.
22. *Ibid.*, pp. 325–6.
23. *Ortschronik von Kummersdorf Gut.* [Rolf Kaim to author].
24. Bartmann in the author's *Death Was Our Companion*.

25. Wilke, *Am Rande der Strassen*, p. 86.
26. Lakowski/Stich, *Der Kessel von Halbe 1945*, pp. 122–4.
27. Brand in the author's *Death Was Our Companion*.
28. Helmut Jurisch in correspondence with the author..
29. Wilke, *Am Rande der Strassen*, pp. 65–9.
30. *Ibid.*, p. 70.
31. *Ibid.*, pp. 83–5.
32. *Ibid.*, p. 70.
33. *Ibid.*, p. 57.
34. Wilke archives. The 'Wolchow club' was made of hard wood and was a souvenir of Porsch's involvement in close-quarter fighting in the area of that name (usually spelt as Volkhov in English) east of Leningrad.
35. Tieke, *Das Ende zwischen Oder und Elbe*, p. 328.
36. Busse, 'Die letzte Schlacht der 9. Armee', p. 168.
37. Lakowski/Stich, *Der Kessel von Halbe 1945*, pp. 125–8.
38. Wilke, *Am Rande der Strassen*, p. 99.
39. Gellermann, *Die Armee Wenck*, pp. 86–7.
40. Wenck, 'Berlin war nicht mehr zu retten', pp. 66–7; Strawson, The *Battle for Berlin*, p. 146. Neither von Dufving nor Refior mention it in their accounts.
41. Wenck, 'Berlin war nicht mehr zu retten', p. 68.
42. *Ibid.*, p. 66; Gellermann, *Die Armee Wenck*, pp. 93–4.
43. Gellermann, *Die Armee Wenck*, p. 176.
44. *Ibid.*, p. 177.

TWELVE

12TH ARMY WAITS

30 APRIL 1945

A t 0100 hours on 30 April Field Marshal Keitel replied to Hitler's signal of the previous evening with:

1. Wenck's attack has stopped south of the Schwielowsee. Strong Soviet attacks along the whole of his east flank.
2. Consequently 12th Army is unable to continue its attack towards Berlin.
3. & 4. 9th Army is surrounded. An armoured group has broken out to the west; location unknown.
5. Corps Holste has been forced on to the defensive from Brandenburg via Rathenow to Kremmen.[1]

Later General Wenck sent the following radio message to 9th Army: '12th Army now engaged in heavy defensive fighting. Speed up your breakthrough. We are waiting for you.' This was a clear call for haste, for in fact Wenck's divisions were only holding on to their positions with difficulty.[2]

Erika Menze continued her story of the break-out from Halbe:

At dawn on 30 April we could see how many soldiers there were in the crowds ahead of and behind us. Civilians were scattered between all the groups of soldiers, moving along with them. The rumour was that we would come out near Baruth.

In the middle of the woods was a farmstead, that was said to be the Baruth forest warden's lodge. We went on for hours, forwards, ever forwards. But there was also some firing, even from the treetops. The soldiers had long lost their will to carry on fighting. They also knew that this war had become nonsensical in the government's final desperation.

Then came some officers, one here, another further off: 'Where is your weapon?' 'Lost in battle!' Then the soldiers had to take the officers' carbines and were ordered up front. One of them did not want to follow orders and was sworn at and threatened with a pistol.

It must have been past midday when we came to Luckenwalde. We had to keep moving, though we seemed to be going round in a circle. Shot-up trees, broken-down vehicles, lost or discarded equipment, pieces of clothing and other items were all lying around. Again we saw dead German soldiers. A young girl wearing a steel helmet sat leaning against a tree. One soldier said that she was asleep, but she was dead.

That afternoon we had to cross a railway line that was under heavy fire. We crossed it singly, always during the pauses in the firing. There was another wood on the other side. A shell made a big hole about 15 metres from me, and I looked back in shock.

Some soldiers came crawling out of the white sand uninjured. Then I reached the wood. On the right was an open expanse like a broad road. There were already many foxholes among the tall pinetrees, and two Volkssturm men called out to me. They dug away the sand industriously with their small spades to make enough room for the three of us. It became a little quieter once more.

We had to move on again at dusk. When night came we were already long on our way. I slept while walking, moving along totally exhausted. One of the pair put a piece of Schoka-cola in my mouth from his iron rations. 'You mustn't fall asleep, girl, we have to go on!' the men said.

We reached Märtensmühle and Ruhlsdorf. Women came towards us from the first houses. 'For goodness sake, you're still in uniform! Come quickly into the yard and we'll give you some civilian clothing!' So the three soldiers became civilians again at the next farm.

On the morning of 3 May the new mayor came and told us to use our common sense and find our way home by the shortest route.[3]

Meanwhile in the main group, SS-Lieutenant Bärmann was still pushing on:

At dawn we came to the station for the Kummersdorf Training Area. Again anti-tank guns were everywhere. The station, workshops and fuel depot were on fire. We broke through to the station, the dead remaining where they fell. A couple of lads rolled up a barrel of fuel. We still had five tanks left and each needed its share. One tank commander who had lost his vehicle, appropriated a T-34, marked it with a swastika flag and SS pennant and took over the lead.

We went round the ranges in a big curve and hid ourselves in the woods. A bit of peace at last, but nothing to eat.[4]

Individual groups were involved in heavy fighting in this area. SS-Captain Lobmeyer reported:

We fought our way across the Kummersdorf ranges, having to deal with some *Seydlitz* units, who kept pressing us to surrender, but we fought on to the west. More and more tanks and other vehicles had to be blown up and abandoned due to fuel or ammunition running out.[5]

As day broke, the last Tigers of 502nd SS Heavy Panzer Battalion moved across the eastern firing range and then crossed over to the western firing range and stopped in the Trebbin Forest north of Schöneweide. There was an industrial railway track on the second firing range, so the wounded were loaded on wagons and towed along to the end of the ranges by a Tiger.

The exhausted troops needed a rest and the various combat teams, all that remained of the original battlegroups, wanted a chance to reorganise. A security screen was established and reconnaissance patrols sent out, which reported back that there was a strong Russian cordon with tanks and anti-tank guns deployed along the line of the Trebbin–Luckenwalde road (Reichsstrasse 101). Once more the fuel tanks of other vehicles were emptied to keep the last Tigers mobile and in action, for which SS-Captain Klust was given a written authority by General Busse.

There was a surprise addition to the group with the arrival of XI SS Panzer Corps' rearguard, commanded by SS-Major May, who had fought their way through from Halbe along a route to the north of the main body. SS-Colonel Kempin, commander of 32nd SS Panzergrenadier Division who was with the rearguard, later commented:

Before we reached the 12th Army's rearguard near Beelitz we attacked a Russian artillery position, with the help of some armed women. The guns were aimed to the west and they were unable to bring them to bear on us. We were totally exhausted, as for two weeks we had had neither sleep nor rations, nor any kind of supplies.[6]

The lead was handed over to V Corps, as communications with XI SS Panzer Corps had now been lost. Command and control – according to various reports from the few sources – was now reduced to having groups stay within shouting distance of each other.

SS-Lieutenant Bärmann went on:

> It wasn't long before the Ivans found us again and attacked us with bombs and machine-gun fire from their ground-attack aircraft, so we had to move on. Those not wounded had to march, only the wounded being allowed on the tanks. I was lying on the rear of a Jagdpanzer and fell asleep from exhaustion next to SS-Sergeant-Major Everding, who had been hit in the hip.[7]

They set off again towards evening. One group, which included elements of Panzergrenadier Division *Kurmark*, was detailed as the northern flank guard and moved off to the north before turning west just south of Wiesenhagen. This group was overtaken by Soviet tanks and was fired on by anti-tank guns and mortars, but each time the self-propelled flak gun travelling with them proved its worth, and by nightfall they had reached the area of Märtensmühle.

Meanwhile the main group, which included the Königstigers of 502nd SS Heavy Panzer Battalion and the SPGs of 920th SPG Training Brigade, as well as armoured vehicles of Battlegroup *Lobmeyer* and 32nd SS Tank-Hunting Battalion, crossed the Trebbin–Luckenwalde road and the railway beyond it to reach the vicinity of Liebätz.[8]

SS-Lieutenant Klust, commanding one of the Tigers, reported:

> We came up to the Trebbin–Luckenwalde road. I went forward to reconnoitre the situation. The road was dead straight, and left and right of it at some distance were a few well-camouflaged anti-tank guns or tanks.

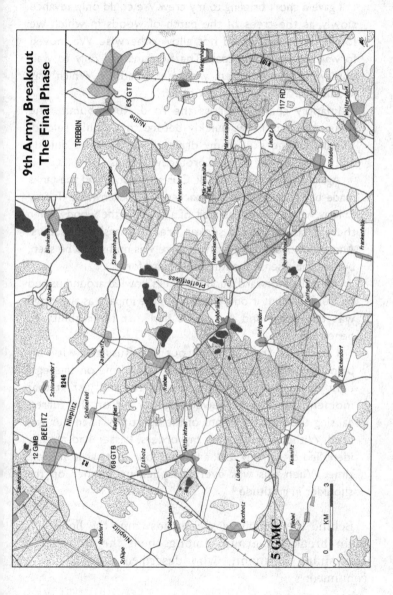

I gave a short briefing to my crew. We could only advance slowly, as the trees of the patch of woods in which we found ourselves would not allow otherwise. We moved forward as if on hot coals. The Russians had only to wait until we presented them with our broadside. Which way should I turn the turret, right or left?

Infantry charged across the road. Rummbumm. The Russians fired. Now, quickly before they could reload. Thanks to the skill of my driver, Fink, we were quickly across and moving into the protective woods.

Again on a woodland track. Our spirits rose and the tanks made better speed. We approached the Luckenwalde–Teltow railway, where there was a bit of a break in the woods. Over there a stream and a sunken area of marshy meadows. Another short reconnaissance. There was nothing to be seen, but we could sense the Russians waiting for us.

We rolled forward. Suddenly shells howled around us and hit our Tiger, but it only shook with the impact, as the range was too great and the shells had lost their ability to penetrate.

I carefully tried to pick out the Russians with my binoculars, then Lasser, my gunner, tapped me on the leg. I bent down towards him in the turret and just at that moment our Tiger received another hit on the turret, causing the glass to fly out of the apertures. Then our gun fired. Without waiting for my orders, Lasser had already identified the enemy tank and fired four shots at it in short time. When this was over, I clapped my gunner on the shoulder in gratitude.[9]

Behind the armoured spearheads came the flood of the main break-out group, among them the wounded SS-Lieutenant Bärmann, who described how the ordeal continued:

We reached the Luckenwalde–Trebbin road at dusk. During a short halt, I climbed off and went into the bushes. I had eaten a piece of turnip and now had diarrhoea. When I returned, they had all gone. I tagged on to the stream of soldiers and civilians making their way to the west, and reached the road, where two well-camouflaged Russian anti-tank guns had the road under fire at short range. In the short pauses as the Russian crews reloaded, crowds rushed across the road, but the effects of the turnip were such that I could hardly move.

As I looked around, I saw an APC hidden behind a bush. The five men of its crew were discussing what to do, and then went with hand grenades and a machine gun to deal with the two Russian anti-tank guns. After a while I heard a short burst of fire and the explosions of hand grenades – but then the anti-tank guns started firing again.

It was hopeless for me to try and get across the road. I still had my pistol and wanted to make an end of it. Then, like a guardian angel, the cook from our Supply Company, SS-Corporal Fahrenkamp, appeared and helped me up and on.

Just short of the road we made a pause under cover to get the feel of things, and lying there were several lads from my battalion, who gave me the comforting feeling that I would not be left behind. Then a senior Flak officer appeared and asked why we were not moving on – the roar of the anti-tank guns gave him his reply.

Immediately the shells had exploded, two of our men picked me up and took me forwards; a whole mass of men crossed the road and vanished into the woods beyond. After several hundred metres we came to the multi-track railway line. We picked up a wounded man and went past a shot-up Königstiger.

We went further along a woodland track, then from behind came a whole crowd with cars. The vehicles were driven by senior officers and fully loaded behind with their belongings. They only shook their heads at the requests from the wounded; not once did one of them take one of those with them that were lying on the roadside unable to move on.

Then we met up with our group again. They had had to make a detour round a wooden bridge (near Liebätz) and were only making slow progress across the marshy meadows. There were still two Jagdpanzers and a 105-mm self-propelled howitzer.

We reached Märtensmühle as night fell. The village was under fire from heavy artillery and anti-tank guns were firing into the village from the north-east. Once it was dark, we moved on.

In the woods we came across our battalion commander, SS-Captain Krauss, who directed us to the Märtensmühle forest warden's lodge, where the divisional command post was supposed to be. We had long since given up believing that there would still be one.

Then our divisional commander, SS-Colonel Kempin, appeared at the forest warden's lodge, and with him was Wache, his Intelligence Officer. We heard that one break-out group had already made it. Kempin pressed for an immediate break-out so as to complete the breakthrough during the night. Hörl and I said our good-byes to Kempin and gave him our home addresses.

There were several bangs outside. A sentry reported excitedly that Seydlitz people were blowing up the last of our vehicles, but whether they were really Seydlitz people, no one could tell. Most vehicles had completely run out of petrol.

One of our youngsters appeared with 40 litres of fuel, which we poured into the tank of our last SPG. Following a short discussion, we decided to drive on as long as the fuel lasted. We set off after midnight.[10]

By midnight the group containing General Busse had reached the Märtensmühle–Berkenbrück sector. They were now within ten kilometres of the positions held by 12th Army's *Hutten* and *Scharnhorst* Divisions.[11]

Ever since passing through Halbe the remaining troops of the 23rd SS Panzergrenadier Division *Nederland* had been in the lead of the infantry breakthrough, and there were still about a hundred of them left at Märtensmühle, including their divisional commander, SS-Major-General Wagner, and the commander of the 1st Battalion, 48th SS Panzergrenadier Regiment *General Seyffarth*. They had also brought their injured along with them in their own vehicles, but these had now run out of fuel and some 40–50 badly wounded had to be left behind in the village school. The survivors moved on to the Märtinsmühle forest warden's lodge to prepare for the last bound.[12]

The main group had survived the day, despite heavy losses in men and equipment – 1st Ukrainian Front claimed to have taken 20,000 prisoners.

Ernst-Christian Gädtke with the 32nd SS Tank-Hunting Battalion was also in this area later that day:

Dry, sunny spring weather. We rolled on through the woods on tracks and fire-breaks, myself luckily still sitting on the assault gun. Along the route was the occasional dead body, equipment discarded in heaps, abandoned vehicles, and once even a Volkswagen jeep squashed flat in the middle of the road.

In the evening we reached Märtensmühle, between Trebbin and Luckenwalde. Russian troops had passed through here days before on their way to Berlin. Next to the dead soldiers lying in the gardens and alongside the road were civilians, old men and women, and in the ditches discarded plunder, broken suitcases and washing baskets with scattered items of clothing.

We took cover in the Märtensmühle barns. Bread was shared out with canned dripping, which we washed down with *ersatz* coffee from our mess tins. Someone said that in the morning we would be attacking Beelitz, which was occupied by the Russians. We would break through their positions and then meet up with the troops of General Wenck's 12th Army west of Beelitz, where they were waiting for us.[13]

Other splinter groups were not so lucky. The 117th Guards Rifle Division encountered a group of about 5,000 Germans near Luckenwalde, of whom eventually 4,500 were captured. Other groups were eliminated by 3rd Guards Army east of Staakow, and by 28th Army east of Kummersdorf Gut.

That night, to prevent 9th Army getting through, Marshal Koniev ordered the redeployment of some of 4th Guards Tank Army into the area east of Beelitz. This included elements of 68th Independent Guards Tank Brigade, 7th Motorcycle Regiment, 71st Light Artillery Brigade, 61st Guards Tank Brigade of 10th Guards Tank Corps, 12th Guards Mechanized Brigade of 5th Guards Mechanized Corps, together with some corps troops. They were given the task of blocking the Michendorf–Treuenbrietzen road (Reichsstrasse 2).

Those elements of Marshal Koniev's forces fighting in the woods north and north-west of Staakow were relatively successful and by the evening of 30 April had closed up to the line Zesch–Radeland, but in the Baruth area 28th Army and 50th and 96th Guards Rifle Divisions were less successful. Their attacks north of the Hammerfliess depression were met with strong resistance and only reached the line Mückendorf–northern edge of Baruth–Radeland. The 13th Army's 395th Rifle Division also met strong resistance near Kummersdorf Gut and was unable to penentrate any deeper into the woods. This perhaps reflects the Red Army soldiers' weariness with the war. In order to prevent the

German groups pushing south on Luckenwalde, 280th Rifle Division was redeployed from Jüterbog and was ordered to attack towards Gottow–Schöneweide. It reached these places by evening but without fully completing its task.[14]

A member of Battlegroup *Schill*, forming part of the rearguard of the Halbe pocket, reported on this day:

Late on the night of 29/30 April, the *Schill* Battlegroup abandoned its positions east of the Dahme, other combat units having left hours previously. The order for leaving was already 20 hours overdue. Mobs, unarmed of course, and refugees were wandering around in vast numbers, some of them with vehicles, which hindered our progress. What was intended, we had no idea, we only knew and wanted to reach our goal, if necessary by force, which was the 12th Army's position this side of the Elbe. We first clashed with enemy forces near the Klein Hammer forest warden's lodge. Then came enemy tank probes, in which we lost heavily, even though we were reinforced by gunners from the 1st Battalion of 32nd [SS] Artillery Regiment. Those men still capable of fighting reassembled for a break-out to the south-west, but without success. Because of the flood of other shattered troops fleeing back, our hastily-prepared positions were almost overrun. We only held on to the position by the hardest resolve and even won some additional combatants. Those in uniform unwilling to fight vanished into the woods and ran into the next Russians only a few hundred metres away. The day was filled with minor skirmishes with Russian scouts, who withdrew immediately they encountered the least resistance. There were constant air attacks.

During the course of the afternoon, enemy air activity and tank attacks concentrated on an area about three kilometres south-west of us. Occasional 20-mm flak fire indicated that our own troops must be holding out there.

The constant firing of white flares by the enemy indicated their targets.

They closed in on us from three sides, our weak perimeter defences being virtually untenable, so that we had to abandon our original intention of fighting our way through the Russian positions during the night, and had to move immediately. After a somewhat hesitant start, the will to fight on prevailed, and we charged with a thunderous 'Hurrah!' right through the Russian positions, which promptly gave up all resistance and collapsed.

Our next move was in the direction of the flak fire we had identified. Abandoned items, from water bottles to intact 88-mm flak guns, including their towing vehicles and ammunition, indicated that we were on the same escape route as the units in the days before us. The peaceful heathland here had become a deathtrap for many thousands of brave soldiers and at least as many refugees. Within a few days we had gone from barely negotiable tracks to roads of death and horror. Women and children who had sought safety in flight from the enemy forces and the horrors of war had been overrun here and crushed, just like the thousands of soldiers who had abandoned their fighting and protective roles, thinking only of saving themselves by fleeing.

Communication with the combat team south-west of us was soon re-established and we discovered that it was the remains of SS-General Kleinheisterkamp's XI SS Panzer Corps group, which included the Panzergrenadier Division *Kurmark*. This group was getting itself ready for the final breakthrough. The unifying password 'Freedom' was given out and the military column set off. The first part of the route was reconnoitred by scouts, and the civilians and wounded placed in the centre. The enemy immediately followed up on both sides as well as at the rear. We saw a barrier in front of us that we had to overcome. It was clearly of Russian construction, and not up to the usual Volkssturm standard. A storm troop was detailed to clear the way and mine detectors were already in operation, despite heavy enemy fire from the flanks exacting a considerable number of casualties. The barrier was taken by assault and the Russian troops gave in.

We were now standing on the outskirts of Halbe and had to redeploy. With all the shooting going on all around us, we were taking considerable numbers of casualties among those in uniform as well as the waiting refugees and wounded, so we reinforced our cover on the flanks. Meanwhile it had become dark, and we could clearly see the flashes of the Russian artillery and rocket launchers firing to the north, south and west of us, so could also see a little of what lay ahead. We could definitely make out the outlines of T-34 and Stalin tanks with a Tiger in between, among the stacks of timber in the sawmill in front of us. Our anti-tank guns opened up, but it was a waste of time as these were already wrecks from the previous days.

From above us came the tacking of the Lame Ducks[15] as they fired one flare after another, so that it became almost as light as day. However, this came in useful in deploying our weapons to the best advantage.

We were hardly reacting to the explosions from shells and mortars, but the Stalin-Organs always caused a disruption. Heavy Russian machine-gun fire was raking us from a certain place in the village; it could not fail to hit something. Halbe village had become a place of death and horror. Equipment, vehicles and corpses of all kinds and many nationalities were lying about alongside and on top of each other, reaching as high as the roof gutters of the smaller village cottages. The buildings were almost all burnt out, little better than ruins. There must have been some fearful fighting here during the last few days, and the village must have changed hands several times.[16]

The remaining groups in the central pocket were pressed by four divisions from the south, while all the armoured forces attacked from the north. The 63rd Guards Tank Brigade set off south from the area south of Trebbin–Klein Schulzendorf while 28th Army's 71st Mechanized Brigade and 61st Guards Rifle Division advanced on the Sperenberg area, thus blocking the Trebbin–Sperenberg road to the German groups with strong forces. These Soviet attacks created a stable defensive front, but they were unable to split up the German groups any further, and 54th Guards Rifle Division failed to block the Wünsdorf–Baruth road (Reichsstrasse 96), its advance being stopped on the Zossen–Baruth road between Zesch and Neuhof. Meanwhile Marshal Zhukov's troops had continued clearing the woods around Halbe and by 1730 hours could report the complete destruction of the German units found there.[17]

NOTES

1. Gellermann, *Die Armee Wenck*, pp. 97–8; Gorlitz, The Memoirs of Field Marshal Keitel, p. 223.
2. Lakowski/Stich, *Der Kessel von Halbe 1945*, p. 128.
3. Helmut Jurisch in correspondence with the author. Schoka-cola was a form of chocolate containing an energising substance.
4. Tieke, *Das Ende zwischen Oder und Elbe*, p. 327.
5. *Ibid.*
6. Letter to Dr Lakowski, cited in Lakowski/Stich, *Der Kessel von Halbe 1945*, p. 183.
7. Tieke, *Das Ende zwischen Oder und Elbe*, p. 327.
8. *Ibid.*, p. 334.
9. *Ibid.*, p. 335.
10. *Ibid.*, pp. 335–7.
11. Lakowski/Stich, *Der Kessel von Halbe 1945*, p. 129.
12. Tieke, *Das Ende zwischen Oder und Elbe*, p. 337.
13. Gädtke, *Von der Oder zur Elbe*, p. 36.
14. Lakowski/Stich, *Der Kessel von Halbe 1945*, pp. 128–30.
15. This was a nickname for the Po-2, sometimes also called the

Sewing Machine because of the distinctive sound of its engine. The Po-2 was a biplane, armoured against infantry fire, and used extensively for night bombing, the observer dropping either clusters of hand grenades or light bombs by hand in First World War style. Many of the crews were female.

16. Wilke, *Am Rande der Strassen*, pp. 71–4.
17. Lakowski/Stich, *Der Kessel von Halbe 1945*, p. 129.

THIRTEEN

THE LAST LEG

1 MAY 1945

By midnight the leading elements of 9th Army were in the woods between the Märtensmühle forest warden's lodge and Berkenbrück. Discussion about when and how the break-out should continue was interrupted by the armour moving off and the rest automatically following.

Relatively weak Soviet resistance in Berkenbrück was rapidly overcome and the road to the west was open. At about 0330 hours the leading elements broke through Hennickendorf, where a barrier was crushed by a Tiger. The fighting here was again described by SS-Lieutenant Bärmann:

> We took over the lead at about 0400 hours. The woods were full of the exhausted and wounded. Just before Hennickendorf we had to go over a little hill that was defended by Russian anti-tank guns. A few shells and these anti-tank guns were silenced and the Russians withdrew. We drove on through Hennickendorf, where some houses were burning. After a few hundred metres we came to a barricade at the Pfefferfliess stream. Karl Hörl drove the SPG to the edge of the woods on the left and took up a firing position where we had a good view. On both sides of the stream in front of us lay a swampy meadow, and about 1,500 metres away there was a hill with a few buildings and

the Dobbrikow windmill. In between were Russian tanks and anti-tank guns, and some Stalin-Organs to the right of the windmill.

There was a Königstiger near us, still in the lead, and an eight-wheeled armoured car of 10th SS Armoured Reconnaissance Battalion. About fifteen of our men advanced across the meadows, making a start, and a flood of soldiers and civilians streamed out from everywhere, thousands of them, across the Pfefferfliess stream towards Dobbrikow.

The Russians let fly with all their barrels from the windmill hill. Our SPG, Tiger and armoured car returned the fire. Then, as ammunition and stacks of rockets began exploding alongside the windmill, the enemy fire faltered and the Russian tanks started to withdraw.[1]

Major Otto-Christer von Albedyll, commander of the Armoured Reconnaissance Battalion *Kurmark* was killed near Hennickendorf when going to the assistance of his wounded adjutant. He was a brave, wise and much loved officer, whose men stopped to bury him by the roadside.[2] The last vehicles of 561st SS Tank-Hunting Battalion ran out of fuel at this point, and Lobmeyer's men had to go on as infantry.[3]

Hermann Pätz, a soldier at home on sick leave in Hennickendorf as the result of an eye injury, remembered these events:

The Russians came on Sunday 22 April, at about noon, having occupied Luckenwalde. We had all hidden ourselves, everyone having a bunker in their garden. They even set up a command post in Hennickendorf and many Russian positions were prepared.

The firing started early on 1 May, when German troops chased out the Russians. Three T-34s were shot up, one towards Märtensmühle, one towards Stangenhagen and the third towards Schönhagen. German soldiers were here all day; the leaders went along the road from here to Dobbrikow. At about 0700– 0800 hours a half-tracked APC stopped in front of our house with several others behind it.

In the first was General Busse. Busse's APC was fitted with aerials and large batteries, and manned by six or seven men. I remember Busse as an imposing person wearing the Knight's Cross. They got out and spread out a map. I offered them some milk, which they drank. I plucked up my courage and asked the general: 'Where do you want to go to?' He replied, pointing to the map: 'Here near Rieben is a large wooded area; we will stop there and break through at night.' And: 'We must find out how strongly Dobbrikow is occupied.' To one of his officers: 'Find an NCO and a few men for this!'

He had hardly finished speaking when the Soviets fired from the direction of the village. Busse and his people quickly jumped back into the APC and raced off towards the woods that began about a kilometre away from us. Then came several wounded Germans and shortly afterwards the Russians. These were the last of the 9th Army. For days afterwards the Russians were pulling German soldiers out of the woods.[4]

SS-Sergeant-Major Streng also described his experiences here:

Our tanks rolled along the Hennickendorf–Dobbrikow road. Half-way along we came under artillery fire from a copse on the right. Anti-tank guns? We couldn't tell for certain. Suddenly a heavy blow struck our Tiger and the track mudguards fell to the road with a clatter.

Our gun roared at the copse some 330 to 400 metres away. There were some bright, explosive flashes and branches and treetops whirled into the air.

Like lightning came a second direct hit on the hull of our tank. A shell hit the right side of the hull with enormous force and shot upwards. Then followed another frightful bang. We clenched our fists and gritted our teeth. 'Hit on right side of turret! Driver, hard left! Quick, go, go!' I screamed on the intercom. Our tank reared itself up and rolled left into a field sloping down to a small lake. After going several hundred metres, we turned back to the right. Meanwhile the other tanks had overcome the Russian anti-tank guns and the march of thousands continued.

Our fuel ran out. Somehow we got hold of some petrol and drove on. As we were climbing aboard, our tank received a direct hit from half left across the lake from a Russian tank standing there that we had not seen. I was wounded in the left upper arm and left thigh. They laid me down inside the tank, which Läbe took over. The Wenck Army was only a few kilometres away, but here at Wittbrietzen–Rieben–Zauchwitz the Russian cordon seemed impenetrable.

The whole column, including the remains of the 2nd Battalion, Panzergrenadier Regiment *Kurmark*, moved via Dobbrikow on to Rieben. Russian bombers and ground-attack aircraft kept attacking, each time leaving more dead and wounded.

Rieben was taken by storm, but the break-out group kept coming up against more and more Russian blockades. The mass of German soldiers and civilians, not bound to the roads and tracks like the vehicles, swarmed their way westwards between Zauchwitz and Rieben. *Seydlitz-Troops* were particularly active in this area, leading unsuspecting splinter groups into Soviet captivity.[5]

Streng then went on to describe the fighting between Rieben and Schönefeld:

Warm spring sunshine was streaming over the land. It was 1000 hours. We moved on. Some wounded emerged from an asparagus field[6] and clung tightly to the exterior of our Königstiger, these unfortunates lying all over the tank from our gun to our stern. Actually we were feeling quite happy, being hopeful of reaching Wenck's Army during the course of the day.

We rolled along the road to Beelitz. Troops came out of the woods and asparagus fields and marched behind us. We speeded up. If only we had had better communications inside the tank; every order had to be shouted.

The tank stopped again. An anti-tank gun on the road was swept aside with a blast of high explosive. Half left stood a Russian tank. 'Armour piercing!' The Tiger's turret turned slowly left. Fire! Hit! Clouds of smoke obscured the view.

Suddenly there was a metallic crack on the tank's right side and a long drawn-out hissing. A blinding whiteness sprayed in from outside. There was dead silence for a second. We must have overlooked a Russian tank on our right. A white cloud of smoke filled the interior of the tank and a wave of heat took our breath away.

The tank was on fire. Everyone fumbled for the escape hatches to get to the open air. Tongues of bright flame burned our unprotected hands, upper bodies and faces. Heads and bodies collided with each other as hands unfastened the hot escape hatches. Vital air entered the lungs as racing pulses hammered in the throat and brain. A purplish blackness pierced by green flashes filled my eyes.

I grasped the hatch with flying hands, wriggled and thrust myself through, standing on the breech shield and gun. Two heads met in the hatch. I instinctively pulled Läbe up and pushed him out of the top of the turret with my head and body. I caught my leather jacket on a hook, ripping it off my body and it fell back into the burning tank with a final flash of silver from the Iron Cross.

I let myself fall head over heels from the three-metre high turret, pushing myself away from the sides with my hands as I fell. In falling I saw that the skin of my left forefinger had been torn loose, so I tugged it off, leaving a bloody something.

The burning, reeling figure of the radio-operator jumped right in front of me. Hartinger, Neu and Öls ran past. Was anyone still inside? The tank exploded behind us, the 18-ton turret lifting off and being hurled aside. This was the end.[7]

Rudi Lindner also witnessed this event, as he described in his account of his experiences that day:

We had to cross several open spaces during the night, and each time the infantry and tanks were called forward. There was repeated fighting and shooting. When we had to take cover we tried to make sure that we five stayed together. With this came great fatigue, hunger and thirst. We wanted simply to remain lying there with the consequent danger of falling asleep. It cost us much effort to keep forcing ourselves on and stay awake. We avoided the open spaces and tried to remain in the woods, which was not always possible. I am still amazed today that we managed to maintain contact with the leading tanks in this unholy turmoil.

Everywhere there was gunfire and cries from the wounded. The dead lay around as we overcame several enemy positions and cordons. The 12th Army's front line should be immediately behind the last Russian cordon, but would we ever reach it alive? Our leading tank drove out of the woods, was immediately engaged by the Russian anti-tank guns, and pulled back again. There was now artillery fire on our edge of the woods and we had to turn south to get away from the road. About 15 minutes later our last two Tigers attacked out of the woods to the north of us and a broad stream of soldiers and refugees poured over the open ground to the west and north-west.

Unfortunately, as we discovered later, that was the most strongly manned sector of the Russian cordon between Schönefeld and Wittbrietzen. The Russians fired flat out with tanks, anti-tank guns, Stalin-Organs, artillery and mortars on the defenceless people in the open ground, and bombers and ground-attack aircraft joined in. Death struck viciously again and reaped a rich harvest. There was no cover for the soldiers and civilians, who were completely exposed to this murderous fire. Mercilessly, the remains of 9th Army were being given their death blow only a few hundred metres from the protection of 12th Army's front line.

Of the heavy tanks we now only had Klust's Königstiger from No. 1 Company and Streng's from No. 2 Company. Streng's tank had been hit several times during this decisive breakthrough. Even so, he was still able to engage in a tank duel and knock out three T-34s, but then his tank was hit by an anti-tank gun and burst into flames. After a dozen severe hits, this time the tank could not be saved. It was the tank that I had been on in Halbe and which had been hit by a phosphorous shell and caught fire there. A few minutes later SS-Second Lieutenant Klust's tank was also knocked out, thus writing off the last of the 14 Tiger tanks which 9th Army had sent to join up with 12th Army.

For the first time I held my four comrades of the 1241st Regiment back from attacking as we had done so often in the last days and weeks. We remained lying at the edge of the woods and watched the course of the uneven fight. It was not fear or cowardice, but military common sense and combat experience that led me to this decision, its correctness being demonstrated only a few minutes later.

An APC with Hitler Youth leaders appeared from the left flank and drove into cover near us. They had the task of warning the remains of 9th Army about this strong enemy cordon and were meant to direct us south-west towards Wittbrietzen. These youngsters looked just like *Seydlitz-Troops*. What an irony of fate for the many who had fallen on this open ground and the soldiers and civilians who had been wounded.

While death awaited north of Wittbrietzen, the way south of it was 'an easy walk' to 12th Army's front line. Had this APC with its certainly courageous crew arrived only two or three hours earlier, 9th Army's spearhead could have been directed in this direction.

With unfortunately so few soldiers, we turned to the south-west and within about 1,200 metres reached the described spot under cover of the woods, from where it was only a short distance over open ground to the woods opposite. The men of 12th Army dug in on the edge of the woods were expecting us and directed us back behind the railway line.

We could hardly believe that we had managed to make the last section alive, and without having fired a shot. It was only later that we realised how often death had stretched out a finger towards us, in the purest sense our constant companion, and what enormous luck we had had to belong to the few to have survived the fighting on the Oder Front, the Hell of Halbe and the death march to 12th Army's lines.[8]

SS-Lieutenant Klust, commander of the other Königstiger in this group, gave a slightly different account of his experiences during this final stage:

We approached Schönefeld. The engine of our Tiger started spluttering, being about to run out of fuel. There was none to be had anywhere. Then we learned from local civilians that there should be some stored at the transmitter south of Schönefeld, so we struggled on there on the last drops in our fuel tank.

We found, as described, a 200-litre barrel and put the contents into our fuel tank, but when the engine started up, Bert Fink, my driver, expressed doubts about the fuel. The engine was running unevenly and kept stopping. Only through my driver's technical skill could our Tiger be got moving. We had to keep the engine hatch open with a man pulling on a lever.

The 12th Army's reception point could not be far off. Thousands of soldiers and civilians were streaming across the open ground to the west. But our tank could not go much further either.

We received orders again, but orders had little effect anymore. Our Tiger engine gave up, making bubbling noises. We were then told to dig the Tiger in and to use the gun as artillery to cover the remains of 9th Army but, in view of the situation, I decided otherwise. We made our Königstiger unserviceable and made off to the west with the others. We left our our old wreck behind with pangs of regret, for we had fought so many fights together.

My radio-operator, Heimlich, was killed in a bombing attack on the autobahn south of Beelitz.[9]

Ernst-Christian Gädtke also battled through successfully:

The morning of 1 May was as cold as the night. We prepared ourselves for the attack with some more ersatz coffee and a few cigarettes.

We rolled on towards Beelitz via Ahrensdorf, Stangenhagen and Zauchwitz.[10] Shortly after Zauchwitz the road emerged from a wood on to open fields, and round a bend to the left we could see Beelitz ahead of us and hear artillery and infantry fire coming from there. On either side of the road stragglers were waiting in the ditches for a breach to be forced up ahead. We could see flashes of gunfire coming from Beelitz and then fountains of earth sprang up around us as the shells exploded, splinters whistling through the air.

Our guns received the order to open fire, so we had to get off as the hatches were closed down. I jumped off to the right and tried to keep up with the moving gun at some distance to the side, but the guns speeded up towards Beelitz and I was soon left behind. Russian artillery fire was still falling on the road, so I moved away northwards from the road without noticing I was doing so. The meadows were strewn with clumps of bushes and trees, and here we found cover. There were small groups of soldiers from various units advancing here, but no properly led attack, more of a loose and accidental movement. No one was in command, and no one really knew what was happening. After a few minutes I found myself separated from my group, having got lost somehow. The assault gun had vanished up the road, and with it went my last worldly goods including my carefully packed haversack.

Unwillingly, I let myself be drawn away from the road and the artillery fire. Someone shouted: 'Get round the place to the north', and 'Keep right.' Then we came to a drain that cut right across the land. A wounded man was lying on the bank with his thigh ripped open by shell splinters. 'Take me with you!' he cried. We called for medical orderlies, but there were none around. Finally four of us placed him on a tent-half and carried him through the knee-deep water. We laid him down again at the edge of the woods, by which time he had lost consciousness, and left him there.

The woods were swarming with stragglers, most of them unarmed. They were lying down in groups, apparently having decided not to do anything, just wait for it to be all over.

I joined on to a section of infantry under a lieutenant who were moving purposefully through the wood. 'Come with us, comrade', one of them called out to me, 'You don't look as if you just want to be taken prisoner.'

We went a short distance through the woods to the

north-west and then concealed ourselves in a thick pine plantation. The lieutenant called us together and explained what he proposed doing. According to him the Russians were only holding a thin line here, concentrating on places like Beelitz. An attack on Beelitz was just stupid. North and south of there one had a far better chance of getting past the Russians. We would wait hidden in this plantation until dusk and then make our way through the Russian lines in the dark. Everything depended on sticking together, moving dead quietly, maintaining discipline and, should something happen, acting decisively. This made sense. We set sentries on the edge of the plantation, stretched ourselves out on the ground and got a little sleep.

Once it was dark, we shared out all that we had left to eat, crispbread and tinned cheese. We left the plantation in single file moving silently towards the west. We reached the autobahn without stopping and observed the wide gap from the edge of the woods for a few minutes. Nothing moved. Then we raced across, ducked down, in a body. Not a shot was fired as we disappeared into the woods on the far side.

We reached the Borkwalde settlement unscathed. Light was coming from a cellar window. We went down to the cellar, where a few men and women were sitting. The Russians had passed through here a few days before heading north for Potsdam, but there had been German troops in the area for several days. They had evacuated several hundred wounded and nurses from the Beelitz sanatorium, but had gone again. No Russians had been seen west of the autobahn in the last few days.

Now we were sure – we had got through.[11]

The last of the armoured vehicles kept to the Rieben–Schönefeld road, where several Soviet anti-tank barriers were overcome. But then the leading armour was struck again, as SS-Lieutenant Bärmann remembered:

We saw about ten T-34s near Schönefeld. A Königstiger stood about 400 metres in front of Schönefeld, taking the anti-tank barrier and Russian tanks under fire, and only pulling back when it ran out of ammunition. We couldn't get through on the Beelitz road, so turned off left on a track and drove across open country. Despite enemy fire, we reached a wooded hill on which there was a radio transmitter mast, about 400 metres south of Schönefeld, where we stopped to reorientate ourselves.[12]

Helmuth Jurisch, who was also in this area, reported:

From the radio station near Schönefeld a track led through a wood to the village of Elsholz about two kilometres away. Along this track towards Elsholz were moving soldiers like myself who had fought their way from Halbe. Then in the wood in front of Elsholz I was taken aboard another of our tanks as radio-operator. As we came out of the wood the village lay suddenly in front of us, the houses hidden behind trees, the church back a bit on the right, and green fields in front. Everything was quiet at first, but soon an enemy machine gun opened up rather ineffectively from the church tower on the attacking soldiers, who, according to a witness, were able to take the machine gunners in the tower.

Fortunately the Russians had no anti-tank weapons in the village, so our tank was able to reach the village intact. Ivan took to flight and crept away. After a short stop to ensure all was in order, we rolled on into the village. We then came to the Nieplitz swamp, in which our last four Panthers became stuck fast. This swamp lies west of Elsholz behind Route 2. From here a track went past the railway station, through a wood and over fields to cross some meadows short of the Nieplitz stream. There in the meadows right of the track lay the graveyard of the last remains of our tanks, the four Panthers of 1st Battalion, Panzer Regiment

Brandenburg, which had fought since 4 February 1945 with Panzergrenadier Division *Kurmark*. We bailed out for the last time and had to watch as our four Panthers, virtually out of fuel and ammunition, literally sank into the swamp. We twenty tankmen then marched towards Beelitz, crossed the Nieplitz stream by the nearest bridge, made our way across streams and ditches and finally reached Route 246 south-west of Beelitz, where troops of the Wenck Army were moving towards Brück. After several days we reached Fischbeck on the Elbe and crossed the collapsed Elbe bridge into American captivity near Tangermünde.[13]

Totally exhausted, an estimated 30,000 people, including 5,000 civilians, reached General Wenck's lines, leaving behind 13,000 prisoners and over 5,000 killed.[14] Busse later suggested that some 40,000 men and several thousand refugees reached Wenck's lines. Other figures are lower. Koniev says that about 30,000 of the 200,000 who broke out of the Halbe pocket reached the Beelitz area, but were then set upon again by his forces and that at the most only 3–4,000 could have got through to 12th Army. In any case, whatever the numbers, for those who had achieved their goal, it had been a considerable physical and mental feat.[15]

On 1 May Marshal Zhukov's 33rd Army relieved 13th Army as Koniev's 1st Ukrainian Front redeployed for 'Operation Prague'. By this stage the reduction of the remaining breakthrough groups had become a secondary task and was completed with varying degrees of success.

NOTES

1. Tieke, *Das Ende zwischen Oder und Elbe*, p. 338.
2. He was the heir to the Klessin estate featured in the author's *With Our Backs to Berlin*.
3. Tieke, *Das Ende zwischen Oder und Elbe*, p. 338.

4. Schulze, *Der Kessel Halbe–Baruth–Radeland*, pp. 74–6.

5. Tieke, *Das Ende zwischen Oder und Elbe*, p. 339.

6. The area around Beelitz is famous for its asparagus crops. The asparagus fields with their deep corrugations would provide some measure of cover from fire for the troops sheltering there.

7. Tieke, *Das Ende zwischen Oder und Elbe*, pp. 340–1.

8. Lindner in the author's *Death Was Our Companion*.

9. Tieke, *Das Ende zwischen Oder und Elbe*, p. 342.

10. From Stanganhagen onwards the road was Route 246, the main road from Trebbin to Beelitz, so Gädtke's subsequent moves took him north of the latter town.

11. Gädtke, *Von der Oder zur Elbe*, pp. 36–7.

12. Tieke, *Das Ende zwischen Oder und Elbe*, pp. 339–40.

13. Jurisch to the author. Although he gives the date of this incident as 30 April, it seems most likely to have occurred on 1 May. In a subsequent discussion with the author, Jurisch stated that the driving of the tanks into a swamp just north of Salzbrunn was deliberate.

14. Kollatz: 'Die Front an der Elbe 1945', p. 65.

15. Busse, 'Die letzte Schlacht der 9. Armee', p. 168, describes the break-out as having taken place on the night of 26/27 April and the union with 12th Army on the morning of the 29th, but this is in conflict with Wenck's chronology and that of other witnesses, and allowance should be made for the fact that Busse's article was apparently written in captivity some ten years after the event; Wenck, 'Berlin war nicht mehr zu retten', pp. 68–9. Koniev, *Year of Victory*, pp. 180–2, denies the break-out was effective.

FOURTEEN

RETREAT TO THE ELBE

As soon as General Reymann's troops and the exhausted remains of 9th Army were safely behind XX Corps' lines, General Wenck gave the order for the withdrawal to the Elbe to begin on the night of 1/2 May. The withdrawal was conducted without pause day and night, the screening divisions taking care to conceal their movement and avoid any conflict that would hamper their progress, the rearguards only fighting delaying actions when necessary. As the artillery pieces ran out of ammunition, they were blown up and abandoned. Tanks, APCs and armoured cars covered the flanks.

At first the Soviets did not pursue too strongly. This was probably due to the after-effects of their May Day celebrations and by the need to re-deploy while 1st Byelorussian Front took over the 1st Ukrainian Front's responsibilities to release Koniev's men for the attack on Prague.[1]

The survivors of 9th Army were in no fit state to continue the struggle. Some were fortunate enough to get rides on a shuttle service of trucks and trains to the Elbe organized by 12th Army, but many had to make their own way, as Helmut Jurisch described:

When Bert Fink and I were dropped off by truck in Ziesar, word was going round that the remains of 9th Army were

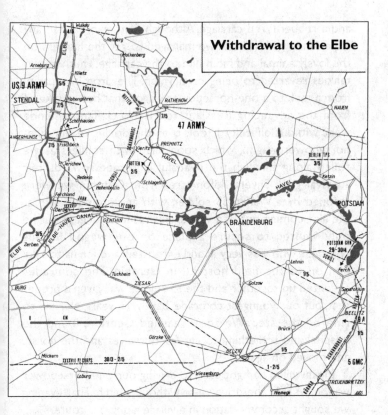

pushing through to the Elbe and going into American captivity.

We both found somewhere to spend the night in Halbe, clean ourselves up and sleep, as we had not done for so long, in soft feather beds. I even had a bit of luck, as the pretty young woman of the house took a fancy to me.

We set off again next morning, and right after Ziesar we stumbled on a paddock with horses belonging to an abandoned farm, and a friendly nag allowed itself to be caught. Inside the farm buildings we found some harness and a rubber-tyred carriage. Although neither of us had any experience with horses, we managed to get the harness on the lovely animal and hitch him to the carriage. Thus we two tankies reverted to being cavalrymen. The drop in capacity from a tank to a one-horsepower wagon that had to take us from the advancing Russians to Fischbeck/Tangermünde went without difficulty. I took over the driving of our one-horsepower wagon, which soon filled with soldiers as we rolled along through the peaceful landscape towards our survival goal. Several kilometres from Genthin we were stopped by a Waffen-SS soldier, with an automatic rifle at the aim, coming out of a wood. This made us uneasy, but he only wanted to secure a place on our wagon for his comrade, who was very ill and exhausted, and for us to take him on to the field hospital in Genthin. The comrades squeezed up together and the SS soldier was given a proper seat, but our youngest comrade, barely 16 years old, had to ride on the step. We soon reached Genthin, found the hospital and something to eat for ourselves and the horse, and moved on again.

Meanwhile I had got used to driving our one-horsepower wagon, so that the drive went without a hitch. That evening we sought accommodation in a village along our route.

Next day I reached Fischbeck in good form with my crew, and turned the horse loose in the green Elbe meadows. We found temporary accommodation in a barn and spied out the land. We found all that we needed for survival in vehicles abandoned in the Elbe meadows: food, underwear, bits of uniform, and also equipment. Only a few soldiers had come across this 'army supply depot' so far, as most were streaming directly to the crossing place, where a mass of soldiers were crammed together. We looked for everything that a soldier going on a journey needed; haversack, blankets, tent-half, underwear, long-life sausage, and so on.

On the morning of the next day, it could have been either 4 or 5 May 1945, we joined a column moving towards the Elbe bridge. Far from the bridge the column became stuck and did not move on for a long time. Using my boy-scout experience, I made a reconnaissance of the place with Bert Fink, and when we reached the Elbe bridge we saw the reason for the hold-up. The bridge had collapsed in the middle as a result of demolition, and a plank spanned the gap between the two sections of the bridge sticking up from the water, allowing only a single file of soldiers to pass. As we were so near to our long-desired goal, we tagged on to the head of the column. We were soon across on the other side in Tangermünde, and once more we had made it!

The American soldiers standing on the roadway received us in friendly fashion. They were interested in our watches and cameras but didn't force us to give them up. I had to hand over my pistol. After a rest in the station area, the march to Stendal was the next stage to prisoner of war camp.[2]

Wenck sent Lieutenant-General Maximilian Reichsfreiherr von Edelsheim, commander of XXXXVIII Panzer Corps, to negotiate the surrender to the American Ninth Army, as the Ninth Army Chief of Staff, Major General James E. Moore reported to his commander, Lieutenant General William L. Simpson, in the following memorandum on 7 May (with original spelling errors):

1. On 4 May 1945, in compliance with your verbal instructions, I proceeded to the Command Post of the 102d Division and, accompanied by Major General Keating, Division Commander, and Brigadier General Fox, Assistant Division Commander, I went to Stendal, for the purpose of interviewing General of the Armored Forces Baron von Edelsheim, representing the Commander-in-Chief

of German armies at the Elbe and the Havel. Colonel Loren Williams, Regimental Commander in that sector was also present.

2. General von Edelsheim had previous presented to Brigadier General Fox a request on the part of the German Commander for the surrender of his forces and evacuation of civilians as indicated on the attached inclosure. This formed the basis of our discussion.

3. General von Edelsheim informed me that the forces which he represented were the Twelfth German Army and remnants of the Ninth German Army which had been fighting on the Eastern Front. He stated that the strength of the force was approximately 25,000 unarmed soldiers, 40,000 men in battle formations and 6,000 wounded. He also stated that there were approximately 100,000 civilians in the area which he wished to evacuate to the west bank of the Elbe. He stated that they had a considerable amount of transport and about a week's supply of food in army stores, plus that which was carried on the individual soldier. He also stated that they had adequate field hospitals and medical personnel to care for their wounded.

4. General von Edelsheim gave his order of battle, the following units:

XX ARMY CORPS
Division Scharnhorst
Division Koenei
Division Schill
Division Hulten
48th PANZER CORPS
KG Radtke
KG Koehler
KG Rugner
MISCELLANEOUS CORPS UNITS
39th PANZER CORPS
Division Berlin

> KG Brandenburg
> KG Ratenow
> 41st PANZER CORPS
> KG Havelberg
> KG Jahn
> NINTH ARMY REMNANTS OF TWO DIVISIONS

5. General von Edelsheim stated that his army had been directed to move to the north and they had started the movement of their service elements, but the Russian drive which made contact with our left flank, had cut off the combat elements of the army from the service troops. He stated that the [American] prisoners (company patrols from the 102d Division), which he had, had been evacuated to the rear and were probably now in Russian hands.

6. General von Edelsheim was told that the Russians were our Allies and fighting against the Germans with us – that we had all the German prisoners that we wanted and more too. He was told, however, that if Germans appeared on the west bank of the Elbe River with their hands up, or under a white flag, under custom of war they would be accepted as prisoners and they would not be fired on while they were crossing the river. It was made clear, however, that we accepted no responsibility for any action on the part of the Russian forces opposing him and, if they cut him off from the river or fired on his troops while they were crossing, that he would have to meet that problem as best he could. He was told that the means for crossing the river would have to be provided by the German forces.

7. The critical food situation with respect to the Germans in our area was outlined to General von Edelsheim and he was told to bring maximum food stocks, kitchens and individual mess equipment with his troops. He was also told that we would put his forces in a wired-in enclosure upon their arrival, and that we would expect them to come over by companies or battalions, properly organized and

controlled by their own officers. In view of the shortage of housing, he was also told that all men should bring their shelter halves with them.

8. With respect to the wounded, General von Edelsheim stated that he had adequate medical personnel and installations to care for them and requested that he be allowed to bring over all his wounded. He was told that if he brought medical personnel and installations over first, and that it was determined by our forces that they were adequate, he would be allowed to bring his wounded across the river. It was explained to him, however, that at that time it was doubtful if any shelter other than that provided by the German army could be provided.

9. The method of crossing the river was to be over the Tangermunde Bridge which, though partially destroyed, could then be used as a foot bridge. It was also expected that floats or rafts would be used to move kitchens, hospital units, etc., and that some of the men would probably swim the river.

10. General von Edelsheim was told that there would be no movement of civilians from east to west bank of the Elbe River.

11. General von Edelsheim agreed to all the foregoing, thanked me, and stated that he would immediately establish liaison with Colonel Williams in order to control his troops as they came over the river.[3]

The decision to refuse to receive any refugees was presumably based on the problems of feeding, but would have resulted in their involuntary abandonment to the vengeance of the pursuing Soviet forces east of the Elbe had not the Soviets themselves intervened.

Heinz Küster, an aircrew candidate drafted to a parachute convalescent battalion in the defence of Brandenburg, described the scene on the east bank of the Elbe on the afternoon of 6 May:

The Elbe was in full flood and dangerous, sweeping everything along in its depths. Opposite us the river formed a big bend and was about 350 metres wide. About 250,000–300,000 soldiers and a vast number of refugees were on the meadows between the Elbe dyke and the river. I reckon there were also some 2,000–3,000 horses.

As time went by, the Russians increased their pressure, firing indiscriminately with mortars, field and anti-tank guns. There must have also been some large-calibre tank guns, for horses and people were being blown apart.

Panic caught hold and there were screams from the wounded and men and animals being torn apart. It was hell. The cries of fear from the horses were frightful. Thousands of people were torn away that afternoon and night by the racing, swirling river. We could hear the endless cries for help and see the raised arms of those trying to swim across the Elbe.

At about 1600 hours that afternoon an inflatable boat came across from the American side. Everyone streamed down to the riverbank and the boat was overloaded. But no one wanted to sit on the side and take a paddle. I took my Luftwaffe comrade by the collar and pulled him on the boat, then jumped on the side and took a paddle.

A sergeant-major with a drawn pistol shouted that he was in command of the boat. With steely gestures and a loud voice he made it clear that he would shoot anyone without pity who did not follow his instruction to the letter. Then he demonstrated how to use the paddles and handed out eight of them. We would have to paddle with all our strength, or we would never reach the other side, and the Russians would shoot us down like rabbits. This was my last chance, and I paddled like a world champion.

The Russians fired at us in the middle of the river, but about ten to twenty metres too short. Incredibly, we got across untouched. There were forty-eight men in the boat and eight paddling; the water level was only five centimetres below the boat casing. The sergeant major said he would row back again and wanted us to row back with him, but the 64-year-old NCO and myself took off. We were both soaked through to the skin and freezing in the ice-cold wind. The sun peeked through the clouds from time to time, but we were freezing.[4]

At about noon on 7 May, Soviet tanks broke through to the Elbe about five kilometres south of the Tangermünde railway bridge and started shooting at the crossing points. The Americans fired flares to mark their positions, but the Soviets continued firing, killing one American soldier and wounding three others. As a result of this, the Americans withdrew their troops two kilometres back from the river, and the Germans seized this opportunity to get civilians across. There was a similar occurrence at Ferchland, where the Soviets brought the west bank under mortar fire; once again the Americans withdrew and the German civilians were able to cross.[5]

The evacuation of 12th Army from the east to the west banks of the Elbe was successfully completed on the night of 7/8 May. General Wenck later gave a figure of over 100,000 soldiers and about 300,000 civilian refugees. General von Edelsheim reckoned 90,000–100,000 troops, of whom 40 per cent were unarmed. General Moore recorded 40,000 fighting troops, 25,000 unarmed soldiers, 6,000 wounded and 100,000 civilians.[6]

However, on the morning of 8 May a number of American tanks and armoured cars surrounded the prisoner of war camp opposite Ferchland and announced that the prisoners were to be handed over to the Soviets. Panic broke out and many prisoners committed suicide and others were killed or wounded. The units involved were:

- The whole of the *Friedrich Ludwig Jahn* Infantry Division;
- Part of the *Ferdinand von Schill* Infantry Division;
- Part of the Potsdam garrison;
- Five officers and 65 men of the 243rd SPG Brigade;
- Part of HQ Battery, 1170th SPG Brigade;
- The last ten officers and men of 541st Volksgrenadier Division;
- Female Flak and Signals auxiliaries;
- Probably also some members of XXXXVIII Panzer Corps.[7]

The inclusion of the female auxiliaries is astonishing in view of the record of Soviet troops, but one must presume that this was not known to the Americans, or they would not have done this.

The prisoners who remained in American captivity had a rough time. The discovery of the Nazi concentration camps so enraged the Americans that they obliged their prisoners to remain in open fields, resulting in a high death rate. Those who were handed over to the French and Belgian authorities to assist with the post-war recovery also had a hard time, being obliged to work and live under severe conditions. The lucky ones were handed over to the British, who tended to allow the German units to administer themselves until such time as they were able to release individuals by their civilian categories to meet the demands of restoring the German economy.

On 2 May 1st Ukrainian Front reported to Moscow:

1. On 1 May 1945 the front's troops finally concluded the destruction of those encircled elements of the enemy's 9th Army in the area east, north and north-west of Luckenwalde.

On 30 April 1945 the encircled elements of the enemy's 9th Army, with a combined strength of up to 25,000 men, were at first split into three groups and then completely destroyed or captured during the course of the day. Individual enemy soldiers were captured in the woods. During the course of the day 18,500 prisoners were brought in, mainly from the encircled groups.

2. The main forces of 3rd Guards Army, together with elements of 28th Army, destroyed the enemy east of Luckenwalde during the course of the day ...

During the day the army brought in up to 9,000 prisoners and captured 58 tanks, 100 guns and 600 vehicles.

4th Guards Tank Army

10th Guards Tank Corps and 5th Guards Mechanized Corps conducted fighting with part of their forces and eliminated the encircled enemy south-east of Beelitz and north of Luckenwalde. During the course of the day they brought in up to 4,000 prisoners.

13th Army, with four rifle divisions, fought to liquidate the encircled enemy north-east and north of Luckenwalde, as a result of which the enemy was destroyed. During the course of the day up to 4,500 prisoners were brought in.[8]

According to Soviet accounts – there are no German ones available – 60,000 dead were left behind in the fighting south-east of Berlin, and 120,000 took the difficult path into captivity, including seven generals. All the army's equipment was lost.

There are no details available on Red Army losses in the fighting for the reduction of the Halbe pocket, but during operations from 16 April to 8 May, 1st Ukrainian Front lost 113,825 men killed, wounded and missing; 1st Byelorussian Front lost 179,490 in the same period.[9]

Notes

1. Gellermann, *Die Armee Wenck*, p. 105.
2. Helmut Jurisch in correspondence with the author.
3. Gellermann, *Die Armee Wenck*, pp. 186–8.
4. Küster, *Geschunder Leibe*, pp. 155–7.
5. Gellermann, *Die Armee Wenck*, p. 119.
6. *Ibid.*, p. 111.
7. *Ibid.*, pp. 121–2.
8. Lakowski/Stich, *Der Kessel von Halbe 1945*, pp. 133–5.
9. *GPW*, p. 385; Lakowski/Stich, *Der Kessel von Halbe 1945*, p. 138.

FIFTEEN

AFTERMATH

Immediately after the fighting ended the Soviet writer Konstantin Simonov was on his way to Berlin by jeep. As he drove along the autobahn past the Halbe break-out point near Teupitz he came upon an unforgettable sight:

Shortly before reaching the great Berlin Ring, I came across a sight that I will certainly never forget. In this area the autobahn is enclosed on both sides by thick woods that had been split by a cutting whose ends were out of sight.

The German troops that were still holding out on the Oder, when the fighting in Berlin had already started, had used this route to try and thrust their way across the autobahn. Before dawn, only a few hours previously, the intersection of the cutting and autobahn that we had reached had apparently become the site of their final defeat. In front of us lay Berlin, on our right the cutting completely blocked with quite improbable scenes – a pile of tanks, cars, armoured cars, trucks, specialized vehicles, ambulances, all literally piled up on top of each other, tipped over, sticking up in the air. Apparently while trying to turn round and escape, these vehicles had knocked down hundreds of trees.

And amid this chaos of iron, wood, weapons, baggage, papers, lay burnt and blackened objects that I couldn't identify, a mass of mutilated bodies. And this carnage extended all along the cutting as far as I could see. All around in the woods there were dead, dead and yet more dead, the corpses of those who fell while running around under fire. Dead and, as I then saw, some alive among them. There were wounded lying under blankets and greatcoats, sitting leaning against trees, some bandaged, others bleeding and not yet bandaged. Some of the wounded, as I only later noticed, were lying along the side of the autobahn. Then I saw some figures moving among the wounded, apparently doctors or medical orderlies. That was all on the right-hand side.

The autobahn ran down the centre, a broad asphalted road that had already been cleared for traffic. Along a stretch of 200 metres it was pocked with small and large craters that the military vehicles driving to Berlin were having to zigzag round.

The cutting continued on the left-hand side, and part of the German column that had already crossed the autobahn was destroyed here. Again, as far as the eye could see, there was a mess of burnt-out, smashed, overturned vehicles. Again dead and wounded. As an officer hastily informed me, the whole of this vast column had come under fire from several regiments of heavy artillery and a few regiments of Katyushas that had previously been concentrated in the vicinity and had fired on the cutting on the assumption that the Germans would try to break through here.

We left this scene of horror and after a few kilometres saw a convoy of five or six ambulances coming towards us. Apparently someone had summoned reinforcements from our medical battalions but, considering the scale of the slaughter, these five or six vehicles would be no more than a drop in the ocean.[1]

This was the situation that faced the victors in May 1945. Apart from evacuating prisoners and tending to the vast numbers of wounded, the dead had to be buried as soon as possible, a gruesome task that was passed on to the local population, consequently mainly to women and teenagers, to which were added teams of former Nazi officials and prisoners of war.

Elisabeth Schulz gave her account regarding the fate of the wounded:

I was then nineteen years old and working as an auxiliary nurse in Schloss Baruth. At about 0900 hours on 20 April 1945 we were told that it was everyone for themselves. The wounded could not be taken along with us. We were three nurses, two medical orderlies and two *Hiwis* [Russian volunteers]. We decided to stay until all the wounded were gone. Some left on wagons with the nurses and doctors.

With part of the Schloss already on fire, we put the last eighteen severely wounded on a haycart. They were only wearing shirts, as the quartermasters had shut up shop and made off. What the poor boys had to suffer was indescribable, but there were no complaints. They were grateful for being saved, as they thought. The *Hiwis* had found two horses and we set off across the Schloss park. By the time we reached the meadows, the Russian tanks had already passed us, and there was firing from all sides. We quickly laid the wounded down on the grass and took cover. Everything then happened very quickly. We watched the Russians charge across the meadows and shoot medical orderlies, nurses and wounded. I have to thank my fellow nurse, Hedwig Steicke, for saving my life. She ran back with me across the park.

We lay there all night long and then joined the refugees from Baruth next morning, running for our lives across the meadows and being shot at by low-flying aircraft. We came to Radeland, where white flags already hung from the windows, and were most kindly taken in by the Hillebrands family, fed and clothed. Then the first Russians arrived and fighting started in the woods. We were hidden as well as possible in the hayloft. We two nurses then tended the German wounded that the local people brought to us in an abandoned farmhouse, laying them on straw, cutting off their blood-crusted uniforms, destroying the Waffen-SS uniforms, washing the wounded and trying to tend to them without medicine or bandages. Everything we could find was used. The people from the village helped with food, whatever they could find, for the hunger was very great. Even a doctor appeared from somewhere. We amputated with a handsaw. There was a terrible stench. All the amputees and the dead were put in a barn. There were 145 men with head or stomach wounds and they all died. Soldiers even died of tetanus from small wounds. We could only comfort them as they died. The youngest was only just sixteen years old. He died from a shot in the kidneys – very slowly. About 100 lightly wounded we treated as walking cases and sent them on. We worked day and night, and only slept in hiding. Whenever Soviet controls came, we would literally hold out the excrement buckets under their noses so that they would give up.

We did not record the names of the dead, as we had nothing to write with, and also no time. Apart from that, none of us believed that we would get back home alive. One of our doctors collected their identity discs. Hopefully, they reached the right place.

About mid-May Soviet officers made it clear to us that everyone that was half fit to work, or would soon be fit to work, would be deported to the Soviet Union. Several of us quickly got away, including myself. I only wish that some of them survived, so that our help had not been in vain.[2]

Expediency resulted in many of the dead being buried without any record of name or location being made, the bodies being dragged to and tipped into the nearest trenches and shellholes.

Herr G. Fonrobert, an inhabitant of Halbe, where some 4,000–5,000 had been killed,[3] wrote:

After the surrender was finally achieved on 1 May, we inhabitants of the village were immediately put to burying the dead, and for weeks there was nothing else to think about, as thousands of bodies had to be buried, mainly in quickly-dug makeshift mass graves. And, as a result of the warm spring sunshine, it was necessary to do it quickly. Afterwards there were many months of superficial clearing up of the roads and woods of the war materiel of all kinds lying around, including shot-up army vehicles, guns and tanks that had to be towed away. But everywhere in the woods around for an even longer time there was a smell of decay and fire that persisted for months.[4]

Erwin Hillebrands, then twelve years old, related:

I remember 600–700 dead being buried in three layers in a U-shaped grave at the entrance to Radeland, civilians, soldiers and even children. They were carried out together from the fields and woods around, only a few from the village itself. This quick burial was carried out on the instructions of the Soviet commandant responsible. An epidemic had to be avoided. Sometimes the corpses fell apart or had been eaten by foxes. It was a nauseating task. They pushed the bodies with poles into a suitable or shallow hollow, or simply covered them with sand. If Soviet soldiers were present, it was strongly forbidden to remove the identity discs; the dead were to remain anonymous. The exhumation of this mass grave took place at night in about 1951.[5]

Hilde Neufert, who was twenty-two at the time, vividly recalled the horrors of this task:

When the fighting was over in Märkisch Buchholz, the Russians immediately ordered the men and women, the boys and girls too, to bury the dead, although 'bury' was hardly the right word for it.

There was a mobile workshop in our yard, and the Russians were recovering all kinds of vehicles from the woods. On one occasion there was a Wehrmacht ambulance full of corpses. We had to unload them, all of whom, apart from their wounds, had had a bullet in the back of the neck. We had to throw their bodies mostly into bomb craters, pits and trenches under the eyes of the guards, and then cover them over.

There was a big bomb crater near our house. Once it had been filled to the top, Christmas decorations that an officer had found in our house, balls and ribbons, were strewn over it and trampled in.

I can still recall today when we removed the dead from the woods outside the village and laid them down in a row on the roadside to await transport; it was quite a long row. Suddenly a tank appeared, which changed course from the middle of the road and rolled back and forth several times over the row of corpses. But that was not enough. Finally the tank swivelled around on the remains, mashing them into the sand, and the commander, an officer, shouted at us as we looked on in horror: 'Gittler kaputt! Deitschland kaputt! Wehrmacht kaputt! Soldat kaputt! Nix mehr da! Ha-ha-ha!'

Then we had to pick up the squashed remains out of the sand with bloody hands and put them in a shell-hole.[6]

Willi Klär concluded his account of events he witnessed at Kummersdorf Gut:

On the morning of 30 April the inhabitants left the cellar of the old folks' home and returned to their own homes, only to be met by an horrific scene. Corpses were lying all over the place, about 2,000 of them, men, women and children who had been killed in the woods, in the village and on the ranges.

On the morning of 1 May all the men remaining in the village were rounded up at the old folks' home, whose hall was crammed with wounded German soldiers. All who could walk, whether soldiers or civilians, were led off as prisoners to Sperenberg, where the square between the chemist and the station bar was crowded with them all. They were then divided up into large groups and marched off under escort towards Rehagen, Mellensee, Zossen, Nächst Neuendorf and Glienick to Gross Schulzendorf, which they reached at about midnight. The heavy firing in the battle for Berlin could be seen well from here.

The prisoners were then put in a camp behind barbed wire, a former German Army training camp on the road to Jühnsdorf, and everyone was given a small packet of crispbread.

Next morning, 2 May, most of the civilians were allowed to return home after being interrogated. It was a long march on foot from the Kummersdorf Ranges to Gross Schulzendorf and back, about 52 kilometres, and both days without food.

On 4 May the inhabitants of the village and ranges began digging mass and individual graves to get the dead under the earth for fear of an epidemic. The barracks continued to serve as a hospital for several months.[7]

The Soviet commanders responsible for arranging the burial of the war dead varied in practice regarding the treatment of the identity discs and paybooks of the German dead. In most cases it was forbidden to record the names of the dead and their effects had to be destroyed. Witnesses reported that in some instances only members of the Army,

Navy or Air Force were given a proper grave, members of the Waffen-SS and even the Volkssturm being set aside and buried without markers. What happened to the dead policemen, who had fought in their distinctive green uniforms, is not known. In Halbe itself the identity of only about 300 of the dead could be established.

The Soviets saw to their own dead, with few exceptions avoiding the use of German cemeteries on ideological grounds. Instead they usually established their own cemeteries in the centre of villages or other prominent sites. The Soviet cemetery on Reichsstrasse 96 on the northern outskirts of Baruth was officially established on 7 November 1947 and contains some 1,300 of their dead in 22 mass graves, mainly men from 3rd Guards Tank Army, but these are by no means all the Soviet troops who died in the area.

The vast war cemetery at Halbe, the Waldfriedhof, or Woodland Cemetery, as it is discreetly known, came about as a result of the efforts of Pastor Ernst Teichmann and his wife. Upon his return from the war, during which he had been a padre with the Wehrmacht, Pastor Teichmann took over a parish in the Harz Mountains, where he started concerning himself with the graves of the war dead to be found there. He first heard about Halbe in 1947 and went to see for himself. At about the same time Berlin's Bishop Dibelius managed to establish an Evangelical Church commission for the care of war graves in both halves of the city. Although the *Volkssbund Deutsche Kriegsgräberfürsorge* (German War Graves Commission) was anxious to assist, it had no authority in East Germany, and could only provide support from behind the scenes. Then, on 29 July 1948, a war graves commission was established for the state of Brandenburg when the Soviet Military Administration passed the responsibility for this matter to the civilian authorities, ordering all identifications to be passed on to the German Red Cross in West Berlin for registration.

Pastor Teichmann applied and was accepted for the post of parish priest at Halbe in 1951 and eventually the Waldfriedhof was laid out in accordance with his recommendations. Meanwhile, despite the indifference and even hostility of the East German authorities, Teichmann and his wife, with the help of some members of the community, applied themselves assiduously to the task of identifying and reinterring the war dead from the area with reverence and care. He continued this work until his death in 1983. By the end of 1958 the official record showed 19,178 reinterred, and by the end of 1989 this had risen to 20,222 bodies, of which some 8,000 had been identified.

Not all the war dead came from the immediate vicinity, for East German expansion of open-cast coal mining in the Lausitz area resulted in most of the war dead from that area being transferred to Halbe. Remains are still being discovered at a rate of about 200 per year to add to the cemetery's total. It also contains the remains of some 4,500 prisoners who died in the Soviet 'Special Camp No. 5' in Ketschendorf, near Fürstenwalde, during the period 1945–7. The Waldfriedhof is the largest military cemetery on German soil.[8]

The search for missing persons became a major task in post-war Germany, and few enquirers would be fortunate enough to receive such detailed information regarding the fate of a missing daughter, as was given in this letter written by a soldier four months later:

Meanwhile the Russians had surrounded the pocket that we wanted to escape from and we no longer had the slightest peace. We reached the Hammer–Halbe area in stages. I took your daughter, along with six other refugees, to just short of Hammer, where she could wait out the development of the overall situation herself. She returned that night to the place where we were parked, because Hammer was under fire and the cellars there were all full. Towards morning on 28 April we came under heavy mortar fire so withdrew further into the woods. With dawn all hell broke out from all sides. The first barrage went over us as we lay in a slit trench. At about 0840 hours there was another barrage during which a bomb from a heavy mortar hit a tree behind our trench and we were unlucky enough to have all the splinters shower down directly on our trench. I felt a piercing pain in my left shoulder and said to your daughter: 'I've had it.' Then I noticed that Traudel had started crying, and so had your daughter.

At first it looked like the effects of shock, until your daughter started groaning. The whole thing only lasted seconds. When I heard your daughter's breathing, I realised what was wrong. Three large splinters had pierced her back and the air was coming out of her wounds. Comrades sitting in a hole nearby immediately took Traudel to the dressing station that was close by, as she had a small wound in her leg, while I attended to your daughter as far as my wound would let me. As she had lost consciousness immediately after being wounded, I could not communicate with her. Death followed very quickly, as the medical officer who had been summoned confirmed. We then buried your daughter in the trench in which she had so quickly met her fate.

I then went to the main dressing station to look for Traudel and get my wound dressed. I found Traudel there and took her with me to find transport. However, the artillery and mortar fire was so heavy that no transport was possible and we had to spend the whole day sitting in a foxhole. Then, at about 1900 hours that evening, we were taken to the Hammer forestry office. At the same time the Russians attacked us from the rear and we had no choice but to break out to the front.

The wounded who were unable to move remained lying where they were. My wound had become worse in that I now had fever and was shivering. I carried Traudel with my good arm about three kilometres towards Halbe, but my shoulder wound began bleeding from the effort and I lost so much blood that I could not go any further. Some comrades took Traudel on by vehicle to Halbe.

The whole break-out area lay under a frightful hail of fire such as I had never ever experienced before throughout the war. When I reach Halbe several hours later, it was no longer possible to get through. All the streets were jammed with shot-up and burning vehicles. While looking for Traudel at the many wounded collection points, I was wounded again by a shell exploding three metres away from me, getting splinters in the left knee and thigh. With the help of a comrade, I was able to slip into the cellar of the nearest house, where civilians bandaged me. I lay down there and was found by the Russians when they took the village during the course of the evening. A Russian officer had me immediately bandaged by a Russian medical orderly and came back two hours later with a German doctor and two stretcher bearers, who took me to the dressing station. My enquiries about Traudel were unfortunately unsuccessful. Traudel wore a small label with her Cottbus address on it under her coat, as I saw myself. Hopefully she has found her way to you in the meantime.

The whole episode in the Halbe area from 26 to 30 April was a catastrophe. From the 140,000 men who were in the pocket, more than 20,000 were killed and 10,000 wounded.

The fate of Frau Buhlmann and your Traudel has had the same effect on me as if they were my nearest kin. And during the few hours that I sat together with Traudel in the foxhole, I grew as close to the child as if she had been mine.[9]

But what happened thereafter to the principal protagonists in this drama?

General Busse (full name Ernst Hermann August Theodor Busse) was released by the Americans in 1947, and from

1950 until 1965 served as the principal adviser on Civil Defence to the Federal German Ministry of the Interior,[10] for which he was awarded the Gross Verdienstkreuz mit Stern upon his retirement. He died at the age of 89 at Wallerstein in Bavaria on 21 October 1986.

Marshal Koniev served on the Allied Control Commission in Austria until he replaced Zhukov as Commander-in-Chief Land Forces in 1946. In July 1955 he was appointed the first Commander-in-Chief of the Warsaw Pact Forces, but had to give up the post through ill health five years later. Fully recovered, he was appointed Commander-in-Chief Soviet Group of Forces in Germany on 10 August 1961, just three days before the construction of the Berlin Wall began. One year later he transferred to the Group of Inspectors upon nominal retirement, and died aged 79 on 20 May 1975.

Marshal Zhukov stayed on as Commander-in-Chief of the Group of Soviet Forces in Germany until 1946, when Stalin appointed him Commander-in-Chief of Land Forces, but soon afterwards downgraded him to commander of the Odessa Military District and later to the Ural Military District, posts normally occupied by a colonel-general. Following Stalin's death in March 1953, Zhukov became Minister of Defence in the new government under Nikolai Bulganin, receiving his fourth star as 'Hero of the Soviet Union' on his 60th birthday in 1956. He supported Nikita Khrushchev's take-over in 1957 and was retained in his post, but upon returning from a triumphant visit to Yugoslavia and Albania in October that year, he was dismissed on charges of high-handedness, establishing a personality cult and obstructing Party work within the army.

Deprived of his positions as a member of the Presidium and the Central Committee, and as Minister of Defence, Zhukov withdrew to the *dacha* outside Moscow that Stalin had given him for life during the war. *Pravda* then published an article by Marshal Koniev that amounted to a scathing attack on

Zhukov's role during the war and as Minister of Defence. In March 1958 Zhukov was further humiliated by his contrived retirement as a Marshal of the Soviet Union, an unprecedented step, for marshals were normally transferred to the Group of Inspectors, whose occasional duties justified the continuation of their active-duty perquisites, such as an aide-de-camp and a chauffeur-driven car. Zhukov was now fair game for his old antagonists, and in March 1964 Chuikov attacked Zhukov in his book *The End of the Third Reich*, the first of the senior commanders' memoirs allowed to be published after the war.

However, in 1965, under the Brezhnev regime, Zhukov was invited to attend a celebration of the twentieth anniversary of the victory over Germany, at which he received a great ovation. The next day he joined his old colleagues in reviewing the victory parade from the top of Lenin's mausoleum. A request then arrived from a French publisher for permission to include a book on Zhukov in a series of twenty books on commanders of the Second World War. Somehow this request managed to get through the system, resulting in Zhukov producing his memoirs, upon which he had been working since his retirement. There followed considerable delays in obtaining official clearance, during which Zhukov suffered a heart attack, his second, but then the manuscript was eventually approved by no less than General Secretary Brezhnev, and by the end of April 1968 the book was on sale in Moscow. Despite an official ban on any form of publicity, Zhukov's memoirs were an instant success, and the feedback from the readers, amounting to over 10,000 letters, encouraged Zhukov to start work on a second edition with his morale greatly enhanced. He died aged 77 in Moscow on 18 June 1974.

NOTES

1. Simonov, *Kriegstagebücher*, p. 105 f.
2. Schulze, *Der Kessel Halbe–Baruth–Radeland*, pp. 87–8.
3. Article by Günter Führling in *Deutsche Militärzeitschrift*, Nr. 14.
4. *Halbe mahnt...!* 1963 pamphlet, p. 17.
5. Schulze, *Der Kessel Halbe–Baruth–Radeland*, p. 54.
6. Schulze to author.
7. *Ortschronik von Kummersdorf Gut.* [Rolf Kaim to author]
8. Mihan article to author; Jörg Mückler in *Deutsches Soldatenjahrbuch 2000–2001*.
9. *Halbe mahnt...!* 1963 pamphlet, pp. 13–14.
10. The author was informed by another general present that Busse was given a very stony reception when he gave an address on Civil Defence to the Bundeswehr Senior Staff College at Hamburg after the war.

SOVIET FORCES ENGAGED AGAINST THE HALBE POCKET

Based on F.D. Vorbeyev, I.V. Propotkin and A.N. Shimanky, *The Last Storm*, with some additional information drawn from various sources.

1st Byelorussian Front	***Marshal G.K. Zhukov***
3rd Army	***Col Gen A.V. Gorbatov***

35th Rifle Corps — *Maj Gen N.A. Nikitin*
   250th, 290th & 348th Rifle Divisions

40th Rifle Corps — *Lt Gen V.S. Kuzynetsov*
   5th Rifle Division
   129th Orel Rifle Division
      438th, 457th & 518th Rifle Regiments

41st Rifle Corps — *Lt Gen V.K. Ubranovitch*
   120th & 269th Rifle Divisions
   1812th, 1888th & 1901st Self-Propelled Assault Artillery Regiments

69th Army — ***Col Gen V.Y. Kolpakchi***

25th Rifle Corps — *Maj Gen N.I. Trufanov*
   77th Guards & 4th Rifle Divisions

61st Rifle Corps — *Lt Gen I.F. Grigorievsky*
   134th, 246th & 247th Rifle Divisions

91st Rifle Corps — *Lt Gen F.A. Volkov*
   41st, 312th & 370th Rifle Divisions

Army Troops
   117th & 283rd Rifle Divisions
   68th Tank Brigade
   12th Self-Propelled Assault Artillery Brigade 344th Guards, 1205th,
      1206th & 1221st Self-Propelled Assault Artillery Regiments

Reinforcements

12th Guards Artillery Brigade, 8th & 9th Anti-Tank Artillery Brigades, 293rd Mortar Regiment, 41st Guards Rocket-Launcher Brigade, 75th & 303rd Guards Rocket-Launcher Regiments

18th Anti-Aircraft Division

33rd & 89th Heavy Tank Regiments, 344th Armoured Artillery Regiment

12th & 35th Engineer Brigades, 2nd & 85th Pontoon Battalions, 154th Military Construction Battalion

29th & 40th Chemical Troops Battalions

6th Independent Flamethrower Battalion

273rd General Duties Battalion

33rd Army   *Col Gen V.D. Svotaev*

16th Rifle Corps   *Maj Gen/Lt Gen E.V. Dobrovolsky*
323rd, 339th & 383rd Rifle Divisions

38th Rifle Corps   *Maj Gen/Lt Gen A.D. Tyershkov*
64th, 89th & 169th Rifle Divisions

62nd Rifle Corps   *Lt Gen V.S. Vorobyev*
49th, 222nd & 362nd Rifle Divisions

Army Troops

95th Rifle Division

257th Independent Tank Regiment

360th & 361st Self-Propelled Assault Artillery Regiments

Reinforcements

115th & 119th Fortified Region Troops

257th Tank Regiment

22nd Artillery Division, 33rd Anti-Tank Artillery Brigade, 360th & 361st Guards Armoured Artillery Regiments, 56th Guards Rocket-Launcher Regiment

64th Anti-Aircraft Artillery Division

1st & 6th Pontoon Battalions, 155th Military Construction Battalion

10th Independent Motorized Flamethrower Battalion

283rd General Duties Battalion

2nd Guards Cavalry Corps   *Lt Gen V.V. Kruhkov*

3rd, 4th & 17th Guards Cavalry Divisions

1459th Self-Propelled Assault Artillery Regiment

10th Guards Rocket-Launcher Regiment

1st Ukrainian Front   *Marshal I.S. Koniev*
3rd Guards Army   *Col Gen V.N. Gordov*

21st Rifle Corps   *Maj Gen A.A. Yamanov*
  58th, 253rd & 329th Rifle Divisions

76th Rifle Corps   *Lt Gen M.I. Gluhov*
  106th & 287th Rifle Divisions

120th Rifle Corps   *Maj Gen S.I. Donskov*
  127th, 149th & 197th Rifle Divisions

25th Tank Corps   *Maj Gen E.I. Fominich*
  111th, 162nd & 175th Tank Brigades
  20th Motorized Rifle Brigade
  262nd Guards & 1451st Self-Propelled Assault Artillery Regiments

Army Troops
  389th Rifle Division
  87th Guards Independent Tank Regiment
  938th Self-Propelled Assault Artillery Regiment

Reinforcements
  11th, 162nd & 175th Tank Brigades
  1st Guards & 25th Artillery Divisions, 40th Artillery Brigade, 262nd
    Guards & 1451st Armoured Artillery Regiments, 296th Guards &
    1528th Artillery Regiments, 459th, 526th & 569th Guards Mortar
    Regiments, 21st Guards Rocket-Launcher Regiment, 179th Anti-Tank
    Artillery Regiment, 2nd Guards Rocket-Launcher Battalion
  69th Anti-Aircraft Artillery Division, 1527th & 1702nd Anti-Aircraft
    Artillery Regts
  2nd Guards Motorcycle Regiment

13th Army   *Col Gen N.P. Phukov*

24th Rifle Corps   *Maj Gen D.P. Onoprienko*
  121st Guards & 395th Rifle Divisions

27th Rifle Corps   *Maj Gen F.M. Chyerokmanov*
  6th Guards Rifle Division   *Col G.V. Ivanov*
  280th Rifle Division
    (to Corps Reserve on 26 Apr)
  350th Rifle Division   *Maj Gen G.I. Vetkin*
    (to 4 GTA on 23 Apr)

102nd Rifle Corps   *Maj Gen/Lt Gen I.M. Puzikov*
  117th Guards, 147th & 172nd Rifle Divisions

Army Troops
  88th Independent Tank Regiment
  327th & 372nd Guards, 768th & 1228th Self-Propelled Assault Artillery
    Regiments
Reinforcements
  88th Independent Tank Regiment
  10th Artillery Corps, 4th & 31st Artillery Divisions, 39th Artillery
    Brigade, 26th Anti-Tank Artillery Brigade, 12th Mortar Brigade,
    327th Guards, 372nd Guards, 768th & 1228th Armoured Artillery
    Regiments, 11th Guards Artillery Regiment, 493rd & 1076th Anti-
    Tank Artillery Regiments, 128th Mortar Regiment, 65th & 323rd
    Guards Rocket-Launcher Regiments
  10th Anti-Aircraft Artillery Division, 1287th Anti-Aircraft Artillery
    Regiment
  19th Engineer Brigade

28th Army   *Lt Gen A.A. Luchinsky*

3rd Guards Rifle Corps   *Maj Gen P.A. Alexandrov*
  50th, 54th & 96th Guards Rifle Divisions

20th Guards Rifle Corps   *Maj Gen N.I. Biryukov*
  48th Guards Rifle Division   *Maj Gen G.N. Korchikov*
    (to 3 GTA)
  55th Guards & 20th Rifle Divisions

128th Rifle Corps   *Maj Gen P.F. Batitsky*
  61st Guards Rifle Division   *Maj Gen K.A. Sergeiev*
    (to 3GTA on 21 Apr)
  130th Rifle Division
  152nd Rifle Division   *Col G.L. Rybalko*
Army Troops
  157th Artillery Brigade, 133rd Guards Mortar Regiment
  530th Anti-Tank Artillery Regiment
  607th Anti-Aircraft Artillery Regiment
  36th Engineer Brigade

3rd Guards Tank Army   *Col Gen P.S. Rybalko*

6th Guards Tank Corps   *Maj Gen V.A. Mitrofanov*
  51st, 52nd & 53rd Guards Tank Brigades
  22nd Guards Motorized Rifle Brigade
  385th Guards, 1893rd & 1894th Self-Propelled Assault Artillery
    Regiments
  3rd Guards Motorcycle Battalion

7th Guards Tank Corps   *Maj Gen V.V. Novikov*
   54th Guards Tank Brigade
   55th Guards Tank Brigade   *Col D. Dragunsky*
   56th Guards Tank Brigade   *Col Z. Slyusarenko*
   23rd Guards Motorized Rifle Brigade
   384th Guards, 702nd & 1977th Self-Propelled Assault Artillery
     Regiments
   4th Guards Motorcycle Battalion

9th Mechanized Corps   *Lt Gen I.P. Suchov*
   69th, 70th & 71st Mechanized Brigades
   91st Tank Brigade
   383rd Guards, 1507th & 1978th Self-Propelled Assault Artillery
     Regiments
   100th Motorcycle Battalion

Army Troops
   16th Self-Propelled Assault Artillery Brigade
   57th Guards & 90th Independent Tank Regiments
   50th Motorcycle Regiment

4th Guards Tank Army   ***Col Gen D.D. Lelyushenko***

5th Guards Mechanized Corps   *Maj Gen I.P. Yermankov*
   10th, 11th & 12th Guards Mechanized Brigades
   24th Guards Tank Brigade
   104th & 379th Guards, & 1447th Self-Propelled Assault Artillery
     Regiments, 285th Mortar Regiment, 11th Guards Rocket-Launcher
     Battalion
   763rd Anti-Aircraft Artillery Regiment
   2nd Guards Motorcycle Battalion

6th Guards Mechanized Corps   *Col V.I. Koryetsky/Col S.F.*
                                 Puthkariev
   16th, 17th & 35th Guards Mechanized Brigades
   28th, 117th & 118th Guards Tank Regiments
   423rd & 424th Guards Self-Propelled Assault Artillery Regiments,
     240th Guards Mortar Regiment, 52nd Guards Rocket-Launcher
     Battalion
   427th Guards Anti-Aircraft Artillery Regiment
   19th Guards Motorcycle Battalion

10th Guards Tank Corps   *Lt Gen Y.Y. Belov*
   61st, 62nd & 63rd Guards Tank Brigades
   29th Guards Motorized Rifle Brigade

72nd Guards Tank Regiment

416th & 425th Guards Self-Propelled Assault Artillery Regiments,
   299th Guards Mortar Regiment, 248th Guards Rocket-Launcher
Battalion

359th Guards Anti-Aircraft Artillery Regiment

7th Guards Motorcycle Battalion

Army Troops

68th Guards Tank Brigade, 13th & 119th Guards Independent Tank
   Regiments

70th Guards Self-Propelled Assault Artillery Brigade, 71st Guards
   Artillery Brigade, 312th Guards Mortar Regiment, 248th Guards
   Mortar Battalion

6th Guards Anti-Aircraft Artillery Division

3rd Guards Motorized Engineer Brigade

7th Guards Motorcycle Regiment

Air Forces   *Air Chief Marshal A.A. Novikov*
2nd Air Army   *Col Gen S.A. Krasovsky*

1st Guards Air Assault Corps
   8th & 9th Guards Air Assault Divisions
   12th Guards Air Fighter Division

2nd Guards Air Assault Corps
   5th & 6th Guards Air Assault Divisions
   11th Guards Air Fighter Division

3rd Air Assault Corps
   307th & 308th Air Assault Divisions
   181st Air Fighter Division

4th Air Bomber Corps
   202nd & 219th Air Bomber Divisions

6th Guards Air Bomber Corps
   1st & 8th Guards Air Bomber Divisions

2nd Air Fighter Corps
   7th Guards & 322nd Air Fighter Divisions

5th Air Fighter Corps
   8th Guards & 256th Air Fighter Divisions

6th Air Fighter Corps
   9th, 22nd & 23rd Guards Air Fighter Divisions

Army Formations
   208th Air Night Bomber Division
   98th & 193rd Guards Air Reconnaissance Regiments
   222nd Air Transport Regiment

16th Air Army   *Col Gen S.I. Rudenko*

3rd Air Bomber Corps   *Maj Gen A.Z. Karavacki*
   241st & 301st Air Bomber Divisions

6th Air Bomber Corps   *Maj Gen I.P. Skok*
   326th & 339th Air Bomber Divisions

6th Air Assault Corps   *Maj Gen B.K. Tokarev*
   197th & 198th Air Assault Divisions

9th Air Assault Corps   *Maj Gen I.V. Krupski*
   3rd Guards & 300th Air Assault Divisions

1st Guards Air Fighter Corps   *Lt Gen E.M. Belecki*
   3rd & 4th Guards Air Fighter Divisions

3rd Air Fighter Corps   *Lt Gen E.Y. Savicki*
   265th & 278th Air Fighter Divisions

6th Air Fighter Corps   *Maj Gen I.M. Dzusov*
   234th & 273rd Air Fighter Divisions

13th Air Fighter Corps   *Maj Gen B.A. Sidnev*
   193rd & 283rd Air Fighter Divisions

Army Formations
   1st Guards, 240th, 282nd & 286th Air Fighter Divisions
   2nd & 11th Guards Air Assault Divisions
   113th, 183rd, 188th & 221st Air Bomber Divisions
   9th Guards & 242nd Air Night Bomber Divisions
   16th & 72nd Air Reconnaissance Regiments
   93rd & 98th Air Observation Regiments
   176th Guards Air Fighter Regiment
   226th Air Transport Regiment

18th Air Army   *AVM A.Y. Golovanov*

1st Guards Air Bomber Corps
   11th & 16th Guards, 36th & 48th Air Bomber Divisions

2nd Guards Air Bomber Corps
   2nd, 7th, 13th & 18th Guards Air Bomber Divisions

3rd Guards Air Bomber Corps
   22nd Guards, 1st, 12th & 50th Air Bomber Divisions

4th Guards Air Bomber Corps
  14th & 15th Guards, 53rd & 54th Air Bomber Divisions

Army Formations
  45th Air Bomber Division
  56th Air Fighter Division
  742nd Air Reconnaissance Regiment

APPENDIX B

ORDER OF BATTLE:
GERMAN 9TH ARMY

9th Army	*Gen Theodor Busse*
XI SS Panzer Corps	*SS-Gen Mathias Kleinheisterkamp*

303rd Infantry Division Döberitz — *Col Albin*
- 300th Grenadier Regiment [2 Battalions] — *Lt Col Helmut Weber*
- 301st Grenadier Regiment [2 Battalions]
- 302nd Grenadier Regiment [2 Battalions]
- 303rd Fusilier Battalion
- 303rd Artillery Regiment
- 303rd Signals Battalion

169th Infantry Division — *Lt Gen Georg Radziej*
- 378th Grenadier Regiment [3 Battalions]
- 379th Grenadier Regiment [2 Battalions]
- 392nd Grenadier Regiment [3 Battalions]
- 230th Artillery Regiment [4 Battalions]
- 230th Fusilier Battalion
- 250th Artillery Regiment

712th Infantry Division — *Maj Gen Joachim von Siegroth*
- 732nd Grenadier Regiment [2 Battalions]
- 745th Grenadier Regiment [2 Battalions]
- 764th Grenadier Regiment [2 Battalions]
- 712th Tank-Hunting Battalion
- 1712th Artillery Regiment

SS-Panzergrenadier Division Kurmark — *SS-Maj Gen Willy Langkeit*
- *Kurmark* Panzergrenadier Regiment [2 Battalions]
- 1241st Officer Cadet Regiment [2 Battalions]
- Brandenburg Panzer Regiment
- Panzer Corps Großdeutschland [2 Battalions]
- *Kurmark* Recce Battalion
- *Kurmark* Tank-Hunting Battalion

Kurmark Engineer Battalion
Kurmark Artillery Regiment [2 Battalions]

23rd SS Panzergrenadier Div *Nederland*　　SS-Maj Gen Jürgen Wagner
　48th (1st Dutch) SS Panzergrenadier Regiment *Gen Seyffarth*
　　　　　　　　　　　　　　　　　　　　　　SS-Lt Col Scheibe
　49th (2nd Dutch) SS Panzergrenadier Regiment *de Ruiter*
　　　　　　　　　　　　　　　　　　　　　　SS-Lt Col Lohmanns
　502nd SS Heavy Panzer Battalion　　　　　*SS-Maj Hartrampf*
　Dora II Tank-Hunting Commando

Frankfurt-an-der-Oder Garrison　　　　　　*Col/Maj Gen Ernst*
Biehler
　1st, 2nd, 3rd, 4th, 5th, 6th & 7th Fortress Regiments
　2nd Police Battalion
　44th Fusilier Battalion
　523rd Artillery Regiment

V SS Mountain Corps　　　　　***SS-Gen Friedrich Jackeln***

286th Infantry Division　　　　　*Maj Gen Emmo von*
Rohde
　926th Grenadier Regiment [2 Battalions]
　927th Grenadier Regiment [2 Battalions]
　931st Grenadier Regiment [2 Battalions]
　1237th Officer Cadet Regiment
　Dresden Volkssturm Battalion
　286th Artillery Regiment [3 Battalions]

32nd SS Volksgrenadier Div *30. Januar*　　*SS-Col Kempin*
　86th SS Grenadier Regiment *Schill* [2 Bns]　*SS-Lt Col Eccer*
　87th SS Grenadier Regt *Kurmark* [2 Bns]　*SS-Lt Col Voss*
　88th SS Grenadier Regiment [2 Battalions]　*SS-Lt Col Becker*
　32nd SS Fusilier Battalion
　32nd SS Field Training and Replacement Battalion
　32nd SS Tank-Hunting Battalion
　32nd SS Motorized Artillery Regt [3 Bns]　*SS-Lt Col Lorenz*
　32nd SS Motorized Signals Battalion

391st Security Division　　　　　*Lt Gen Rudolf Sickenius*
　95th Grenadier Regiment
　1233rd Officer Cadet Regiment
　1239th Officer Cadet Regiment
　SS Battalion *Heyer*

391st Artillery Regiment

156th Infantry Division   *Maj Gen Siegfried von Rekowksy*
   1313th Grenadier Regiment [3 Battalions]
   1314th Grenadier Regiment [3 Battalions]
   1315th Grenadier Regiment [3 Battalions]

Corps Reserve
   561st SS Tank-Hunting Battalion   *SS-Capt Jakob Lobmeyer*

V Corps   **Lt Gen Eduard Wagner**

35th SS Police Grenadier Division   *SS-Col Rüdiger Pipkorn*
   89th SS Police Grenadier Regiment [2 Battalions]
   90th SS Police Grenadier Regiment [2 Battalions]
   91st SS Police Grenadier Regiment [2 Battalions]
   500th SS Storm Battalion

36th SS Grenadier Division   *SS-Maj Gen Dirlewanger*
   72nd SS Grenadier Regiment [2 Battalions]
   73rd SS Grenadier Regiment [2 Battalions]

275th Infantry Division   *Lt Gen Hans Schmidt*
   983rd Grenadier Regiment [2 Battalions]
   984th Grenadier Regiment [2 Battalions]
   985th Grenadier Regiment [2 Battalions]
   275th Fusilier Battalion
   275th Artillery Regiment

342nd Infantry Division   *Lt Gen Heinrich Nickel*
   554th Grenadier Regiment [2 Battalions]
   697th Grenadier Regiment [2 Battalions]
   699th Grenadier Regiment [2 Battalions]

Army Troops

21st Panzer Division   *Maj Gen Werner Marcks*
   125th Panzergrenadier Regiment [2 Bns]   *Col Hans von Luck*
   192nd Panzergrenadier Regiment [2 Bns]
   22nd Panzer Regiment
   21st Armoured Recce Battalion   *Maj Brand*
   155th Armoured Artillery Regiment *Tannenberger* [3 Battalions]
   305th Army Flak Battalion

10th SS Panzer Division Frundsberg   *SS-Maj Gen H. Harmel*
   10th SS Armoured Recce Battalion
   23rd Flak Division
   303rd Panzer Battalion

2nd Tank-Hunting Battalion
1129th Tank-Hunting Company

APPENDIX C

ORDER OF BATTLE:
GERMAN 12TH ARMY

12th Army	**Gen Walter Wenck**
XX Corps	**Gen Carl-Erik Koehler**
Theodor Körner (3rd RAD) Division	*Lt Gen Bruno Frankewitz*
1st *Theodor Körner* RAD Grenadier Regiment	*Maj Bieg*
2nd *Theodor Körner* RAD Grenadier Regiment	*Maj Becker*
3rd *Theodor Körner* RAD Grenadier Regiment	*Maj Menzel*
Ulrich von Hutten Infantry Division	*Lt Gen Gerhard Engel*
1st *Ulrich von Hutten* Grenadier Regiment	*Maj Wesemann*
2nd *Ulrich von Hutten* Grenadier Regiment	*Maj Anton Siebert*
3rd *Ulrich von Hutten* Grenadier Regiment	*Maj Hobra*
2nd Potsdam Grenadier Regiment [2 Battalions] [w.e.f. 20 Apr 45]	
Ferdinand von Schill Infantry Division	*Lt Col Alfred Müller*
1st *Ferdinand von Schill* Grenadier Regiment	*Maj Carstens*
2nd *Ferdinand von Schill* Grenadier Regiment	*Maj Kley*
3rd *Ferdinand von Schill* Grenadier Regiment	*Maj Müller*

Scharnhorst Infantry Division	*Lt Gen Heinrich Götz*
1st *Scharnhorst* Grenadier Regiment	*Maj Mathias Langmaier*
2nd *Scharnhorst* Grenadier Regiment	*Maj Mahlow*
3rd *Scharnhorst* Grenadier Regiment	*Lt Col Gerhard Pick*

XXXIX Panzer Corps — ***Lt Gen Karl Arndt***

XXXXI Panzer Corps — ***Lt Gen Holste***

XXXXVIII Panzer Corps — ***Gen Maximilian von Edelsheim***

Ungrouped Formations

Friedrich Ludwig Jahn (2nd RAD) Division — *Col Gerhard Klein/ Col Franz Weller*

1st *Friedrich Ludwig Jahn* Grenadier Regiment — *Lt Col Gerhard Konopka*

2nd *Friedrich Ludwig Jahn* Grenadier Regiment — *Maj Bernhard Schulze-Hagen*

3rd *Friedrich Ludwig Jahn* Grenadier Regiment — *Maj Dahms*

Potsdam Infantry Division   *Col Erich Lorenz*
    1st, 2nd & 3rd Potsdam Grenadier Regiments

Note: All infantry regiments listed had 2 battalions.

BIBLIOGRAPHY

Books

Baumgart, Eberhard: *Jenseits von Halbe*, Druffel-Verlag, Inning am Ammersee, 2001.

Bradley, Dermot; Hildebtand, Karl-Friedrich; Röverkamp, Marcus: *Die Generäle des Heeres 1921–45*, Biblio Verlag, Bissendorf, 1993.

Chaney, Otto P. Jnr: *Zhukov*, Futura, London, 1986.

Chuikov, Vasilii I.: *The End of the Third Reich*, Progress Publishers, Moscow (Panther Edition, London, 1969.

Eisenhower, Dwight D.: *Crusade in Europe*, Heinemann, London, 1949.

Erickson, John: *The Road to Berlin*, Weidenfeld and Nicolson, London, 1983.

Fey, Will: *Panzer im Brennpunkt der Fronten*, J.F. Lehmanns Verlag, Munich, undated.

Förster, G., and Lakowski, R.: *1945 – Das Jahr der endgültigen Niederlage der faschistischen Wehrmacht*, East Berlin, 1985.

Führling, Günter G.: *Endkampf an der Oderfront – Erinnerung von Halbe*, Langen Müller Verlag, 1996.

Gellermann, Günter W.: *Die Armee Wenck – Hitlers letzte Hoffnung*, Bernard & Graefe Verlag, Koblenz, 1984.

Gorlitz, Walter (ed.): *The Memoirs of Field Marshal Keitel*, William Kimber, London, 1965.

Gosztony, Peter: *Der Kampf um Berlin 1945 in Augenzeugenberichten*, Deutscher Taschenbuch Verlag, 1975.

Great Patriotic War of the Soviet Union, Progress Publishers, Moscow, 1974.

Guderian, Heinz: *Panzer Leader*, Ballantine Books, New York, 1965.

Kampe, Hans Georg: *Wünsdorf – Geburts- und Entwicklungsstätte der deutschen Panzertruppen*, Verlag Dr Erwin Meißler, Waldesruh bei Berlin, 2000.

Koniev, I.S.: *Year of Victory*, Progress Publishers, Moscow, 1984 (Schkeuditzer Buchverlag, 2001).

Kormonicki, Stanislaw: *Polnische Soldaten stürmten Berlin*, Polish Military History Institute, Ministry of Defence, Warsaw, undated.

Koschan, Heinz: *Der Hölle entronnen – Lebenserinnerungen*, Band 2, Schkeuditzer Buchverlag, 2001.

Kuby, Erich: *The Russians and Berlin 1945*, Hill & Wang, New York,

1964.

Lakowski, Richard, and Stich, Karl: *Der Kessel von Halbe 1945 – Das letzte Drama*, Brandenburgisches Verlagshaus, 1997.

Le Tissier, Tony: *Death Was Our Companion*, Sutton Publishing, Stroud, 2003.

Le Tissier, Tony: *Race for the Reichstag*, Frank Cass, London, 1999.

Le Tissier, Tony: *With Our Backs to Berlin*, Sutton Publishing, Stroud, 2001.

Le Tissier, Tony: *Zhukov at the Oder*, Praeger, Westport CT, 1996.

Lucas, James: *Battle Group! – German Kampfgruppen Action of World War Two*, Cassell, London, 1993.

Luck, Hans von: *Gefangener meiner Zeit – Ein Stück Weges mit Rommel*, Verlag E.S. Mittler & Sohn, 1991.

MacDonald, Charles B: *The Last Offensive (United States Army in World War II – The European Theater of Operations)*, Office of the Chief of Military History, United States Army, Washington DC, 1973.

Montgomery-Hyde, H.: *Stalin: the History of a Dictator*, Rupert Hart-Davis, London, 1971.

Noakes, J., and Pridham, G.: *Nazism 1939–1945*, Part 3, University of Exeter Press, 1988.

O'Donnell, James P.: *The Berlin Bunker*, J.M. Dent, London, 1979.

Ramm, Gerhard: *Ein unbekannter Kamerad – Deutsche Kriegsgräberstätten zwischen Oderbruch und Spree*, P. & R. Verlag, Woltersdrof Schleuse, 1993.

Ramm, Gerhard: *GOTT MIT UNS – Kriegserlebnis aus Brandenburg und Berlin*, Verlag Gerald Ramm, Woltersdorf Schleuse, 1994.

Rocolle, Pierre: *Götterdämmmerung – La Prise de Berlin*, Indo-China, 1954.

Ryan, Cornelius: *The Last Battle*, Simon & Schuster, New York, 1966 (Collins, London, 1973).

Schramm, Percy Ernst: *Kriegestagesbuch des OKW 1940–1945*, Vol. IV, Bernard & Graefe Verlag für Wehrwissen, Frankfurt/Main, 1961.

Schulze, Lothar, *Spurensuche Band 9 – Der Kessel Halbe–Baruth–Radeland – Der Durchbruch zur Armee Wenck in April 1945*, Podzun-Pallas-Verlag, Wölfersheim-Berstadt, 2002.

Seaton, Albert: *The Russo-German War 1941–1945*, Praeger, New York 1971 (Arthur Barker, London, 1971).

Shtemenko, S.M.: *The Soviet General Staff at War*, Doubleday, New York,

1977.

Simonov, Konstantin: *Kriegstagebücher*, Band 2, East Berlin, 1982.

Spaether, Helmuth: *Die Geschichte des Panzerkorps 'Großdeutschland'*, Duisburg, 1958.

Stang, Werner, and Arlt, Kurt: *Brandenburg im Jahr 1945*, Landeszentrale für politische Bildung, Brandenburg, 1995.

Steiner, Felix: *Die Freiwilligen*, Deutsche Verlagsgesellschaft, Rosenheim, 1992

Strawson, John: *The Battle for Berlin*, Batsford, London, 1974.

Tessin, Georg: *Verbände und Truppen der deutschen Wehrmacht und Waffen-SS im zweiten Weltkrieg 1939–1945*, Biblio Verband, Osnabrück, 1977.

Thorwald, Jürgen: *Das Ende an der Elbe*, Steingrüben Verlag, Stuttgart, 1950.

Tieke, Wilhelm: *Das Ende zwischen Oder und Elbe – Der Kampf um Berlin 1945*, Motorbuch Verlag, Stuttgart, 1981.

Toland, John: *The Last Hundred Days*, Arthur Barker, London, 1965.

Trevor-Roper, H.R.: *The Last Days of Hitler*, Macmillan, London, revised edition 1972.

Tully, Andrew: *Berlin: Story of a Battle*, Simon & Schuster, New York, 1963.

Vorbeyev, F.D., Propotkin, I.V., and Shimanky, A.N.: *The Last Storm*, Ministry of Defence, Moscow, 1975 (2nd edition).

Wagener, Ray: *The Soviet Air Forces in World War II*, Doubleday, New York, 1973.

Wagner, Gerd: *Der 9. Fallschirmjägerdivision im Kampf um Pommern, Mark Brandenburg und Berlin*, Cologne, 1985.

Willemer, William: *The German Defense of Berlin*, HQ USAREUR, 1953.

Zhukov, Marshal Georgi K.: *Reminiscences and Reflections*, Progress Publishers, Moscow, 1974 (English translation 1985).

Ziemke, Earl F.: *Battle for Berlin: End of the Third Reich*, Purnell, London, 1968.

Other Sources

Busse, Theodor: 'Die letzte Schlacht der 9. Armee', *Wehrwissensschaftliche Rundschau*, East Berlin, 1954.

Chernayev, V.: 'Some Features of Military Art in the Berlin Operation', *Voyenno-Istoricheskiy Zhurnal*, April 1955.

Chronos-Film of Berlin: film *Der Todeskampf der Reichshauptstadt*, 1993.

Domank A.: 'The 1st Guards Breakthrough Artillery Division at Halbe', *Voyenno-Istoricheskiy Zhurnal*, March 1978.

Dufving, Theodor von: personal archives to which the author had access.

Engelmann, Joachim: *Geschichte der 18. Panzergrenadier Division*, unpublished MS, Oldenburg, undated.

Fleischer, Wolfgang: 'Der Kessel von Halbe', *Visier*, 5/90.

Führling, Günter: article in *Deutsche Militärzeitschrift*, Nr. 14.

Gädtke, Ernst-Christian: *Von der Oder zur Elbe – Ein Bericht*, unpublished MS, 1992, in the author's possession.

Halbe Mahnt...!: a locally produced pamphlet, dated 1963, in the author's possession.

Jurisch, Helmut: sundry articles in *Soldat im Volk* magazine.

Kollatz, Karl: 'Die Front an der Elbe 1945 – Endkampf vor den Toren Berlins', *Der Landser*, 1984.

Kortenhaus, Werner: *Lothringen–Elsaß–Ostfront – Der Einsatz der 21. Panzer-Division*, unpublished MS.

Kreisleitung Jüterbog: *Dank Euch Ihr Soldaten zur Befreiung des Kreises Jüterbog 1945*, 1985.

Küster, Heinz: *Geschunder Leibe*, Gebrandmarkte Seelen, unpublished MS, 2000, in the author's possession.

Mihan, Werner: correspondence with the author.

Mückler, Jörg: article in *Deutsches Soldatenjahrbuch 2000-2001*.

Novikov, A.A: 'The Air Forces in the Berlin Operation', *Voyenno-Istoricheskiy Zhurnal*, May 1975.

Ortschronik von Kummersdorf Gut, copy of a handwritten document provided by Herr Rolf Kaim.

Refior Berlin Diaries, Federal Military Archives, Freiburg.

Timmons, Lt Col: 'Command and Control in the Wehrmacht', *Parameters*, US Army War College.

Voyenno-Istoricheskiy Zhurnal, April 1965.

Wenck, Gen. Walther: 'Berlin war nicht mehr zu retten': *Stern Magazine*, 16/95.

INDEX

Page numbers in bold refer to maps. Page numbers followed by 'n' (eg 228n) refer to notes